IDENTITY INVESTMENTS

CULTURE AND ECONOMIC LIFE

IDENTITY INVESTMENTS

Middle-Class Responses to
Precarious Privilege in Neoliberal Chile

JOEL PHILLIP STILLERMAN

STANFORD UNIVERSITY PRESS
Stanford, California

Stanford University Press
Stanford, California

Printed in the United States of America on acid-free, archival-quality paper

Library of Congress Cataloging-in-Publication Data
Names: Stillerman, Joel (Sociologist), author.
Title: Identity investments : middle-class responses to precarious privilege in neoliberal Chile / Joel Phillip Stillerman.
Other titles: Culture and economic life.
Description: Stanford, California : Stanford University Press, 2023. | Series: Culture and economic life | Includes bibliographical references and index.
Identifiers: LCCN 2022015869 (print) | LCCN 2022015870 (ebook) | ISBN 9781503634398 (cloth) | ISBN 9781503634404 (paperback) | ISBN 9781503634411 (ebook)
Subjects: LCSH: Middle class—Chile. | Group identity—Chile. | Privilege (Social psychology)—Chile. | Social status—Chile.
Classification: LCC HT690.C5 S75 2023 (print) | LCC HT690.C5 (ebook) | DDC 305.5/50983—dc23/eng/20220523
LC record available at https://lccn.loc.gov/2022015869
LC ebook record available at https://lccn.loc.gov/2022015870

Cover design: Jason Anscomb
Cover images: from a photo by the author
Typeset by Elliott Beard in Minion Pro 10/14

In memory of Ricardo Santander and Rodrigo Salcedo,
two dear friends dedicated to social justice in Chile.

Contents

Figures and Tables

Figures

Tables

Acknowledgments

THIS BOOK ORIGINATED WITH a conversation I had with my friend and colleague, Guillermo Wormald, in July 2007. I was eligible to apply for a sabbatical that fall, and asked if he thought I should write a proposal to continue research on street markets (I had already published several articles and chapters on this topic) or on the middle class. He replied, "Definitely study the middle class. They are a changing group, and a lot of people are interested in their development." That turned out to be excellent advice, which I very much appreciate.

This project has benefited from the support of many individuals and organizations, and I am enormously grateful for all the assistance I received to help make it a reality. I apologize in advance to anyone I may have missed, but please know that your support benefited this project. Leslie Gates, Dorinda Welle, Peter Winn, Juliet Schor, Heidi Tinsman, Jeff Rothstein, Omar Lizardo, Ronald Breiger, Francisco Sabatini, Gonzalo Cáceres Quiero, Rosario Palacios, and the late Charles Tilly provided helpful guidance during the project's initial stages. This project would not have been possible without generous funding and assistance from several organizations. Field research in Santiago during 2008–2009 was supported with a sabbatical from Grand Valley State University and a U.S. Department of Education Fulbright-Hayes Faculty Research Abroad fellowship (Award Number: P019A080002). I declined a Fulbright Commission Award to receive the above fellowship. In 2016, I received a second sabbatical award from Grand Valley that provided essential writing time. The Grand Valley State University Human Research Review Committee (project number 07–232-H) approved the field research for this book. My wonderful students Autumn Chorney and Natalie VeCasey kindly provided much-needed bibliographic assistance.

In Chile, I was fortunate to receive institutional support from the Instituto de Estudios Urbanos y Territoriales, Pontificia Universidad Católica de Chile, where I served as visiting professor from 2008 to 2009. Institute directors Claudia Rodríguez, Pedro Bannen, and Roberto Moris graciously hosted me, and Elizabeth Lizama provided wonderful support and friendship. I benefited from the opportunity to join a research team studying shopping malls in La Florida, including the late Rodrigo Salcedo, Gonzalo Cáceres Quiero, Liliana de Simone, Miguel Pérez, Jordan Harris, and Justine Graham. Rodrigo Salcedo, Gonzalo Cáceres, and Francisco Sabatini provided ongoing guidance with my project. I also appreciated the opportunity to exchange ideas with Jonathan Barton, Francisca Márquez, Carlos de Mattos, Alejandra Rasse, María Sarella Robles, Ana Parraguez, and María Elena Ducci. Miguel Pérez and Leila Juzam did a fantastic job transcribing the interviews for this book.

My family and I had the surprising and wonderful opportunity to spend a second year in Chile while I served as chair of the Escuela de Sociología, Universidad Diego Portales (UDP). I first met some of my future colleagues there thanks to a chance encounter with Don Slater, who was in Santiago to give a lecture. Rodrigo Salcedo encouraged me to apply for a teaching spot there, while María Luisa Méndez and Manuel Vicuña (dean of History and Social Sciences) urged me to seek the chair position. There, I benefited from stimulating conversations and collaborations with friends and colleagues Ana Cárdenas Tomazic, Felipe Link, Tomás Ariztía, José Ossandon, María Luisa Méndez, Florencia Herrera, Berta Teitelboim, Modesto Gayo, Mauro Basaure, Antonio Stecher, Juan Pablo Toro, and Lorena Godoy, several of whom were also conducting research on Chile's middle classes. My stay at UDP also gave me additional time in the field, which allowed me to expand the dataset for this project. Personal circumstances unfortunately required me to cut short my time at UDP, but I am grateful to have had the opportunity to work with such wonderful colleagues and friends. Dean Frederick Antczak of the College of Liberal Arts and Sciences, Grand Valley State University, kindly granted me a leave so I could spend a second year in Chile.

Several individuals provided crucial connections with research participants. Leyla Flores (my spouse), Consuelo Figueroa, Francisco Sabatini, Gonzalo Leiva, María Luisa Méndez, and Roxana Oyanedel provided contacts for the snowball samples in the two communities. Gonzalo Cáceres Quiero, Leyla Flores, the late Ricardo Santander, Carolina Santander, José Ossandon, and Ana Parraguez provided invaluable assistance with gaining entrée into the five schools I studied. Emmanuelle Barozet and Vicente Espinoza kindly shared their expertise on Chile's middle classes as I developed the project. I am especially grateful to all the research participants who opened their homes and shared their experiences with me. I would like to thank Víctor, Aniluap, Evelyn, Deyda, and Luis for taking the initiative to connect me with other participants and providing suggestions for activities that would enrich the project.

I presented draft portions of this book at the American Sociological Association annual meetings, Latin American Studies Association congresses, International Sociological Association conference, Pontificia Universidad Católica de Chile, Universidad Diego Portales, Universidad Católica de Valparaíso, Cornell University, and Grand Valley State University. Diane Davis, Gay Seidman, Daniel Fridman, María José Alvarez-Rivadulla, Rachel Sherman, Carolina Bank Muñoz, Omar Lizardo, Rachel Sullivan Robinson, Leslie MacColman, Marshall Battani, Jeffrey Rothstein, Elizabeth Hutchison, Rachel Campbell, and Laurel Westbrook provided helpful feedback on chapter drafts.

Portions of the manuscript originally appeared in the following publications and are reprinted with permission:

Stillerman, Joel. 2017. "Housing Pathways, Elective Belonging, and Family Ties in Middle Class Chileans' Housing Choices." *Poetics* 61 (April): 67–78. (Elsevier)

Stillerman, Joel. 2016. "Art in the Chilean Living Room." *Consume This!* Blog sponsored by the American Sociological Association Section on Consumers and Consumption. https://asaconsumers.wordpress.com/2016 /12/11/consume-this-art-in-the-chilean-living-room/.

Stillerman, Joel. 2016. "Educar a niñas y niños de clase media en Santiago: Capital cultural y segregación socioterritorial en la formación de mercados locales de educación." *EURE* 42(126): 169–186. (Pontificia Universidad Católica de Chile)

Stillerman, Joel. 2010. "The Contested Spaces of Chile's Middle Classes." *Political Power and Social Theory* 21: 209–238. (Emerald)

At Stanford University Press, I am grateful for the expert guidance and assistance of Marcela Maxfield, Sunna Juhn, and Tiffany Mok as well as *Cul-*

ture and Economic Life series editors Frederick Wherry and Jennifer Lena. The manuscript benefited enormously from feedback provided by the editorial staff, series editors, and three anonymous reviewers. Catherine Mallon did an excellent job copyediting the manuscript. It is a wonderful honor to have the opportunity to publish this book with Stanford.

Moving a family to Chile and enrolling our two daughters in school and daycare was a challenging task, and we very much appreciate generous help from colleagues and friends. Heidi Tinsman, Gonzalo Cáceres Quiero, Ana María Farías, Consuelo Figueroa, Francisca Márquez, Raúl González, Francisca Muñoz, Gonzalo Leiva, and Partricia Aravena are amazing friends that helped us get settled and provided warm companionship. As always, the Flores Morales family was a constant source of support and joy. Our daughters Gabriella and Micaela graciously endured the challenges of adapting to Chile and the return to the U.S. This was difficult at times, but I am happy they are now fully immersed in Chilean culture and more deeply connected to family there. I would like to thank my family members for their ongoing support and encouragement: Frieda, Audrey, Marcia, Jonathan, Annette, and David Stillerman; Sidney Simon; and David, Maxine, and Sophie Freedman. Leyla Flores, my wife and companion, provided invaluable support in all aspects of this project. She shared her connections, historical expertise, moral support, and most importantly, willingness to endure my many years' dedication to this project. Thank you for all you do for me and our family.

IDENTITY INVESTMENTS

Introduction

TAMARA AND LUIS ARE members of Santiago, Chile's upper-middle class, and yet they defy the common view that members of this affluent group focus on hoarding opportunities[1] for themselves and their children. Tamara, a pharmacist working for a government agency, and Luis, an architect, live in La Florida, an up-and-coming mixed class district in southeastern Santiago. They have Italian ancestry, grew up in downtown Santiago, and attended elite public schools. Tamara's father was a factory worker that later opened a small business, while Luis's father was a dentist. Their children attend a secular, alternative private school, though they feel it approximates their experiences in elite public schools. Their home is full of Latin American crafts, a few original paintings purchased at a charity auction, several art reproductions, and a poster of a young Fidel Castro (see Figure I.1). They enjoy their relationships with neighbors and "the smell of country air." Their leftist beliefs are central to their identities. Tamara comments, "We married under democratic rule after dating for five years. We refused to wed until Pinochet [Chile's dictator from 1973 to 1990] stepped down. We waited a week [*laughs*]."[2] Tamara later comments that even if she had the money, she would never live in one of Santiago's richest neighborhoods because it would make her uncomfortable given her principles.

Ledda and Miguel are also members of the upper-middle class, but their religious beliefs and childhood experiences marked by the horrors of Chile's dictatorship make them sensitive to the plight of the poor and Chile's political

1

Figure I.1 Tamara and Luis's Living Room. Source: photo taken by author.

Figure I.2 Ledda and Miguel's Living Room. Source: photo taken by author.

dissidents. Ledda is a physical therapist and Miguel is a physician. Her parents were teachers while his father was a public university employee. They live with their children in the upper-middle-class community of Ñuñoa, located in eastern Santiago. They send their children to a private Catholic school near their home, and often hold school-related parties there. Their home includes original artworks as well as several prominently located Bibles and crosses: "It's like a cemetery," Ledda jokes (see Figure I.2). Her childhood under the dictatorship profoundly shaped her adult experiences: "In the North, I went to an elitist school in Antofagasta, but the priest was forced into exile because he protected people [from the military] . . . People talked about the proletariat in my school and home even though my family wasn't political . . . this was because my mother's fellow teachers were disappeared."[3]

Marcela is a member of the lower-middle class, and hence she worries about the risks of her family's frequent contacts with the poor for her fragile class standing. She is a single mother that drives a truck transporting produce from a large wholesale market. She hails from northern Chile, but after a falling out with her father, she migrated to Santiago to finish her high school education. Her living room includes artworks depicting homes and harbors in regional cities, including her hometown, highlighting her provincial origins (see Figure I.3). While her eldest daughter attended an elite public high school, received a degree, and is now a professional, she sends her younger children to a Catholic charter school to protect them from violence: "There are other public and charter schools near my house, but they're terrible. I'd need to teach my kids to use a knife or a gun if I sent them there. So, I make a superhuman effort to send my kids to a private charter school that I can afford."[4]

Mickey and her husband are members of the upper-middle class, but they are younger than the above interviewees and exhibit distinct lifestyles and values. Mickey, a history teacher, and her husband, a pharmacist, hail from southern Chile. They currently live in Ñuñoa and send their children to a secular alternative school. When I interviewed her in late 2008, she was thirty-seven, making her five to ten years younger than Tamara and Ledda. She and her husband like rustic decorations, including family heirlooms, that reflect his rural upbringing (see Figure I.4). When exploring schools in the community, Mickey found most options unappealing: "We looked at a religious school run by nuns, but our teenage daughter is totally anti-religion. We considered Akros [a secular private school], but it was too elitist. We could tell by the girls standing at the entrance and the despotic way they treated the cus-

Figure 1.3 Marcela's Painting of Valparaíso, Chile's Historic Port City. Source: photo taken by author.

Figure 1.4 Mickey's Rustic Cabinet. Source: photo taken by author.

todians and the secretary. We didn't like it at all." While she found the alternative school appropriate for her daughter, she considered sending her younger
son elsewhere: "I was a student teacher at Manuel de Salas. Their test scores are
just average, and since they have a system of alternative conflict resolution, the
kids are hard to manage. I doubt we'll send our son there."[5]

In this book, I develop a typology of middle-class groups, each with a distinct history and value orientation. Tamara is an example of a group I call
"activists." Members of this group either came from leftist families or participated in student activism under the dictatorship. Some have parents that
were leftist activists and suffered imprisonment, torture, assassination, and/
or exile. Parents' political commitments and intergenerational trauma resulting from political repression profoundly affected activists. Others in this
group became party members as college students during the dictatorship and
faced blocked mobility in the labor market due to their "high-risk" activism.[6]
These highly educated teachers, arts professionals, and public employees
experienced political trauma and assert humanistic and artistic values as part
of their sharp critiques of free market policies imposed under the dictatorship.
These values place a stamp on their market choices—they explicitly asserted
or implicitly acknowledged political identities and intellectual values through
their choices.

Ledda is an example of the group I call "moderate Catholics." These individuals grew up in Catholic families and attended religious schools. Many
of their parents were small business owners, bank employees, and public servants. While some in this group draw on traditions of liberation theology
dominant in Chile from the 1960s to the 1980s, others are politically conservative. They work in the liberal and technical professions, sales, and in their
families' businesses. They are united by their deeply help religious values and
support for tolerance toward divorced couples, single parents, and others, in
contrast to more staunchly conservative Catholics and evangelical Protes-
tants. Moderate Catholics examine markets through an ethical lens. Morality
is the North Star of their market choices as they criticize hostile interpersonal
behaviors, excessive competition, and materialism. They, too, criticize the Pinochet regime's market model and/or its consequences, but they do so differently than do activists.

Marcela represents "pragmatists"—lower-middle-class individuals. Some
pragmatists experienced downward mobility from middle class or affluent
families, while others rose up from poverty. Pragmatists work in lower-paid

clerical, sales, and service jobs. Although some pragmatists espouse religious values, they mainly focused on hard work, decency, and discipline. Pragmatists often lived near poor people, and they were the most vocal among the four groups in their criticisms of the poor. Where activists emphasized political identities and moderate Catholics highlighted morality, pragmatists fundamentally valued achievement and criticized what they perceived as poor people's morally dangerous behavior. Pragmatists' market decisions centered around individual achievement, distancing themselves from the poor, and complaining about the social exclusion they experience.

Mickey is an example of youngsters. While she and others have college educations and relatively high incomes like activists and moderate Catholics, they espouse distinct identities that I hypothesize reflect their birth under the dictatorship. They were not socialized in political parties or established religious organizations prior to the dictatorship, and some have experienced upward mobility as young adults. Youngsters migrated to Santiago from the provinces and/or came from working- and lower-middle-class homes and work in a variety of professions. Thus, while they do not articulate strong ideological identities, they are especially sensitive to elitism and discrimination. Their market choices are less explicitly articulated than those of the other three groups. I summarize characteristics of each group in Table I.1.

The contrasting backgrounds, experiences, and perspectives of these four middle-class groups inspire a series of questions that animate this study. First, why do members of the upper-middle class criticize market-based competition and elitism rather than focusing on securing or improving their economic positions? Second, why do lower-middle-class individuals pursue individual advantage in contrast to their more affluent counterparts? Third, how do middle-class individuals express their value commitments through their market behavior? Finally, how have the diverse perspectives of middle-class groups affected recent Chilean politics?

This book develops the concept of *identity investments* to answer these questions. This concept allows us to understand how different groups within Chile's middle classes developed their identities as adults through their family, educational, and work experiences, and how these identities then shape their investments in the employment, school, housing, home decoration, and leisure markets. The idea of identity investments deliberately combines the term *identity*, which we usually associate with an individual's personality, cultural background, family background, and group affiliations, with *invest-*

Middle-Class Group	Education	Average Age	Occupation	Ideological Orientation
Activists	College or junior college	40s	Education, public service, science and technology, arts	Leftist
Moderate Catholics	College or junior college	40s	Medicine/health, law, engineering, finance, sales	Religious
Pragmatists	High school or technical certificate	40s	Clerical, retail, services	Meritocratic
Youngsters	College or junior college	30s	Graphic arts, social services, accounting, education	Anti-elitist

Table I.1   Characteristics of Middle-Class Groups

ments, which we commonly associate with wealth accumulation based on self-interested rational calculation. I define identity investments as the set of motivations and practices that guide economic decisions so that they affirm individuals' deeply held values.

The concept of identity investments draws on the seminal work of sociologist Pierre Bourdieu.[7] He argued that individuals develop a class-based *habitus* (a set of attitudes) based on their childhood socialization that builds on their parents' class-based resources (education, social connections, money, and status). He contended that individuals' social position (class location based on habitus and capital possession) shapes their investments in different markets (or fields). To illustrate: a teacher would likely offer similar explanations for why she prefers art films to Hollywood blockbusters as those she uses to articulate why she prefers organic to processed food. He argued that an individual's habitus will lead them to use the same principles for investing in different consumption markets (what he calls "the homology between positions and position-taking"), and that competition in these markets often takes on a symbolic form as people with different habiti, or ways of viewing the world, clash over defining the stakes in these markets.

This book builds on Bourdieu's comparison of different fields in his major work, *Distinction*, to examine how individuals in different segments of Chile's middle class make investment decisions within markets that are decisive for economic survival and prosperity (employment and housing), the market that influences children's prosperity as adults (education), and markets through which families display specific lifestyles (home decoration and cultural/ leisure pursuits). Each of these fields operates as a site of symbolic display and competition. While other multimethod (statistical and interview-based) studies have compared distinct fields in the UK,[8] Australia,[9] Scandinavia,[10] and among upper-middle-class Chileans,[11] this is the first qualitative study of Chile's middle classes that examines these five fields.

This study extends an aspect of Bourdieu's analysis that has gained less attention than his work on education, cultural consumption, and class reproduction. Much of the development of Bourdieusian analysis has focused on these areas, leaving discussions of politics and ideology relatively undeveloped.[12] In this context, I will argue that religious and political identities tend to attenuate purely class-based self-interest under specific circumstances. The concept of identity investments also highlights how Chile's political history has influenced individuals' market behavior.

Additionally, the concept of identity investments complements other analyses of the cultural roots of market behavior. Viviana Zelizer argues that the economic and cultural dimensions of consumer behavior are inextricably bound together so that it is a mistake to describe economic practices as "purely economic," "solely status driven," or "only cultural."[13] Similarly, Frederick Wherry argues that individuals often engage in economic behavior based on morally acceptable norms or guidance within their group.[14] Identity investments highlight the importance of the cultural and moral dimensions of economic life.

Identity investments are distinct from the related terms of *identity markets* and *identity work*. The term identity markets refers to job discrimination based on employers' racist assumptions.[15] In contrast, the concept of identity work describes homeless individuals' stigma management strategies.[16] Departing from these two related concepts, I understand identity investments as the means through which individuals draw on preexisting identities and values as guides for participating in and interpreting distinct markets. Rather than focusing on discriminatory practices and stigma management—both sociologically important processes—identity investments help us understand how individuals bring cultural, moral, and political frameworks to their market behavior to achieve meaningful goals that may stretch beyond or come into conflict with self-interested wealth accumulation.

The concept of identity investments provides a useful tool for interpreting the attitudes, practices, and relationships of activists, moderate Catholics, pragmatists, and youngsters. Identity investments offer a powerful alternative to common scholarly interpretations of middle classes in Chile focused on opportunity hoarding, strategies seeking upward mobility, or fragmented identities (described below). Through an examination of middle-class individuals' pathways into the labor market, school choice, housing choice, home decorations, and consumer behavior, I find consistent patterns within each of these four groups reflecting deeply held identities shaped through experiences in the family, education system, political organizations, and religious institutions. Where others see middle-class people as largely self-interested, I discovered deeply held religious, political, and anti-elitist beliefs within the upper-middle class.[17] Further, I observed a strongly held meritocratic mentality through which lower-middle-class individuals sought to disassociate themselves from the poor as a stigma management strategy while criticizing the upper-middle class's economic advantages and symbolic dominance. Table I.2 describes each group's core identity investments.

In addition to identity investments, I use the concept of *precarious privilege* to understand the fragility of the middle class in contemporary Chile as well as middle-class Chileans' motivations for constructing symbolic boundaries with other groups.[18] While others have used the concept of precarious privilege to understand lifestyle migration[19] or labor activism,[20] I deploy this idea to examine the contradictory circumstances of middle-class families in Chile's free market context.

The term *precarity* was initially developed to understand the growth of "non-standard, unprotected" work arrangements in the contemporary world.[21] Here, I use the term *precarious privilege* to describe middle-class families'

Middle-Class Group	Principal Identity Investments
Activists	Expressions of political identity, artistic consumption
Moderate Catholics	Symbols of religion and family lineage; family-friendly practices
Pragmatists	Expressions of resourcefulness; communion with extended kin
Youngsters	Pride in occupational success; appreciation of commercial and consecrated art forms

Table I.2 Middle-Class Identity Investments

relative prosperity alongside their fragile hold on their occupational positions. As explored throughout this book, middle-class adults change careers because they have downgraded professions, undergo bouts of unemployment, may be pushed out of desirable residential areas, and observe demographic transitions in their children's schools that they believe undermine the schools' sense of community. These threats to middle-class status reflect weakly regulated labor, housing, and education markets alongside a slowdown of economic growth beginning in the 2000s.[22]

Consequently, members of the middle classes feel that their status is threatened and respond to those threats by constructing symbolic boundaries with other groups. Lamont developed the concept of symbolic boundaries to understand how upper-middle-class men distinguish themselves from others.[23] These men construct cultural, socioeconomic, and moral boundaries with others to safeguard their own sense of moral worth. In the Chilean context, each middle-class group constructs a specific set of symbolic boundaries reflecting their social position and core values.

Activists who changed careers or work in downgraded professions criticize the wealthy and upwardly mobile members of the middle class for their ostentation and focus on money rather than the values of solidarity and education. Moderate Catholics who work in more stable, high-paid professions feel excluded from the elite because they cannot afford their lifestyle and criticize the upwardly mobile for their competitive and antisocial behaviors. Both these groups feel their existing status is threatened by the growing influence and prosperity of more business- and consumption-oriented segments of the middle class. Youngsters, who work in a variety of professions but are newcomers to the upper-middle class, criticize wealthy individuals' and school administrators' discriminatory behaviors toward immigrants, children with disabilities, and those with more modest incomes. This attitude reflects their desire for inclusion in the upper-middle class as they have experienced upward mobility but are not incumbents in this group. Finally, pragmatists experience hostility from upper-middle class people and criticize the "moral depravity" of the poor, largely because they are wedged between these two groups and work in low-paid, unstable jobs. Table I.3 outlines each group's conditions of precarious privilege and the symbolic boundaries members construct.

To understand middle-class identity investments and their relationship to precarious privilege, we must define the middle classes and move beyond the here and now to examine how Chile's recent history of political struggle and

Middle-Class Group	Condition of Precarious Privilege	Principal Symbolic Boundaries with Others
Activists	Proximity to the wealthy/ upwardly mobile; career changes; work in downgraded professions	Reject ostentation, competitiveness, and consumerism among wealthy and upwardly mobile
Moderate Catholics	Proximity to the wealthy/ upwardly mobile; risk of unemployment	Feel excluded by the wealthy and criticize the competitiveness and immoral behavior of upwardly mobile people
Pragmatists	Low-paid, unstable employment; proximity to the poor	Resent hostility from upper-middle class and fear the poor
Youngsters	Social exclusion from upper-middle class due to recent entry to this group	Challenge discriminatory attitudes of upper-middle class

Table I.3 Precarious Privilege and Symbolic Boundaries

unresolved conflicts shaped middle-class identities that guide their market behavior and public practices.

Why Study the Middle Classes in Contemporary Chile?

While scholars of Chile have historically focused on political parties and political change,[24] working-class and poor people's movements,[25] economic development,[26] and the upper class,[27] scholars have recently shifted their attention to the middle classes.[28] This focus reflects the middle classes' substantial growth in countries of the Global South (postcolonial and non-European countries) during the 1990s and 2000s. Beginning in the early 2000s, economists noted that rapid economic growth had led to declining poverty and a growing middle class in Asia, Latin America, Africa, and Eastern Europe.[29] Around the same time, political scientists and sociologists began to revisit questions raised in the mid-twentieth century about the potential of middle classes to promote democratic government.[30] Others explore middle-class participation in social movements in the Global South.[31]

Because Chile experienced impressive economic growth beginning in the 1980s (with short recessions in 1999 and 2009 and slowing growth in the 2000s), and poverty has declined since the 1990 resumption of civilian rule, Chile has experienced substantial expansion of the middle classes, which made up approximately 59 percent of the population in 2017.[32] Given Chile's historically high poverty rates and unequal income distribution, the growth of the middle classes has important implications for Chileans' capacities to save money, purchase homes, consume more sophisticated goods, and increase their educational levels (all of which might increase business profits and contribute to economic growth); and an expanded middle class has the potential to become a powerful political actor whose newfound prosperity may influence members' political orientations and decisions. Middle-class growth also creates the potential for intensified conflicts with the wealthy and the poor, who both may resent middle-class people's growing incomes. Additionally, growing differences *within* the middle classes based on changing employment patterns and lifestyles can intensify conflict between segments of this group. The changing economic and occupational positions of middle-class people may also contribute to cultural change in Chile. All of these factors suggest that studying the middle class is paramount for understanding contemporary Chile and may provide insights for cultural and political change in other countries.

Will the Real Middle Class Please Stand Up?

If scholars claim that middle classes have grown in Chile and elsewhere in the Global South, this raises the question of how we define the middle classes and determine their boundaries with the rich and the poor. As scholars since the mid-nineteenth century have discovered, defining the middle classes is easier said than done because middle classes represent a heterogeneous set of occupational groups with distinct experiences and worldviews. Additionally, "middle class" provides wealthy and lower income people with a convenient way to label themselves that reduces the stigma associated with being rich or poor.[33] Unlike large business owners and blue-collar workers, who in principle can construct a collective identity based on their respective shared interests, members of the middle class might find it difficult to identify common ground with their peers. I cannot claim to have identified a definitive answer to the vexing question of how to define the middle classes and demarcate their boundaries with other social classes, but I do lay out some of the main approaches to defining and studying middle classes and articulate how I understand this group.

Economists tend to study middle classes by analyzing their incomes in relation to the top and the bottom of the distribution. The rationale for this approach is that it facilitates comparisons across countries and examination of changes in incomes across time. While there is considerable debate about which income measure is most accurate, most economists studying Latin America argue that the middle classes are those families with a per capita (per person) income of between 13 and 70 dollars per day. The lower cutoff for the middle class means that this category includes those that have only a 10 percent risk of falling into poverty. Scholars have included a category between the middle class and the poor—the vulnerable—those earning between 4 and 10 dollars a day / per capita and whose incomes place them at risk of falling into poverty. The upper limit of the middle class excludes the highest 2 percent of income earners from this class. While this seems like a very high threshold for dividing the middle class from the wealthy, scholars find that moving the cutoff lower only changes the size of the middle class by a few percentage points. Use of this method demonstrates that since the early 2000s, Chile's middle class has grown substantially as a portion of the income structure.[34]

A broad definition based on incomes does not allow us to examine differences across occupations and their relative permeability to newcomers. In this light, a second approach adopted by sociologists examines middle-class occupations under the umbrella of the "service class." This classification system arranges different occupational groups based on whether they are business owners, salaried employees, or hourly workers.[35] This approach divides the middle class into an upper service class (professionals and managers), a lower service class (clerical and routine nonmanual workers), and small business owners. Using this method, analysts of Chile noticed a significant movement from the poor into the middle class and short range mobility within the middle class during the 1990s,[36] more restricted upward mobility into the middle class in the 2000s,[37] and downward mobility out of the middle class during the 2019–2021 COVID-19 pandemic.[38] Bourdieu's model outlined above describes a more internally differentiated middle class by highlighting variations in attitudes and lifestyles across professions subsumed under the service class.

A focus on occupations alone does not allow us to observe how middle-class individuals access and accumulate material and symbolic resources like housing, consumer goods, or social status. In this context, a third approach among sociologists looks at the *assets* middle-class families secure and accumulate. Middle-class individuals use their education, business ownership, and or occupational positions to access resources.[39] Scholars studying Chile, often drawing on the work of Bourdieu and Lamont, find that middle-class families use access to educational institutions, property ownership, and social connections to cement their control over prized material and symbolic resources.[40]

A singular focus on resource accumulation strategies may overlook how middle-class people participate in politics and public life. In this vein, a fourth approach examines middle-class politics. Here, scholars look back to Aristotle and Confucius, both of whom argued that the middle class serves as a balancing force between the rich and the poor and also tends to support democratic government.[41] This approach began in the 1950s, when researchers saw middle-class expansion as portending the rise and consolidation of democracy.[42] Contemporary studies of middle classes in the Global South ask whether or not the middle classes are a democratizing force, with some highlighting the middle classes' leadership of prodemocracy movements.[43] Others argue that middle-class members' dependence on public employment discourages them from challenging authority[44] or that their economic privileges make them unlikely to promote the rights of all citizens.[45] Scholars also point to political divisions across middle-class occupational groups.[46] Finally, recent work examines how U.S. Cold War era foreign policies sought to bolster Latin American middle classes to encourage economic development and democratization, as well as to prevent revolution.[47]

Middle-class practices and identities are also place-specific. A fifth approach examines middle-class participation in housing markets as well as the distinct characteristics of different kinds of middle-class communities. Scholars contrast middle-class families' cultural orientations in working-class suburbs, bedroom suburbs, and gentrifying urban communities;[48] explore middle-class tendencies to settle in central urban areas near family;[49] and examine the extent to which middle-class residents form ties with the poor in mixed-class communities.[50]

Finally, scholars consider how different middle-class age cohorts develop distinct cultural orientations, and how these differences reflect broad-scale social changes. Abramson and Inglehart argue that rising levels of education and prosperity among younger age cohorts have led them to adopt "post-materialist values" and to participate in new social movements focused on gender equality and environmentalism, for example.[51] Others contend that different patterns of democratic transition in Spain and Portugal affected younger age cohorts' cultural practices. The process and outcomes of democratization impacted educational policies, thus exposing younger people to different artistic traditions in the two countries.[52] Thus, we can anticipate that different middle-class age cohorts will display distinct identities and cultural orientations.

The concepts of identity investments and precarious privilege examine two types of variation across middle-class groups: cultural and ideological differences between occupational and age cohort groups, and differences in middle-class identities and practices across communities. As noted above, this book builds on Bourdieu's analysis of the different worldviews held by members of distinct occupations based on their respective asset portfolios (property, education, and connections).[53] Through statistical analysis, Bourdieu developed a "map of social space" that located different occupational groups based on their total wealth (capital volume) and their asset portfolios (capital composition, most notably education versus property ownership). I build on the work of qualitative scholars that find inspiration in Bourdieu's theoretical argument to explore contrasting consumption styles among middle- and working-class people,[54] distinct working- and middle-class child-rearing patterns,[55] and different worldviews among distinct middle-class occupational groups.[56]

I find Bourdieu's analysis of capital volume and composition particularly helpful in understanding different forms of identity investment across distinct segments of Chile's middle classes. Thus, I observe important horizontal differences based on capital composition between activists (public employees, artists, educators) and moderate Catholics (liberal and technical professionals, employees of family businesses). I also observe differences between these first two groups and youngsters, who have similar occupations but belong to a different age cohort.[57] Finally, these three groups have a larger capital volume than pragmatists, which leads to important vertical differences between professionals and clerical workers or lower-income freelancers.

While Bourdieu provided inspiration for the classification of these groups, I draw on analyses of middle-class politics to explain the source of their different lifestyles and worldviews. I argue that as Chile's occupational structure has shifted from the public to the private sector and toward more profit-centered businesses, traditional middle-class occupations like teaching and civil service positions have faced a decline. Members of those groups were the most vocal opponents of the Pinochet regime in my sample. Hence, these individuals strongly adhere to their political identities as a symbol of group membership and a form of resistance to market-based social policies. While doctors, lawyers, and technical professionals were not so sharply affected by Chile's economic changes, their strong religious beliefs help explain their resistance to the unbridled logic of markets. Youngsters, whose occupational life began in the 1990s and 2000s, had little involvement in Chile's political polarization under the dictatorship, but they resent their social exclusion by more established members of the upper-middle class. Finally, pragmatists either moved into the lower-middle class due to downward mobility or climbed up to the lower-middle class through dint of hard work. They do not enjoy the educational, network, or economic privileges of the upper-middle class, and hence see hard work as the only means to their own and their children's success.

In addition to integrating asset, political, and age cohort perspectives on the middle class, I also examine differences across communities, building on studies of housing. As described in more detail below, I studied middle-class families in the traditional, upper-middle-class community of Ñuñoa and the mixed-class, suburban community of La Florida. I found that members of a single group (e.g., moderate Catholics) displayed different market practices in the two communities reflecting distinct housing, education, and cultural markets as well as the different populations in each area. Table I.4 summarizes these differences.

The concepts of identity investments and precarious privilege shed light on status conflicts in the workplace, neighborhoods, and schools, as well as the symbolic contests materialized in home decorations and consumer behavior. The resulting analysis offers a different interpretation of Chile's middle classes than most scholarship focused on upper-middle-class opportunity hoarding and lower-middle-class pursuit of upward mobility. Rather, individuals in this

Community	Housing	Schools	Leisure Practices
Ñuñoa	High prices displace families or compel them to live in apartments.	Private schools; parents avoid elite schools.	Public cultural consumption; neighborhood activism.
La Florida	"Ñuñoa diaspora" follows others to more affordable homes.	Charter schools; parents avoid low-quality private and public schools.	Domestic cultural consumption; limited local participation.

Table I.4 Differences across Communities

sample were profoundly marked by the Chilean dictatorship's free market policies, and their identity investments explicitly or implicitly challenge Chile's class and political system. The common focus on opportunity hoarding and upward mobility overlooks how middle-class lives are rooted in Chile's polarized politics and the complex, and at times contradictory ways, that some middle-class families have developed a cultural and political critique of Chile's free market society through their market practices.[58] Through identity investments, individuals use market practices to articulate and advance political, ethical, cultural, and emotional values that at times contradict or attenuate profit-oriented goals and behaviors.

History, Politics, and Chile's Middle Classes

Thus far, I have argued that to understand the attitudes, practices, and identities of Chilean middle-class adults, we need to examine their recent economic transformation in the context of Chilean history and politics. This context is essential to our analysis because middle classes benefited from and helped forge educational and social welfare policies for much of the twentieth century, free market policies and political repression under the 1973–1990 dictatorship had profound effects on the middle class, and many participants in this study suffered during the dictatorship and engaged in prodemocracy activism.

From the early twentieth century until Chile's 1973 military coup, the middle classes benefited from social reforms designed to expand the scope of public education, create a domestic industrial base, and initiate social welfare policies. Simultaneously, members of the middle classes helped develop these policies through their participation in centrist and leftist political parties and their roles as government officials. While a small middle class of business owners, professionals, and employees emerged in the middle of the nineteenth century and gained political representation through the secular Radical Party (PR), these occupational groups began to expand in the 1880s after Chile defeated Perú and Bolivia in the War of the Pacific (1879–1882), thereby gaining territory in its northern region with valuable nitrate mines that served as an export engine for its economy.[59]

Radical Party government officials helped lead the expansion of public elementary and secondary education in the late nineteenth and early twentieth centuries. Public education expanded through a 1925 law establishing mandatory primary education. The PR saw the educational system not just as satisfying a practical need, but also as a means to educate Chileans as citizens and thereby resolve the intense class conflicts that emerged at the beginning of the twentieth century. As such, Radical President Pedro Aguirre Cerda (1938–41), a former teacher, president of the Teacher's College, and education minister, coined the slogan "to govern is to educate" (*gobernar es educar*) and enacted educational policies promoting patriotism via school curricula including Chilean literature, folk music, dance, and poetry. Through the PR focus on reformist nationalism, middle-class teachers and government officials sought to wrest ideological legitimacy from the landowning, mining, and banking elites that had long controlled Chilean politics.[60]

The PR's leadership of educational policymaking and administration during the first half of the twentieth century (and three presidential administrations from 1938–1952) expanded educational access, creating greater opportunities for students' upward mobility into the middle class as well as growing employment for teachers and government officials.[61]

The PR's public policies benefitting the middle classes coincided with middle-class labor activism. In the late nineteenth and early twentieth centuries, anarchists and communists founded industrial workers' unions,[62] while teachers and employees followed suit. Members of these professional unions helped form the Socialist Party (PS), some joined the Communist Party (PC), and others joined the left wing of the PR. Teachers, employees, and small business owners gained government support for legal reforms that benefited their members, and many of their leaders would later become high-level officials in the PC and PS. As such, these groups helped shape the left-wing nationalist and Marxist ideologies that captured an important segment of the Chilean electorate until the 1973 military coup.[63] Female teachers, healthcare providers, and social workers developed professional associations and helped design social welfare policies.[64]

With the PR push for Import Substitution Industrialization (ISI) beginning in the late 1930s that used government subsidies to jump-start manufacturing, a new cadre of industrial managers and technicians joined the middle class. While many in the middle class supported the PR and Marxist parties during the 1930s and 1940s, their criticisms of Radicals' self-serving practices led them to support populist and conservative presidents in the 1950s and early 1960s.[65]

By 1964, Eduardo Frei, a member of the reformist Christian Democratic Party (PDC), was elected president. The PDC had roots in progressive breakaway elements of the Conservative Party. These groups were inspired by the late nineteenth century papal encyclical, *Rerum Novarum*, which called on Catholics to support the working class and to encourage workers and employers to harmonize their interests. By midcentury, the PDC had strong connections with industrial managers and engineers, and offered policies to address the stagnation of Chilean industry during the 1950s. The party actively appealed to the middle class.[66]

In 1970, socialist physician and former senator Salvador Allende was elected president with 36 percent of the vote against PDC and conservative National Party competitors. In addition to U.S. government hostility, as his presidency progressed, the middle and upper classes (via the PDC and National Party) asserted their opposition to inflation, product shortages, and his use of executive decrees to nationalize industries, eventually joining protests calling for his ouster.[67]

In September 1973, the military junta overthrew Allende, with support from upper- and middle-class citizens and clandestine U.S. aid. The coup ended four decades of democratic rule: stable democracies had been relatively uncommon in the Latin American region. After the coup, the Pinochet regime sought to eliminate the political left through assassinations, arrests, exile, blacklisting, and the suspension of political parties. Additionally, University of Chicago–trained economists joined the junta to implement free-market policies that led to shrinking public sector employment and privatization of state-supported manufacturing. Beginning in the late 1970s and especially after the promulgation of a 1980 constitution approved through a sham referendum, the junta began to apply market principles to labor law, education, healthcare, and pensions. By the 1980s, sociologists noticed an important restructuring of middle-class occupations through which private-sector employees, small-business owners, and freelancers occupied a larger share of employment than teachers and public employees.[68]

Education reform had profound consequences for class inequality in Chile. In early 1981, unequal educational access was intensified by the decentralization of public school funding and the creation of charter schools in the K–12 sector, as well as incentives for the creation of private universities. Public school funding declined, affluent students attended private and fee-charging charter schools (fees were permitted in 1993), and those not admitted to traditional elite universities could pay to attend less selective private universities. The social fallout from these reforms (segregation of students between charter and public schools and students graduating from low-quality private universities with crushing debt) led to massive protests a quarter century later under democracy.[69]

Members of the Catholic Church were among the first to aid victims of human rights abuses, followed by activism among family members of disappeared persons, and middle-class college students. A severe recession in 1982–1983 left one-third of Chileans unemployed and detonated three years of prodemocracy protests led by the unemployed, women, and students. While protesters failed to topple the Pinochet regime, they sparked reforms allowing exiled political leaders to return. Additionally, although the Pinochet dictatorship had harshly repressed the Communist Party, its cellular structure and clandestine organization allowed it to play a central role in social protests, even while its erstwhile Socialist Party allies became more moderate. The regime held a plebiscite on Pinochet's rule in 1988, and the non-Marxist opposition (the *Concertación* or Coalition of Parties for Democracy, including the PDC, and leftist parties except the Communists) succeeded in defeating him as well as the regime's hand-picked presidential candidate the following year.[70]

The post-1990 center-left presidential administrations including the Socialist Party, Party for Democracy, and the Christian Democrats attempted to build consensus to heal political wounds generated under the dictatorship and to prevent coup attempts from restive generals. In the negotiations to extricate the generals from power, the opposition parties felt compelled to accept "authoritarian enclaves"—nondemocratic laws that provided institutional power to the military and outsized legislative influence to the political right.[71] The Concertación was cautious about pursuing human rights cases and sought to legitimate its authority through careful economic management that avoided the inflation of the Allende years. The coalition also sought to demobilize social movements that might make costly demands for government programs. The Concertación held the presidency for twenty years during which it presided over a sustained economic boom, declining poverty rates, and relative social peace. The Communist Party regained influence in national unions (teachers, healthcare workers) but did not join the Concertación (renamed New Majority) until Bachelet's second administration beginning in 2014.[72]

While Christian Democrats held the presidency during the 1990s, Socialist presidents Lagos and Bachelet were elected in 2000 and 2006. Their election fed hopes for greater social and constitutional reforms, though these aspirations were not realized. They continued the free-market policies pursued under the dictatorship and did not pursue constitutional reforms, though they passed modest unemployment, healthcare, and pension reforms that benefited the very poor.[73]

Despite murmurs of discontent, there was no sustained national movement that successfully challenged the legacy of Pinochet's economic and social policies during the first two Concertación administrations. The exceptions were indigenous mobilizations and public employee strikes, but social movements that had supported the prodemocracy struggle were largely quiescent during the 1990s. Some attribute this decline in activism to heightened individualism fueled by growing consumption, indebtedness, and disaffection from formal politics,[74] while others suggest it reflected Concertación voters' pragmatic support of their government.[75]

In contrast, the first Bachelet administration (2006–2010), during which I conducted research for this book, was a crucial *inflection point* in Chilean politics. During the 2000s, Chile, like other countries in Latin America, was buoyed by high international commodity prices that led to growing wealth.[76] Nonetheless, Concertación governments continued free-market policies and did little to redistribute wealth or address the "authoritarian enclaves" established in the twilight hours of military rule. Additionally, beginning in 2000, economic growth decelerated, affecting wages and employment.[77]

Protests ensued from 2006–2008, including subcontracted workers in export sectors, critics of the botched rollout of a new public transit system in Santiago, and most importantly, among middle and high school students. In 2006, Chilean high school students staged a national mobilization known as the "Penguin Revolution" demanding a reform of the dictatorship's educational policies.[78] Students' street protests and school takeovers demanding the return to the old public education system as well as the prohibition of profit-making by charter schools brought President Michelle Bachelet's administration to the bargaining table.[79]

Interestingly, the Penguin Revolution and later college student movements were not exclusively poor people's movements, as some might imagine, but were led by middle-class youths who sought upward mobility through Chile's "pay-to-play" education system and who felt stymied by the debts they incurred. Upper-middle-class youths opposed to Chile's free market model also participated. Further, activists called into question the idea that education could or should function as a commodity rather than a public good. Bachelet's education minister created a commission to study the situation, which initially led to the demobilization of the protesters, though protests returned in 2008 because Bachelet's legal reforms did not address students' main demands.[80]

The 2010 election of conservative Sebastián Piñera to the presidency after twenty years of Concertación rule was equally surprising. Piñera is a billionaire whose brother wrote Chile's labor law under Pinochet and who benefited from privatizations under the junta. It seemed unlikely that after turning away from the military for two decades, voters would elect one of its most successful beneficiaries. Here, too, the middle classes played a crucial role. During the presidential campaign and in postmortem analyses, scholars noticed that many middle-class people who had supported the Concertación shifted their vote to the right. This reflected disappointment with the government's focus on antipoverty policies that did not appear to benefit the middle class. It also signaled the emergence, in Chile and throughout Latin America, of a lower-middle class that had climbed out of poverty as a result of economic growth and social spending during the 1990s and 2000s and that had adopted a meritocratic belief that economic success results from individual initiative.[81]

Piñera's administration did not bring social peace, however. In 2011, college students exploded into a sustained national mobilization that eventually led to a major reform of both K–12 and college education under the second Bachelet administration (2014–2018). In this mobilization, college students demanded the end to profit in charter schools, free college so that students could avoid crushing debt, and a new Constitution.[82] In October 2019, under Piñera's second administration, middle school students in Santiago called for a massive subway fare evasion, which led to a multi-issue national mobilization that lasted for months and forced the government to accept a late 2020 referendum on drafting a new Constitution to replace Pinochet's 1980 charter. The referendum received massive support, and Chileans elected members of a new Constitutional Assembly in May 2021.[83] That same year, leftist former student leader Gabriel Boric was elected president in a runoff election against far-right congressman José Antonio Kast, who had garnered the most votes in the first-round election. Boric's meteoric rise from a college student activist to the presidency in a single decade was both remarkable and reflective of Chile's profound political shifts.[84]

I conducted research for this book during these tumultuous changes. From 2008 to 2010, during the first Bachelet administration and the first Piñera government, I conducted interviews with middle-class adults, observed their school activities, and photographed their living rooms (more on the study design below). The interviews revealed the above historical and political processes as they intersected with the middle class: legacies of pre-1973 middle-class reformist political activism among my study participants' parents, college student activism under the dictatorship, bubbling discontent under the Bachelet administration, and political and moral divisions within the middle class. While this research was not intended to study the Penguin Revolution, nor could I have anticipated the 2011 student movement, the 2019 to 2020 social explosion, the successful Constitutional referendum, or Boric's 2021 presidential election, the tensions and conflicts I observed among my middle-class subjects reflected and anticipated those consequential political conflicts. Indeed, interviewees noted their children's participation in the Penguin Revolution, its effects on their schools, and its broader importance.

As indicated above, far from being an apolitical group in search of wealth and status, some segments of the middle class constructed their identities based on intergenerational practices of social and political activism, while others offered implicit support for the Piñera administration. While my research relied on a nonrandom sample, other scholars have demonstrated middle-class students' central role in the 2006 and 2011 student movements. Additionally, a survey during the largest protest of the 2019 social explosion found that a third of participants had college degrees, and residents of Ñuñoa and La Florida (the two communities studied) were among the top five communities participating in the protest.[85] Additionally, a representative survey conducted in late 2019 found substantial middle-class support for and participation in the protests, though most middle-class respondents rejected protesters' use of violence.[86] The concepts of identity investments and precarious privilege outlined above and my integration of asset-based, political, age cohort, and place-based approaches to studying the middle class, provide a unique and powerful *interpretation* of Chile's middle class, which reveals the *centrality* of middle classes to political conflict and change in contemporary Chile, a perspective that has only recently gained support from other researchers.[87]

The Study

This book explores the distinct identity investments of different middle-class fractions by comparing parents whose children attended Catholic and alternative schools in Ñuñoa, a traditional, urban middle-class community; and La Florida, an emerging middle-class suburb (see map and images in Figures I.5,

I.6, and I.7). The study is based on sixty-eight interviews with seventy-seven individuals (in some cases, both spouses were present); photographs of thirty-one living rooms; as well as participant observation at school social events, parent-teacher conferences, and in participants' homes (see the appendix for more details on the study's design and methodology). I studied two schools in Ñuñoa (one secular alternative and one traditional Catholic) and three in La Florida (two secular alternative and one traditional Catholic).

I studied parents in two types of schools in these communities with specific goals in mind. Examining these two communities allows us to contrast

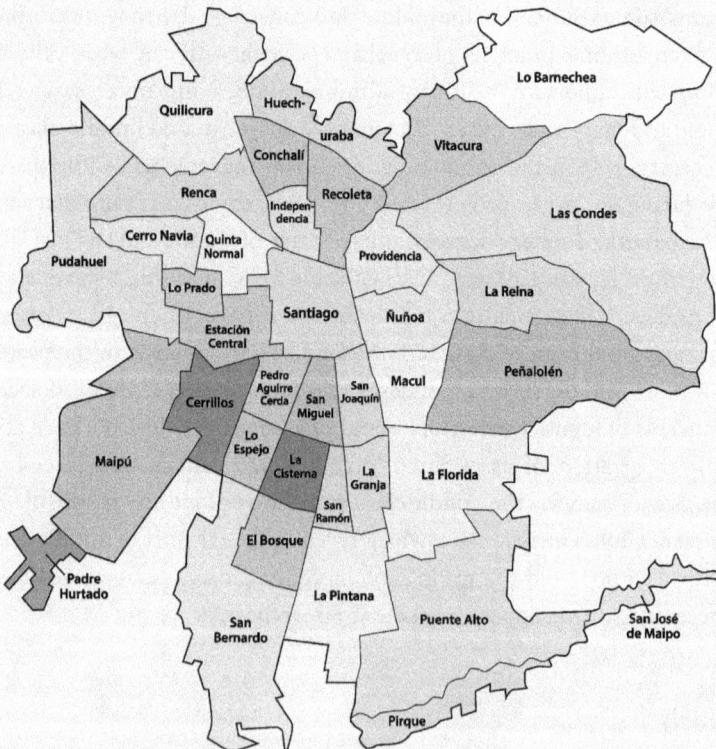

SANTIAGO DE CHILE

Figure I.5 Map of Santiago. Source: Dreamstime

Figure I.6 Photo of Plaza Ñuñoa. Source: Carlos Figueroa. Wikimedia Commons

Figure I.7 Photo of La Florida Main Plaza. Source: Farisori. Wikimedia Commons

middle-class families in an established, upper-middle-class urban area with those in an emerging, mixed-class suburban community. This comparison provides insight into how middle classes vary across distinct communities with different populations and cultural infrastructures. Second, I was interested in occupational and cultural differences among parents whose children attend secular and religious schools given church-state conflicts over education dating back to the nineteenth century in Chile.[88] Much scholarship on middle classes argues that schools are engines of social reproduction because they reward affluent children and marginalize working class or nonwhite children. Hence, focusing on schools was important for considering how school administrators and middle-class parents may hoard resources and thereby intensify economic and social segregation. In contrast, schools can be important crucibles of social change, as evident in interviewees' college activism in the 1980s and some of their children's participation in the Penguin Revolution. As is often true in qualitative research, I did not anticipate the salient differences I discovered across age cohorts, a third source of division I detected in my middle-class sample.[89]

To locate my research subjects within Chile's class structure, I draw on quantitative scholarship on social stratification in Chile as well as other qualitative studies comparing middle- and working-class research participants.[90] I classified individuals as upper-middle-class that held a college or technical degree and whose family incomes were in the top 60th to 90th percentiles of the distribution. These families had annual earnings between $30,000 and $112,000 US dollars and represent approximately 25 percent of the population.[91] In contrast, I classified individuals as lower-middle-class who had a high school diploma or technical certificate (and in a few cases a college degree) and received earnings between the 40th and 50th percentiles of the income distribution. Their annual earnings were between $12,000 and $25,000 US dollars and they represent approximately 25 percent of the population.[92] Including these two groups within the middle class allows us to compare highly paid professionals whose primary income is from employment rather than investments with a rising lower-middle class that has escaped poverty and accesses a growing range of consumer goods and educational options.[93]

I used schools as the focal point for recruiting participants to this study, though interviews examined their family, education, and work histories; processes of school choice and participation in school activities; housing choices and tastes; home decorations and daily uses of the home; as well as consumption and leisure activities. Photographs and participant observation provided additional perspectives from which to understand these families.

While I could have studied middle classes in other Santiago communities whose population characteristics were typical of "average" middle-class families (for example, those with incomes in the middle of the distribution), the advantage of qualitative studies is that they allow researchers to discover new insights rather than to identify an "average" or "typical" population. In this context, I utilized a "case logic" to iteratively develop categories based on each new interview and research site I explored.[94] My decision to highlight theoretically important contrasts across segments of the middle classes, different types of schools, and different communities proved fruitful, while also yielding unanticipated insights.

As will be evident in upcoming chapters, two of the alternative schools I selected became important focal points for participation in the Penguin Revolution, college student movement, and social explosion. Activists' progressive mindset contrasted with youngsters' and moderate Catholics' centrist and conservative views. Similarly, the contrasts between the two communities highlight how members of some segments of the middle class see the wealthy as their main rivals, while others are primarily concerned with distancing themselves from the poor.

These contrasting patterns highlight an important oversight in much of the research on middle classes in Chile: how ideological and political commitments influence adults' investments in distinct fields, and, in turn, how these investments have broader connections to national cultural and political life. I leave it to other researchers to determine whether the patterns I found are unique to these research sites or exemplars of broader phenomena, though the evidence above indicates these sites do reflect broader political trends. In this regard, qualitative research can be used to refine or rectify existing theories, like those developed by Bourdieu,[95] as well as to develop new ideas, like the concepts of identity investments and precarious privilege.[96]

This book diverges from other studies in Chile due to the specific populations I studied and the questions I asked. First, it is different from studies of conservative Catholic sects and their private schools.[97] This segment of conservative Catholics predominates among the very wealthy who have a different class habitus than that of the Catholics studied here. Additionally, the older generation studied here had experiences with a progressive Catholic church prior to the conservative shift with Pope John Paul II. They also observed progressive Catholics that shielded the dictatorship's victims and supported female agricultural workers, among other groups.[98] Similarly, the groups studied here are less prosperous than those residing in Santiago's wealthiest communities,[99] and this likely helps to explain my research participants' condition of precarious privilege and resulting criticisms of competition and materialism.

However, the divergence of my findings from these other studies does not only reflect the specific characteristics of my study participants. Most sociological research on Chile has given less attention to how historical processes influence contemporary middle classes. Additionally, very few sociological studies examine political conflict within the middle classes as well as between the middle classes and the rich and poor.[100] This oversight may reflect the influential view that since the 1990 democratic transition, most Chileans have become more individualistic and their participation in social and political organizations has declined.[101] While this view may have been sustainable during the 1990s when social protest was in decline, I do not think it helps explain the post-2006 protest cycle that included significant participation of middle-class youth and adults. Moreover, after 1990, researchers were captivated by ostensibly new trends in consumer behavior, political apathy, and lifestyles.[102] However, this focus on the novelty of post-1990 Chile overlooks the powerful stamp the pre-1973 era and the dictatorship placed on Chileans. This book unearths how biographical and political legacies are linked to contemporary identity investments.

Chapter Summaries

This study offers an interpretation of how middle-class adults' identities constructed during childhood and in school shape their identity investments in the employment, educational, housing, aesthetic, and cultural consumption markets. It further considers the implications of these decisions for their children's educational and occupational paths as well as Chile's contemporary culture and politics. Each chapter addresses a different field of consumption or investment, but all chapters are tied together through their connection to the typology of *activists, moderate Catholics, youngsters,* and *pragmatists.* The book is structured by a set of three paired chapters that each focus on a different form of investment. Chapters 1 and 2 examine families' access to economic capital via employment and home ownership. Families' possession of economic resources creates key opportunities and constraints for their capacity to invest in other markets and their relationships to other groups. Chapters 3 and 4 focus on school choice and social relationships in schools. I find that schools are a central field linking all the others as they hold the potential to provide economic stability for children in the future and are the sites of parents' most emotionally intense investments and aspirations. Chapters 5 and 6 explore families' aesthetic tastes and practices in the home and through their leisure activities. Families' aesthetic practices are powerful sites for their identity investments and also function as fields of symbolic conflict with other groups. The conclusion integrates insights from the book's substantive chapters and considers their broader implications.

In chapter 1, I explore the challenges middle-class families face due to a weakly regulated labor market. I find that many middle-class families experience precarious privilege through their employment in downgraded professions like teaching, experiences of unemployment in technical fields like engineering, limited access to high-paid employment among those with high school educations, and the gender-based employment barriers women face. Former political activists, who were highly educated, faced a slow path to stable employment due to their "high-risk activism" under the military government.[103] Finally, activists and moderate Catholics who changed careers constructed symbolic boundaries with their more competitive coworkers due to the mismatch between their educational backgrounds and current jobs. Their criticism of colleagues foreshadows their identity investments in the housing, education, and consumption fields.

In chapter 2, I examine individuals' access to housing and preferences for homes and neighborhoods. Housing access and housing taste reveal the importance of extended family as a source of capital and as central to housing choices. Identity investments are evident in families' desire to live near extended kin and to relive their childhoods through their housing choices. Depending on how they accessed housing, middle-class adults understood housing as an investment, a gift, a debt burden, a shared resource, or a source of vulnerability. Upper-middle-class families also faced constraints regarding where they could live—several families from Ñuñoa found the community unaffordable and had to migrate to neighboring communities. Within those constraints, families used the availability of amenities, a sense of place, and the presence of attractive schools as criteria for selecting communities. Finally, in Ñuñoa, activists criticized ostentatious homes and communities, and moderate Catholics avoided high density and gated communities. Pragmatists in La Florida selected housing that allowed them to evade poverty. Individuals constructed symbolic boundaries with distinct groups in the two communities based on their different class compositions. In contrast, youngsters were largely satisfied with their homes and neighborhoods. These families' construction of symbolic boundaries with gated community residents and the poor are similar to boundaries constructed in the workplace and foreshadow the development of community ties and boundaries in schools.

Chapter 3 explores school choice and parental involvement in education. I build on the literature showing how choice systems advantage middle-class families. However, I identify less-studied areas of analysis to explore identity investments in the educational field: school market variation across communities and parents' use of enrichment activities to offset educational deficiencies in their preferred schools. I first describe the choice process. Activists, moderate Catholics, and some youngsters selected schools that were not "too competitive" or "too elite," that treated children as individuals, and that reflected their political or religious values. This decision to reject elite schools shows that parents prioritized their values over maximizing their children's academic achievement or social connections that might benefit their employment opportunities. However, these parents "hedged their bets" by supplementing schoolwork with enrichment activities. Pragmatists saw schools as a platform for their children's upward mobility and hence selected schools they believed provided children with skills, networks, or status that could foster success.

This process played out differently in the two communities due to their locations and educational infrastructure. Ñuñoa families selected among a wide variety of fully private schools (which were the majority of options in the area), some of which they had attended. The presence of established schools with favorable reputations characterized the market. Activists and moderate Catholics selected schools that reflected their values while opting out of schools catering to wealthy families and elite public schools given these families' residence near wealthy communities and their previous educational experiences. In La Florida, upper-middle-class parents followed their values by selecting charter schools (the majority in the community), while avoiding expensive private schools they saw as academically deficient. In contrast, pragmatists selected charter schools they believed protected them from "polluting" contact with the poor.

Chapter 4 explores how schools functioned as communities and sites of intense symbolic conflict. Activists and moderate Catholics were intensely involved in the three most class-homogeneous schools; all groups had more distant ties to the two mixed-class schools. Symbolic conflicts were present in all five schools studied. Activists complained about youngsters' conservatism, materialism, and lack of intellectual curiosity. Moderate Catholics criticized youngsters as ill-mannered, materialistic, and unwilling to participate in school affairs. In contrast, some youngsters found alternative and Catholic schools disorganized and believed that school authorities ignored bullying. Pragmatists felt excluded by upper-middle-class parents and complained about their micro-aggressions while simultaneously distancing themselves from the poor. These patterns played out differently in each school reflecting their unique characteristics. These symbolic conflicts illustrate how group identities are activated within schools as individuals contrast themselves with stigmatized "others."

Second, in contrast to many scholars' view of "against the grain choosers"[104] as ultimately self-centered, middle-class parents, this chapter shows how activists engaged in political mobilization in their children's schools, while moderate Catholics participated in social action with the poor. Additionally, some activists encouraged their children's participation in student movements. Two of the schools studied produced national leaders in student organizations. Hence, parents steeped in activist or progressive subcultures do engage in collective action directed toward greater social equity. Youngsters and pragmatists criticized student activism, highlighting polarization within schools related to the student movement.

Chapter 5 explores identity investments in home decorations through which middle-class adults represent their core values and social connections. I found three patterns of aesthetic taste. Middle-class families displayed a *common aesthetic* focused on handmade wood furniture, family heirlooms, and practical decorations that satisfied children's needs. This common aesthetic reveals how homes operate within a gift economy. In contrast, each middle-class group also displayed a distinct set of tastes based on individuals' identity investments: moderate Catholics had traditional, religious tastes; activists displayed progressive, cosmopolitan tastes; youngsters preferred genre-spanning decorations; and pragmatists displayed a DIY aesthetic. Third, families participated in a *shared discursive field* in which they alternately expressed distastes for minimalist and "gawdy" decoration, while sharing an anti-consumption discourse criticizing materialism and ostentation.

Chapter 6 examines identity investments in cultural consumption and leisure activities. Here, too, we found three distinct patterns. Middle-class families shared common practices: time and financial constraints limited their access to live performances, they preferred educational consumption activities, and they criticized morally suspect "ostentatious" consumption. In contrast, each group's identity investments took a distinct form through their leisure activities. Activists displayed omnivorous tastes with an accent on art film, diverse musical styles, and attendance at public performances. They were especially passionate about *nueva canción* (New Song) artists who play "anti–status quo, politically purposed" music[105] reflecting their political identities. Moderate Catholics' focus on ethical behavior guided their preferences for commercial family films, religious-themed travel, and family- or school-centered activities. They were less interested in visual arts than in using cultural activity to broaden their children's education. Youngsters attended museums and local public performances, but otherwise did not express strong aesthetic tastes. Pragmatists, in contrast, had more limited engagement with cultural consumption and spent much of their free time participating in family activities like barbecues or watching television.

Importantly, cultural consumption varied by location, with those living in Ñuñoa and other centrally located municipalities adopting an urban pattern of leisure activities, including public cultural consumption. They also criticized shopping malls as vulgar, commercialized environments. Those living in La Florida evidenced a suburban pattern of "ordinary consumption,"[106] watched films and browsed for books in shopping centers, and visited with family in or near their homes. They also attended contemporary pop music concerts with their children rather than enjoying the "niche" styles Ñuñoa residents preferred. Finally, Ñuñoa activists participated in local social movements, while La Florida residents had low levels of neighborhood participation, reflecting a widespread fear of crime in that community.

The conclusion synthesizes the book's findings on middle-class identities, strategies, and tastes in the employment, education, housing, home decoration, and cultural consumption fields; considers the study's contributions to comparative analyses of middle classes; and examines Chile's current political environment. I consider how the patterns of identity investment and precarious privilege I observed in the Chilean middle class are similar to or different from findings on middle classes in other national settings and hypothesize about possible explanations of these patterns with the goal of advancing comparative knowledge of middle classes beyond Chile. Additionally, I point to the implications of the split between activists, moderate Catholics, youngsters, and pragmatists for the rise of the student movement and social explosion as well as the election of conservative President Piñera in 2010 and 2018. I also highlight how the activists', moderate Catholics', youngsters,' and pragmatists' identity investments reveal dissent from the opportunity hoarding practices so often associated with middle-class Chileans.

1   Perilous Pathways to Middle-Class Employment

MARIO HOPED TO BECOME a history teacher when he attended college during the dictatorship. However, he was expelled due to his political activism and subsequently worked for the Communist Party. "I was getting paid a pittance, but I was happy [*laughs*]!"[1] After the democratic transition, he returned to college to study computer science and got a job working for a government ministry. While he and his wife, a local education official, earn comfortable salaries, he struggles to get along with his coworkers whom he finds conformist and materialistic. Like others I interviewed, Mario's educational and work experiences are central to this book's broader argument because they influence his identity investments in the four fields explored in later chapters.

Let us first contextualize Mario's experiences within broader changes in Chile's job structure during the last three decades. While the Chilean middle class has grown alongside declines in poverty and income inequality,[2] approximately one-sixth of middle-class families risk falling into poverty.[3] Further, middle-class employment has become increasingly fragile in the 2000s, following the 1998 Asian financial crisis, the 2007–2009 mortgage crisis, and most importantly the COVID-19 pandemic. Additionally, in the 2000s and 2010s, income growth was more modest, and unemployment began to grow.[4] In this context, this chapter explores individuals' career pathways and experiences on the job market.

Middle-class identity investments often reflected childhood experiences and relationships developed in college. This chapter primarily explores individuals' labor market experiences, but also examines how early life and college experiences shaped individuals' identities, social networks, and preferences for their children's schools. Additionally, I examine how middle-class adults navigate a labor market with weak job protections.[5] Upper- and lower-middle-class individuals I interviewed had to adapt to the downgrading of specific professions, retool to pursue a second career, shift from a stable job to freelancing, or face unemployment. This was true even for those that received degrees at prestigious institutions. Additionally, women face barriers to occupational success based on segmented labor markets, the wage gap, patriarchal beliefs, and inadequate financial support for single mothers.

In addition to these labor market patterns, this chapter also explores how individuals' political experiences as children and young adults influenced their job trajectories. Those that engaged in "high-risk activism" during the dictatorship faced barriers completing college and entering their careers during Chile's dictatorship (1973–1990) and often risk unemployment today when working as government subcontractors. Activists' identity investments in party activism had long-term consequences for their career pathways.[6] Most scholarship on the middle classes examines how political activists opt-in to specific professions. In contrast, this chapter follows social movement research showing the biographical consequences of high-risk activism for individuals' careers and family life. Chile's dictatorship played a pivotal role in activists' career trajectories.

Finally, individuals' successful adaptation to new careers led them to clash with coworkers in work settings with unfamiliar occupational cultures. Activists and moderate Catholics that switched careers experienced hysteresis[7] in the workplace as their educational, professional, and ideological identities clashed with their competitive coworkers' ambitions and attitudes. Consequently, these individuals were unable to "use culture for coordination"[8]—they struggled to find common themes of conversation with coworkers that could make work more appealing and create opportunities for upward mobility. Those that changed careers, therefore, tend to *disidentify* with work and focus their identity investments on their children's education, their homes, and their leisure pursuits—fields explored in subsequent chapters. In contrast, youngsters had more stable career paths and did identify with their jobs but were less emotionally engaged in their nonwork lives. Finally, pragmatists saw work in instrumental terms, in part because of its chronic instability or negative effects on physical and mental health. Pragmatists' identity investments focused on their extended kin groups and their children's academic success. Through this chapter, we begin to see how experiences in the family, school, and in the workplace shape the character and settings for identity investments and how these investments are consequential for cultural fissures within the middle classes.

Educational and Career Pathways

Most of the activists, moderate Catholics, and youngsters interviewed in this book were successful professionals earning salaries that placed them in the top two quintiles of income earners. Pragmatists struggled more on the labor market but were able to avoid poverty as adults. However, many of the upper-middle-class individuals I interviewed developed a vocation for professional and public service by observing their parents or through their college experiences. Many adults did not work in their area of study, but their professional vocation was largely shaped prior to entering the labor market. Their identity investments emerged from family and educational experiences rather than through their current occupations.

Before exploring these issues, let us briefly examine the broader context for these career pathways. Scholarship on Chile has traced the evolution of the middle class since the 1970s when it was composed of public and private sector professionals and small business owners.[9] After the military regime's (1973–1990) economic opening led to a financial crisis in the early 1980s, the country entered a long period of economic growth punctuated by two brief downturns in the late 1990s and in 2009.[10] Analysts have explored the implications of Chile's sustained growth and pervasive income inequality for the changing characteristics of its middle classes.

A study relying on 2001 data showed that Chile's occupational structure exhibited closure at the top but considerable short-distance mobility opportunities from farming into clerical jobs, yielding an "unequal but fluid" occupational structure.[11] A subsequent study compared 2001 and 2009 data and found that in the latter period, there was little mobility out of the farm sector or into high-paid professional occupations, suggesting that social mobility had become less fluid than the earlier analysis indicated.[12] Others find that during the 1990s and 2000s, sustained economic growth pulled many Latin Americans out of poverty into small business and clerical occupations.[13] Finally, research finds that in spite of two decades of persistent inequality, from 2003 to 2015 the country's Gini coefficient (that measures income inequality) had declined moderately,[14] though the COVID-19 pandemic erased many of these gains.[15] Chileans experience considerable job instability. Studies of middle-class vulnerability find that about 16 percent of middle-class families sank into poverty between 2001 and 2015. Factors that could trigger downward mobility include the high costs of healthcare or college tuition, accidents causing chronic disability, or unemployment.[16] Thus, the middle class experienced significant expansion during the 1990s, but during the 2000s, segments of this class increasingly risked downward mobility due to weak job and social protections.

Education

Many of the activists and moderate Catholics I interviewed who were Santiago natives attended elite public high schools:[17] public schools in affluent municipalities like Las Condes or Vitacura; or high-performing private schools like El Hispanoamericano, Calasanz, or Redlands. In several cases, multiple generations attended schools like Calasanz and Manuel de Salas (see chapter 3). Many of those hailing from the provinces attended elite public schools or private Catholic schools in their place of origin. Both groups described above graduated from elite universities like the Catholic University, the University of Chile, the University of Santiago (USACH), or regional branch campuses of these universities. Some attended technical schools and achieved economic and career success. This outcome may reflect the fact that these fields tend to favor technical skills over family-inculcated cultural capital and soft skills.[18]

Activists often looked to their parents' careers and political participation, as well as their own educational experiences, as important guides for their adult identities. Ricardo, a judge and former history teacher, comments, "There was a weird tradition at the National Institute with the recess monitors (*inspectores de patio*). They were all college students from the provinces, but the school fed and housed them in exchange for their working some shifts. My dad was studying law and Patricio Aylwin, a teacher that was elected senator [he became president in 1990], said to my dad, 'Francisco, you understand law, why don't you take over my classes?' He stayed there, got a teaching degree, and eventually became vice principal. He was fired after the coup, but we lived on campus while he was vice principal."[19] Thus, Ricardo, who began his career as an educator, absorbed the ethos of the top boys' high school in Chile through his father's employment and residence there.

Others built important social ties in college that influenced their political participation and subsequent educational decisions for their children. Clara, whose father was a Communist activist, remarks, "My whole family went to the University of Chile so it was weird for me to study theater at the Catholic University. I was an atheist. I met Víctor [another activist] there, and I found my footing participating in political activism, which I had begun in high school."[20] Clara and Víctor would later send their children to the same school. Aniluap studied advertising at the University of Santiago: "A couple of my classmates studied at Manuel de Salas and they told me their school was marvelous, they shared their experiences, and commented that they still get together with their high school friends. That's why I sent my daughter there."[21] Thus, college was an important setting for constructing a professional identity as well as developing social networks that influenced decisions later in life.

Moderate Catholics learned guidelines for ethical conduct and found role models through the Catholic schools they attended. Marcelo, a pharmaceuticals salesman and former teacher, remarks, "The school lets the custodial staff's children study there for free. I remember a classmate was the son of one of the cooks that prepared food for the priests that lived on campus. That's super important for me."[22] Dany, a former special education teacher, comments, "I like Catholic schools because their educational model is personalized and focuses on values."[23] These early experiences were important for activists and moderate Catholics both because they clashed with the workplace environments they encountered and because they informed their identity investments in other fields.

Youngsters experienced an upwardly mobile educational trajectory. They attended a mix of elite and middle-tier universities, as well as junior colleges, and enjoyed employment stability in technical fields, education, and human services. To illustrate, Rafael, a youngster who works in educational evaluation, comments, "I attended the National Institute and then received a sociology degree at the Catholic University. Coming from Lo Prado [a low-income community in western Santiago], it was a huge leap to make it into the Catholic University!"[24] Nelson, an accountant, recalls with pride that "I started at the Technical Metropolitan University but then got a high score on the college entrance exam and transferred to the University of Santiago."[25] Youngsters did not have strong affective ties to their high schools or colleges and often had a more credential-oriented view of education as a means to well-paid employment.

In contrast, most pragmatists had high school diplomas and less market-able technical certificates (e.g., secretarial) or attended lower tier universities like the Central University or Cardenal Raúl Silva Henríquez University. Some attended the elite high schools noted above, while others went to local public schools.

Pragmatists were unable to use an elite high school education as a plat-form to attend an elite college and enjoy a high-paying career. Iván, who grew up in a working-class family, attended middle school at the National Insti-tute, but "I had played soccer in the youth league for a professional sports team. The demands of school weren't compatible with sports training, and my grades suffered. I begged my parents to remove me from the school so I could play soccer, and they sent me to a local public high school."[26] His working-class background may have influenced his decision to prioritize sports over academic achievement, and his departure from the National Institute likely limited his chances of attending a more prestigious university.[27]

Several women from working- or lower-middle-class backgrounds at-tended elite high schools (El Liceo #1 de Niñas, Carmela Carvajal) but never completed college. They pursued technical certificates after attending these se-lective schools. For example, Pamela, a pragmatist who works in a call center, became pregnant and married in high school. After her marital separation, "I got a certificate as an executive bilingual secretary because I needed to get a credential quickly so I could make money."[28] She later attended college but was unable to complete her degree due to work and parenting responsibilities. Child-rearing often pulls Chilean women out of the labor market and restricts their wages and employment opportunities once they return to work, as detailed below.[29]

Teaching

We now move from these broad differences in how individuals' family and ed-ucational backgrounds influenced their adult identities to examine how career pathways varied across occupations. Several of the individuals in the sample were trained as teachers. For a few, teaching served as their primary career. In two cases, teaching offered financial advantages because these individu-als' children attended the school where they teach so they received a tuition reduction. However, several of the teachers found the occupation paid poorly and ended up pursuing different careers. This reflects the downgrading of teachers' salaries and benefits under the dictatorship.[30] However, democratic governments increased investment in public education so that salaries began to rise after 1990.[31]

Some teachers made a successful career switch to a better paying field. Although this pathway provided financial security for their families, it often caused emotional distress because they were unable to pursue their vocation, and they often clashed with coworkers, as explored in this chapter's final section. Several physical education teachers changed careers. As Marcelo, a graduate of the University of Chile, comments, "I got a degree in physical education and was halfway through a second degree in physical therapy. My wife was pregnant and expecting twins, so I needed to find a job right away. Since I had some biological training, it was pretty easy to get a job at Merck." Others found relatively low-paying or low-status alternatives. Morgana, an activist who was trained in physical education at the University of Chile, left teaching children to become a part-time adult educator and freelance instructor.[32] Elba was an early childhood educator who tired of the sexual abuse cases she observed and denounced in her workplaces. She also needed to earn more money, so she became a school bus driver.[33]

Others, particularly history teachers, decided to earn a second degree. Ricardo is a graduate of the Catholic University. He remarks, "When I started teaching, the pay was shit—skilled manufacturing workers earned more. While I worked, I pursued a law degree, and a friend told me about a short course to become a judge. I got a job in Valdivia [in southern Chile] shortly afterward." Ricardo's social networks afforded him an opportunity that led to greater job stability and a substantial salary increase. Israel, a Teacher's College (formerly part of the University of Chile) graduate who had been a college political activist, worked for twenty years as a history teacher. He later completed an MA and now works as an urban planning consultant.[34] Víctor, an activist, has degrees in teaching and journalism from the Catholic University and worked as a history teacher for several years. He later pursued a journalism career as an adjunct college instructor and radio employee. He eventually lost his radio job and did freelance work acquired via friends.[35] While none of these teachers experienced unemployment per se, the limited financial and personal rewards of teaching led them to pursue other careers, sometimes after earning a second degree. This reflects the occupational downgrading of teaching, which had been a core occupation within the middle classes during much of the twentieth century.[36]

Without a second degree or studies in a different field, a shift from teaching to another career was a risky proposition. Iván tired of teaching and moved to sales in Herbalife, a multilevel marketing company: "I wanted to give my all to teaching but faced a lot of bureaucratic obstacles. I became a union leader to try to make changes and nothing happened. Then a friend invited me to sell for Herbalife since I was disillusioned with the teaching profession. I knew the business model and the product so I decided to build my own business." Iván saw direct sales as a viable alternative to teaching, and yet it still earned him a modest income. He lacked the business training or social networks (he lived in a working-class settlement) that could provide him with more lucrative opportunities. As outlined in the final section, he had ambitious plans to build another business, but it was unclear whether these plans would succeed.

Liberal and Technical Professions

Liberal professions (medicine, law, accounting) and technical fields (engineering, computer science, finance) are perceived as economically secure, and several moderate Catholics and youngsters in these fields enjoyed prosperous careers. For example, Nelson describes his upward professional trajectory: "I'm an accountant and started out with taxes. I then moved on to audits and have worked for several international accounting firms. I later worked for a national business group on reporting and investments and was recruited back to my original accounting firm. They moved me from auditing to consulting where I am developing a specialization." Doctors, lawyers, and financial analysts had similar experiences.

However, several information technology professionals experienced long periods of unemployment. This likely reflects weak employment protections in Chile that lead one-third of employees to change jobs each year.[37] Carola, an activist and freelance physical education instructor, is married to a computer engineer. She explains that her husband experienced several extended bouts of unemployment, the most recent one for eight months. She comments, "It's been kind of tough, but I think that now we're finally more stable and will be financially better off."[38] Romina, a moderate Catholic and housewife with a computer degree, is married to a computer engineer: "He has been unemployed for four months and he is in the process of founding his own business in Talca [about three hours south of Santiago]. My heart is in Talca, but I know that the educational opportunities are better here."[39] These examples point to the fragility of jobs in technical fields. While none of the upper-middle-class individuals I interviewed fell into poverty, they had to adapt to the unpredictable disruptions of short- to medium-term unemployment.

Lower Tier Service Occupations

Several women in communications or clerical occupations experienced job instability or periods of unemployment because they occupied precarious niches of the labor market. Aniluap, an activist who holds an advertising degree from the University of Santiago, works as a freelance web designer, but she is poorly paid and her income is sporadic. She is a single mother who lives in her aunt's apartment. Nelly had been unemployed for two years when I interviewed her and tried to make ends meet by selling used goods in street markets. "I took early retirement which gives me a small pension. I've looked everywhere for work, but I think because of my age [fifty-nine] no one wants to hire me."[40] These individuals risked falling from the lower-middle class into the "vulnerable" stratum—those making $4–10 per capita daily. While economists argue that middle-class people have a 10 percent chance of falling into poverty, some in this sample were at risk of falling into a vulnerable income bracket and relied on family connections or early retirement to make ends meet. Additionally, precariously employed college graduates like Aniluap experience status inconsistency in that their incomes are not commensurate with their education.[41] The experiences of these educators, liberal and technical professionals, and routine service workers highlight the fragile financial position of many middle-class families during the 2000s.[42]

Gender and Income Earning

Women experienced several barriers to garnering high earnings at jobs and also assumed caregiving responsibilities that led them to leave the labor market. Some moderate Catholic women began careers in high-paying fields like law and computer programming but chose to leave paid work to care for children, reflecting traditional beliefs about gender roles and distrust of paid childcare providers. Additionally, some women, even those with college educations, selected female-coded occupations—such as secretary, physical therapist, early childhood educator, and teacher—that pay less than male-coded jobs. Several women worked as freelancers, which allowed them to combine their caregiving responsibilities with employment, based on the assumption that women are the primary caregivers and that men are the breadwinners. Finally, single mothers struggled to make ends meet. Because women normally received custody after a separation or divorce, they relied on their ex-husbands to provide child support payments. However, with few exceptions, these payments were exceedingly small, so many single mothers experienced declining incomes. Women's absences from the labor market to care for children—based on the high cost of daycare or their preference to stay at home—limited their earning opportunities and financial independence.

These patterns reflect broad trends of gender inequality in Chile's labor market. Women's workforce participation began to increase in the mid-1980s to reach its current level of over 50 percent, which is still low compared to similar Latin American countries.[43] Women face a wage gap and segregated occupations.[44] Nonetheless, declining fertility rates beginning in the 1960s yielded a "demographic bonus" to dual-earner couples as rising wages could be spent on the needs of smaller families. In 2006, approximately 22 percent of children lived in female-headed households. By 2017, 42 percent of households were headed by women. Single-parent households faced a greater risk of falling into poverty during the period under study.[45]

Some professionally successful women chose to leave the labor market after giving birth. In some cases, this reflected health concerns for their children. Claudia, a moderate Catholic and former attorney, comments, "I worked for eight years at a law firm until I had my first child. I tried to enroll her in preschool when she was four, but they demanded a medical certificate to accept her. Since she had severe reflux with vomiting, none would allow her to enroll."[46]

Some women preferred to care for their own children rather than entrust them to domestic employees or childcare professionals. Patricia, a moderate Catholic and businessman's personal assistant, comments, "I put the house in order before I leave in the morning, work part time, and then bring my flash drive home to finish up. I can have lunch with my kids after school. I had bad experiences with domestic employees who ignored my children, so I prefer not to hire one."[47] Claudia and Patricia were both successful women with high earning prospects who accepted their default role as caregivers rather than turning to their spouses or paid caregivers for support, thereby losing potential earning opportunities.[48]

Several women in the sample selected traditionally feminine occupations. For example, two moderate Catholics became physical therapists. Others earned degrees in early childhood education or secretarial certificates. These latter credentials did not offer women well-paid, stable employment. Paulina, a pragmatist with a secretarial certificate, remarks: "I worked twelve years as a secretary and in accounting in a large holding company, and then seven years in banking. When the banking industry had trouble, I left and have not returned."[49] In Chile as in the U.S., female-coded occupations have lower average earnings and are less prestigious than male-coded occupations.[50] While this choice was not inherently problematic if a husband earned an adequate salary to maintain the family, for those women who separated or divorced, becoming a single mother with a low income generated considerable economic vulnerability.

Single mothers devised different strategies to adapt to limited incomes. Marcela, who completed high school and worked as a truck driver delivering produce, comments, "I wanted to have my own home so that I didn't have to worry about paying it off. I inherited some money from my uncle and bought a house I could afford. That put me at ease."[51] Others pooled incomes with family members. Alejandra, a pragmatist, and part-time school custodian, combines incomes with her mother and sister. They all live in the family home, and their brother stays with them on the weekends.[52] Juanita, an activist and government-employed agronomist, earns a relatively high salary, but her son attends an expensive private school and she receives a small child support payment: "My ex-husband left me when my son was eight months old. He has deposited $150 a month in my account for the last three years. There hasn't been a cost of living adjustment [laughs]. I'm an atypical consumer. I buy shoes on clearance at the end of the season. I'm very austere."[53] Rossana, a retail clerk, worked several sales jobs with flexible hours because she could not afford to pay for daycare: "I sold Tupperware for a while, and when I went to parties to sell products I left my daughter with my mother-in-law."[54] These examples illustrate the income reductions and financial challenges single mothers face.

High-Risk Activism and Employment

The preceding two sections explored how individuals move into jobs and professions. In this section, we explore how activists' political participation under the dictatorship affected their long-term employment paths. This section builds on robust scholarship on the political orientations of professionals. Gouldner argued that intellectuals tend to be politically progressive due to the culture of critical discourse present in higher education and their desire for greater power in relation to business owners.[55] Other scholars make more limited claims, arguing that professionals tend to be more liberal than managers or small business owners in spite of their privileged economic position,[56] only a subset of professionals (social and cultural workers as well as public and nonprofit employees) are liberal,[57] or that politically progressive individuals opt-in to public service and creative occupations.[58]

Like these authors, this study finds considerable diversity in political viewpoints across occupations. However, I am here interested in how individuals' participation in "high-risk activism" under the dictatorship influenced their career trajectories. Doug McAdam developed the concept of "high risk/cost activism" to understand why young adults participated in "freedom summer" during the U.S. Civil Rights Movement given the high likelihood that their involvement would lead to bodily harm or death. He found that participants were enmeshed in interpersonal and activist networks prior to joining the campaign.[59] Mara Loveman's study of human rights activism in South America during the 1970s found similar patterns.[60] McAdam did a follow-up study on the effects of high-risk activism on participants' adult lives. There, he found that participation in the movement was transformative and led these individuals to pursue "activist careers" that translated into lower earnings, and that they married later in life or not at all.[61]

The findings on recruitment into high-risk activism and the consequences of participation for individuals' careers dovetail with this book's focus on identity investments. Several activists had parents that were party militants, became deeply committed to political struggle while in college under the dictatorship, and faced difficulties on the job market as a result. They also maintained their political commitments throughout their adult lives. Activists' political affiliation in some cases resulted in their expulsion from college and the need to pursue a second career, an extended period in college due to their focus on political activism, or later access to government jobs under elected center-left administrations after the 1990 return to democracy. However, these government jobs could be double-edged swords: because these individuals were normally hired as independent contractors without job security, when the party coalition in power lost at the polls, they were likely to lose their position and be forced into private sector work. I explore each of these scenarios below.

As noted at the beginning of this chapter, Mario began studying history at the Catholic University of Valparaíso. Even before his entry to college, his father's activism in the Communist Party affected his education: "My dad was imprisoned and disappeared from 1973 to 1976 . . . After his release, he worked as a physician at the Solidarity Vicariate [church human rights initiative] because he couldn't get work elsewhere. He wanted me to go to the National Institute, but it was too dangerous. We had to live in safe houses for a while. He told a priest who was his psychiatric patient about my situation, and the priest enrolled me in Saint Ignatius School [a Jesuit high school]." Thus, his father's activism harshly affected Mario's life as a teen. He would later follow in his father's footsteps: "I was a clandestine activist under the dictatorship. I was expelled for being a student leader. Afterwards, I had the opportunity to do political work with the Communist Party. I received a pittance, but I was happy [*laughs*]! In the 1990s under democracy, I decided to get a computer degree. I worked and studied at the same time. I am now working in the Finance Ministry and have been there ten years." While Mario currently earns a high salary, his experience demonstrates how political repression under the dictatorship made it dangerous for activists' children to attend school and prevented some student activists from receiving degrees, which affected their earnings over time. It also shows how party membership can today be an advantage for individuals seeking government employment.

Israel provides a different angle on this issue. He was a clandestine activist in the Movement of the Revolutionary Left (MIR), a far left party, as a college student. He refers to how his activism impacted the quality of his education and professional progress: "I was a serious party militant but I had to satisfy my parents' working-class expectations. I was the only one of thirty or forty activists in my class that finished the major I began. I only worked two of my first five years out of school; I dedicated the other three to party work. So, I really sacrificed a lot." Israel points to his working-class parents' demands for his professional success,[62] lost wages due to limited early labor force participation, inability to focus on his studies because of his political involvement, and a reduced income early in his career. While he now earns a comfortable salary, he sacrificed his early years in the labor market due to his political commitment.

Luis, an architect, delayed completing his degree because he focused on activism. Because of his comfortable background (his father was a dentist and professor), he did not feel the same pressures to complete his degree as did Tamara, his wife, who came from a working-class family:

Luis: I got my degree later in life. In college, I was busy with other things. We were installing sewers in squatter settlements and organizing volunteer brigades. Then, I entered the workforce and finished college later. I subordinated my personal situation to my social commitments.

Tamara: I might go to a protest, but I couldn't miss any exams. If I was expelled, I wasn't going to become a professional. I knew it was my only chance to graduate—I had to finish or I was screwed. Luis could have his existential crises and change majors. He wasn't afraid of the consequences.

Luis: My financial needs were taken care of.[63]

In this exchange, Luis and Tamara further illustrate the different circumstances of affluent and working-class college students. Affluent students faced lower financial risks resulting from their activism, while working-class students felt compelled to focus on their studies.

A parent's repression under the dictatorship could also affect college plans and occupational paths. Clara describes why she studied psychology after receiving a degree in theater: "I finished my acting degree in 1991. The next year the Rettig Human Rights Report was issued, and because of my father's disappearance, I received a scholarship and pursued a second degree in psychology . . . I separated from my ex-husband at the same time. So, I faced reality and gave up the idea of an acting career." Clara's career change in part reflects some of the challenges teachers faced, as noted above, but it also highlights her personal loss and subsequent policies designed to make amends to the children of the dictatorship's victims.

A third issue refers to the double-edged sword of employment in the public sector. Several upper-middle-class individuals worked in government ministries and had been hired in part due to their political connections. In many cases, administrations hire individuals as independent contractors rather than civil servants to reduce benefits costs and because many civil service jobs are filled by lifelong employees. Once the party coalition in power loses an election, it is very likely they will be dismissed.[64] In this context, Luis was employed in the Ministry of Public Works when I interviewed him. After our interview and Piñera's 2010 presidential election, he told me he had been dismissed and had set up a private consulting business. Thus, these jobs are well paid but lack job security or health and retirement benefits.

This discussion highlights the long-term consequences of high-risk activism for individuals' careers. Under the dictatorship, student activists faced expulsion, lost earnings, and had errant career pathways. Moreover, the children of political activists, in addition to the trauma they experienced due to their parents' suffering, sometimes changed careers when they received compensation under democracy for past human rights abuses. Finally, long-term party activists could parlay their loyalty into public employment, though this came with a catch—jobs could vanish once the administration in power left office. As we shall see in upcoming chapters, political participation under the dictatorship was a key influence on activists' identity investments in other fields with important implications for contemporary Chilean politics.

Symbolic Boundaries in the Workplace

Activists' and moderate Catholics' ideological commitments developed through the family and in college led to clashes with coworkers when they moved into a second career. In this context, Lamont analyzed the workplace as an important site in which upper-middle-class men construct symbolic boundaries with coworkers they view as immoral, social climbers, or dishonest.[65] Similarly, this section illustrates the emotional and cultural struggles activists and moderate Catholics experience in the workplace. Because of their family socialization and education in an earlier era that preceded Chile's wave of market-based growth beginning in the 1980s, they struggle with their coworkers' competitive attitudes and practices. In contrast, I argue that youngsters express satisfaction with their work settings because they did not switch careers nor do they have an earlier cultural "baseline" with which to contrast their current experiences. Pragmatists express resignation about their vulnerability to unemployment or, in a few cases, hope to gain upward mobility through entrepreneurial pursuits.

To understand these different responses to Chile's dynamic workplaces that offer little job security, it is helpful to refer to two concepts. Bourdieu uses the term *hysteresis* to describe adults that confront situations that contradict their childhood habitus.[66] Here, I would add that these workplace situations also contradict some individuals' *occupational habitus* developed through college and early career experiences. The idea of occupational habitus reflects the argument that specific college majors seek distinct qualities in students and those students, in turn, opt-in to those fields.[67] This observation builds on the discussion in the previous section about the political attitudes of professionals. It complements the view that individuals "self-select" into specific careers, and those occupations foster workplace cultures that reinforce distinctive professional identities.[68]

A second useful idea comes from Erickson's study of culture and social networks in private sector firms. She argues that firms more commonly reward cultural knowledge gained on the job or through diverse social networks than high culture accrued through the family or the educational system. Specifically, men gain influence in firms by talking about sports because this is a "least common denominator" that crosses class lines. Sports talk allows men to use culture for "coordination," offering a common ground among men within different strata in an organization.[69]

Activists and moderate Catholics that experience hysteresis in the workplace lack the "coordinating culture" that could potentially benefit them at work. They do not want to talk to their coworkers about "mundane" topics and are horrified by their peers' competitive zeal. In contrast, youngsters do not feel alienated by their workplaces because their job environments do not contrast with their family or educational experiences. Finally, pragmatists face the more immediate challenges of paying their bills in an unforgiving labor market, so they are unconcerned with fulfillment at work. A few hope to pursue entrepreneurial ventures, though these seem difficult to achieve. The hysteresis activists and moderate Catholics feel in the workplace reflects their ideological allegiances, and it in part explains their stronger identity investments in other fields.

Hysteresis among Activists and Moderate Catholics

Several activists and moderate Catholics that enjoyed successful second careers had negative experiences with coworkers that clashed with their ideological sympathies. Marcelo, who moved from teaching to sales, comments: "My coworkers emphasize a person's IQ—cognitive skills, studying, getting a business degree—rather than their emotional intelligence . . . They have serious difficulties socializing . . . They are worried about climbing the ladder, running around in life to earn a few thousand more dollars . . . These arrogant, aggressive people want to step on you. I can't stand them—the lack of respect." Marcelo comes from an affluent family, but chose to become a teacher. He moved to pharmaceutical sales for financial reasons, but the fierce competition among his peers collides with his strong sense of moral purpose, belief in the importance of building meaningful relationships, and desire to prioritize spiritual growth over material success.

Ingrid is from the older cohort and is positioned in between the activist and moderate Catholic groups (her son attends an alternative school, but she also expresses religious beliefs). She works in visual merchandising for a clothing firm and describes frustrations similar to Marcelo's: "It really bothers me how some people at work try to get ahead by putting down their colleagues. In the past, we didn't have email. So, if I needed to tell you something, I had to call you on the phone. So, now, if we agree to something over the phone, and it doesn't work out, some people are so nasty that they claim I never called them because there is no email to prove it. Whatever happened to values?"[70] Like Marcelo, Ingrid addresses themes of competition, social climbing, and ambition, but she also raises additional issues. Technological change lends itself to dishonesty and conflict but also replaces the earlier concepts of honor and trust based on face-to-face interactions in which each party expects the other to keep their word.

Several activists who were former teachers that work in government jobs expressed a strong sense of alienation from their coworkers. Ricardo comments: "My colleagues think they're special. I believe being a judge is about problem solving, and the law is a tool to achieve that. My colleagues look at it from a distance with conservative opinions and a very dismissive attitude. They have no interest in fiction. I can only talk about novels with a small group of social workers, technical assistants, and psychologists." Ricardo here identifies cultural differences based on age, political orientation, and profession. His background as a history teacher and a left-wing activist places him at odds with his younger colleagues. Later in this exchange, he explains that these differences cause him considerable stress. His experience of hysteresis and inability to engage in "cultural coordination" with his peers are palpable.

Mario offers a similar observation: "I work in the Finance Ministry and it's 'so not me.' Everyone wants to be part of the mainstream [seguir la norma]. We don't go to the movies that much, but we do go sometimes or attend gatherings. They never do any cultural activity. Their only leisure activity is shopping; otherwise, they shut themselves inside their houses." Mario notes a similar sense of alienation from his colleagues as did Ricardo regarding their lack of interest in film or reading. Additionally, he finds that they have no interest in social interaction outside the workplace. Marcelo and Ingrid reacted to competition, hostility, as well as the lack of trust and emotional connections in the private sector. In contrast, Ricardo and Mario emphasize their public sector colleagues' authoritarian attitudes, lack of intellectual curiosity, and disinterest in socializing. Both groups perceive work as devoid of authentic human connection.

Some activists did not describe a hostile work environment but were aware of strong status boundaries separating them from their coworkers. Alicia, a health researcher, describes her workplace: "Where I work at the Universidad del Desarrollo, everyone knows everyone. It's a closed social circle that outsiders have a hard time entering. The people are really posh [*son super cuicos*], they all live up in the wealthy suburbs and rarely come down to Santiago. I've known everyone for a long time there, but there's no way I'd ever get a supervisory position because they know what I'm like and how I think."[71] Unlike Mario and Ricardo, Alicia does not chafe at her coworkers' aggressive competition. Rather, she points to her position as an outsider among coworkers hailing from the upper class. However, in addition to her class and status differences with her colleagues, she also points to their political differences by noting that "how she thinks" prevents her advancement. Thus, her political commitments separate her from her coworkers, much like Ricardo and Mario.

Alicia's astute observation merits a brief digression because it anticipates an intense public debate that occurred just two months after the interview. The issues raised in the debate were surely "in the air" when we spoke. In January 2009, Father Felipe Berríos, a Catholic priest that led a volunteer agency, Un Techo para Chile (A Roof for Chile), wrote an opinion editorial in the conservative *El Mercurio* daily newspaper.[72] In the article, he describes leaving downtown Santiago where he observed a college student protest to give a presentation at a private university in the Andes mountains where several wealthy Santiago suburbs are located. He describes it as a "1,000-meter university" (*universidad cota mil*) because these universities are located at an altitude of 1,000 meters above sea level, high above Santiago. He criticizes the fact that students can only arrive there by car. He also speculates that most students in these universities attended private schools in the same communities and are unlikely to "descend" to downtown Santiago to encounter the poverty and student protests he observed earlier that day. His remarks replicate Alicia's comment that her colleagues "rarely come down to Santiago." He worries that these students will not become professionals with a social conscience that dedicate themselves to improving Chilean society because they are surrounded by wealth and have no contact with the poor.[73]

The column references private universities (discussed in greater detail in chapter 4) established under the dictatorship that are costly to attend and are less selective than traditional, state-supported universities (the University of Chile, the Catholic University, and the University of Santiago). Because they are not state-supported, students there cannot access low-interest loans and scholarships.[74] Consequently, private universities have a reputation for serving wealthy students unable to gain admission to traditional universities. The column generated a firestorm of criticism from the presidents of private universities, their students, and some scholars who found his analysis inaccurate and that it displayed his ignorance of scholarship and student loan policies that keep lower income students in traditional universities.[75]

Alicia's description of her employer, the Universidad del Desarrollo (one of the *universidades cota mil*)[76] and the public debate about these educational institutions are important because they highlight the perception that these universities and wealthy communities operate like social bubbles that physically insulate the rich from the majority of Santiago's population. While Alicia does not express resentment toward her coworkers who are part of "a closed circle," she is acutely aware of her exclusion from that social group. This sense of exclusion from elite social circles will resurface in upcoming chapters. Additionally, many Chileans *do* resent the privileges of this elite, as evident in the debate Father Berríos's column generated and the wave of protests among different groups that culminated with Chile's 2020 constitutional referendum and Gabriel Boric's 2021 presidential election.

Returning to our interviewees, not all activists or moderate Catholics felt alienated from their workplaces. Some found their career change congenial. Elba, a moderate Catholic, left her career as an early childhood educator to become a school bus driver. She had denounced her coworkers' and supervisors' sexual abuse of children in several workplaces, which took an emotional toll on her. She appreciated her current work environment: "I get along great with the parents. Maybe my job as a school bus driver is looked down upon, but I think my educational background has helped me. If a parent talks to me about medicine, I know a lot about it because I studied physical therapy. If they talk to me about child development, I know about that as well." Elba's greater comfort level working at a private school with affluent parents than in public daycare centers with poor children may reflect her childhood in an affluent home. Additionally, her negative experiences as an early childhood educator may have made her more open to her current career.

Youngsters and Career Satisfaction

Youngsters spoke about their jobs in positive terms. Nelson expresses pride in his rise through the ranks and recruitment by large national and multinational firms. Rafael, who has a sociology degree, has been successful in a related field: "I'm the technical director at an educational consulting firm. I do educational research and evaluate schools." María, a librarian, comments, "I've been working at Cardenal Silva Henríquez University for nine years, but I had several jobs before that at private universities and press services. I left one to work in a newspaper archive because it offered better opportunities."[77] Thus, youngsters experienced a successful and uninterrupted workplace trajectory and did not seem interested in seeking fulfillment through workplace relationships.

Pragmatists and Precarious Work

Pragmatists had more difficult experiences in the workplace because their job changes were often the result of dismissal or illness, and their efforts to develop as entrepreneurs resulted in burnout. Rossana comments, "I had to leave my job in 2000 when I had surgery and treatment for breast cancer. The doctor that detected my cancer offered me a job after I recovered. I thought I wouldn't be able to work again due to the memory loss I experienced. I worked several jobs after that prior to my current position selling cosmetics." Rossana, a single mother with a high school education and little family support, was at the mercy of an unforgiving labor market. Her multiple job changes did not permit upward mobility.

Olga, also a single mother with a secretarial certificate, had a "rags to riches" story until it all fell apart due to burnout: "I worked in events planning. I learned the trade, left my job to work on my own, and a former boss suggested I create my own company. I was able to work as a freelancer in my old office for thirteen years. I suffered several episodes of stress and hospitalizations that affected me emotionally as well."[78] Olga left her freelance position and was able to use savings and real estate investments to make ends meet. She hoped to find a "low-stress" regular job after the nightmare of her freelance position.

Olga's and Rossana's experiences display a very different attitude toward and experience of work than the upper-middle-class groups. Rather than seeking fulfillment or advancement, they are mainly focused on satisfying their children's basic needs at sometimes great personal cost. Workplace relationships are only relevant insofar as colleagues or supervisors can provide opportunities for employment or advancement. They also reveal the limited work options for single mothers without technical or college degrees.

Iván had big dreams of starting his own business: "One of the reasons I left teaching for Herbalife was to make my dream come true. I have used savings to buy three plots of land in northern Chile, and my life project is to move up there in three to five years to operate a minimarket, an ecotourism business, and God willing, a school. The minimarket will provide revenue for the other two initiatives because wherever there are people, they need to eat [laughs]." He developed his own business in response to frustrations he faced as a teacher. Whether or not he would eventually achieve his dream, it is noteworthy that his response to workplace conflicts was not to seek further education (he likely did not have the resources to do so) but to pursue an ambitious business venture with an uncertain future.

Conclusion

This exploration of middle-class individuals' educational backgrounds and work lives offers a series of paradoxes that underscore many middle-class families' fragile positions. While those employed in the liberal professions (medicine, law, accounting, finance) enjoyed stable, well-paid employment, technical professionals experienced bouts of unemployment, many teachers felt compelled to change careers, and routine service workers churned through multiple jobs or unsustainable freelance positions. Although most members of the upper-middle class "landed on their feet," job uncertainty and career changes placed emotional and financial stress on individuals and families. Pragmatists faced greater financial risks but used adaptive strategies to remain in the middle class. These observations suggest that while many middle-class families maintained a comfortable income, their economic position was always at risk. The fragility of individuals' hold on their middle-class status, the product of weak job protections, suggests that the macroeconomic story of Chile's high growth rates in the 1990s and 2000s should be qualified to consider the threats to middle-class stability.

To be sure, this research was conducted during the Great Recession, and Chile's economy had a small contraction during 2009, though the Bachelet administration used government reserves to support the unemployed.[79] Consequently, it is possible that some of the job instability individuals experienced resulted from that short-term recession. However, individuals described long-term experiences of unemployment and career shifts that preceded the 2009 recession. Furthermore, subsequent research found the persistence of middle-class fragility well into the 2010s when the economy was growing and before the coronavirus pandemic devastated economies across Latin America.[80] Thus, these interviews offer an important antidote to overly buoyant views of Chile's "economic model."

This sense of fragility takes on particular form when considering gender inequality in the workplace. In contrast to large statistical studies that measure families' financial status based on the head of household's income, the evidence above indicates that examining women's labor market participation shows the employment challenges they experience. As we observed, women are disfavored on the labor market. They often pursue less remunerative female-coded careers. Additionally, women who separate or divorce experience a loss of income due to the low or nonexistent child support payments they receive. Finally, the expectation that women are the primary caregivers, the high cost of childcare, and some women's distrust of childcare providers lead many women to take on part-time jobs, accept positions with flexible hours, or leave the labor market to raise children.[81]

This picture of labor market outcomes is further complicated when we consider the effects of high-risk political activism on individuals' career paths. Legacies of political repression of the left continue to affect individuals' labor market participation today. Some interviewees were expelled from college due to their political activism, leading them to pursue a second career; others lost potential income due to their party work; and still others lost jobs after elections because they had been hired as independent contractors in government ministries.

Many individuals' turbulent career paths as well as their political and religious identity investments influenced their current work experiences. Activists and moderate Catholics who moved from teaching to private sector employment, or had younger work colleagues, experienced hysteresis in the workplace and struggled to engage in "shop talk" with coworkers with whom they did not fit. The habitus they developed in the family and through their college training clashed with a competitive workplace. Symbolic boundaries erected in the workplace echoed public debates about wealth and privilege in Chile, as evident in the discussion of the *universidades cota mil*. In contrast, youngsters did not feel out of their element in the workplace and experienced an upward trajectory in their professional fields. Pragmatists, for their part, focused on survival in an unforgiving labor market or tried to build their own businesses as a way to escape from salaried positions, with mixed results.

The construction of symbolic boundaries in the workplace sets the stage for the following chapters' analyses of identity investments in schools, housing, home decoration, and cultural consumption. Activists and moderate Catholics who feel like "fish out of water" when they switch careers, feel "at home" in their children's schools, though they experience tensions with youngsters and pragmatists. Their educational training as well as their political and religious commitments lead them to emotionally withdraw from work. They use schools, homes, and leisure practices as settings for more sustained and fulfilling identity investments while constructing similar symbolic boundaries with "others."

In contrast, youngsters' satisfaction with their work life finds its counterpart in more subdued identity investments in these other fields, where their choices and identities reveal a pattern of "ordinary consumption."[82] Finally, pragmatists' difficult work lives coincide with perceived threats in the housing and education fields as they seek to shield their children from the poor. Their identity investments focus on upward mobility projects for their children and cultivating strong relationships with extended family. We next turn to the housing market, which reveals economic inequality within the middle class as well as the search for a sense of place in homes and neighborhoods.

2

Housing, Extended Family, and the Search for a Sense of Place

VÍCTOR AND ALICIA, BOTH ACTIVISTS, live in a comfortable home in Ñuñoa, but they had a rough start on the housing market. They were both just beginning their careers and had limited funds. However, they did not want to ask Alicia's father for financial help. Víctor comments, "Some people might have thought I was marrying her for the money, and she wanted to move away to be independent from her mother." Their first rental property in a modest western Santiago community suited them well until they discovered they had a leaky roof and a dead animal above the ceiling. So, Alicia's father, who had received a large severance payment after being laid off from his job, offered to buy them a home, which they accepted because he explained that he did not expect anything in exchange for the gift.

Claudia, a former lawyer and moderate Catholic, describes her use of housing as an investment. She explains that she and her husband began living in an apartment her mother purchased when she moved to Santiago from her hometown, Puerto Montt (in southern Chile), to attend college. "My mother didn't charge us rent so we could save money to buy a home," she recalls. When she was pregnant with her second child, she and her husband combined their savings with a housing subsidy to access their first mortgage. She explains that after the purchase, "I was very careful with money, so we continued to save." Once they had paid off that home, they purchased a larger, more expensive house in La Reina (close to Ñuñoa) and rented out their former home to help pay off the new mortgage. She concludes, "This was all coldly calculated."

Nelly, a pragmatist, experienced declining fortunes on the housing market. She comments, "My living situation has worsened over time. I used to be able to afford a more comfortable apartment, but things have been going downhill. My husband lives in the house that we co-own. I'm trying to initiate divorce proceedings so we can sell it." Her early retirement and marital separation led her to seek rental housing that was a step below her previous dwelling.

Víctor and Claudia both relied on family support to enter the housing market. Víctor alludes to his wife's and his desire to live independently, and their initial discomfort with receiving the gift. In contrast, Claudia emphasizes her financial discipline, savings capacity, and savvy investments in the housing market. Thus, Víctor highlights the role of family in providing gifted property, while Claudia embodies the middle-class values of thrift, self-discipline, and saving, although she, too, received family support. In contrast, Nelly, who had lived more comfortably while employed and married, experienced downward mobility when her family and job circumstances changed.

These examples illustrate several ways that the middle-class families studied in this book understand housing access. First, like their counterparts in southern Europe,[1] many couples relied on extended family to access housing and often chose to live near family members. This pattern contrasts with classic understandings of gentrification, whereby middle-class adults move away from their childhood neighborhoods to experience the excitement of the city, and points to how the desire for proximity to extended family shapes middle-class families' identity investments. Second, while the access to family capital that many middle-class families enjoyed placed them in a privileged position within Santiago's competitive housing market, they did not acknowledge their privilege when they described their housing purchases as reflecting clever financial planning or self-discipline. Third, while some middle-class families could use the housing market to their advantage, others who experienced precarious privilege could only enter the housing market via inherited property, or were pushed into substandard housing when their living situations changed.

The chapter also considers the different degrees of choice families could exercise on the housing market given their unequal access to economic capital. Many families were priced out of desirable neighborhoods, including those where their children attended school, and those families engaged in complex tradeoffs to determine where to live. This meant that what I call a *Ñuñoa diaspora* of families raised in that community sought housing in nearby, more affordable communities like Peñalolén, La Florida (our second community of focus), and even Las Condes (an elite community where some affordable housing was available). Other families that were not from Ñuñoa would have preferred residing in the community but could not afford to do so. A few families whose children attended school in La Florida also lived in the more affordable communities of Puente Alto and La Granja, though this was less widespread in the sample, likely due to the relatively modest land values in La Florida.

However, families do not make housing choices based on their financial situation and the local housing supply alone; rather, they express their tastes and cultural goals through the homes and neighborhoods they select: housing choice is an identity investment. Upper-middle-class families with greater access to resources selected homes based on a community's desirable reputation, preferred amenities, social characteristics, or the availability of attractive schools. Moreover, families sought a *sense of place* in their community, which could be based on their childhood memories or the presence of extended family, supportive neighbors, and/or a community of peers. Like the widely used concept of *elective belonging*,[2] middle-class families sought a set of meaningful characteristics in the communities they selected. However, many families opted to stay in their childhood neighborhoods, move near extended kin, or select communities that approximated their communities of origin. Hence, many families' sense of belonging reflected their efforts to remain connected to their roots rather than to seek out a new lifestyle.

Finally, families' identity investments are also evident in the homes and communities they reject; like the workplace, the housing field is a site for the construction of symbolic boundaries. Activists and moderate Catholics in Ñuñoa rejected wealthy families' ostentatious homes and standardized mass-produced houses, youngsters felt pride in their success on the housing market, and pragmatists in La Florida and nearby areas saw their neighborhoods as refuges from the dangers of poverty.

This chapter builds on international discussions of middle-class housing. Much of this debate focuses on middle-class flight to suburban gated communities as a means to maintain or secure social status as well as avoid urban poverty, crime, and "disorder."[3] Additionally, scholars examine gentrification, whereby middle-class adults raised in homogeneous suburbs choose to live in urban communities that have experienced disinvestment but provide excitement and proximity to urban amenities.[4] In these scenarios, scholars consider how gated communities reflect the "privatization of public space" and how gentrification leads to long-term working class or poor residents' physical displacement or symbolic exclusion.

The debate in Chile focuses on whether or not gated communities in the poor urban periphery lead to greater small-scale segregation that generates hostility between middle-class and poor residents,[5] or provide the opportunity for greater "social mix" or cross-class integration.[6] Others argue that the boom in high-rise apartment construction in Santiago's inner city leads to increasing land values and displacement of small homeowners that cannot effectively negotiate high sales prices for their homes with large developers seeking to move into communities.[7]

This chapter analyzes how middle-class families understand their housing decisions in relation to the material and symbolic dimensions of their communities and how they construct symbolic boundaries with neighbors and residents of other communities. The focus follows this book's broader goal to examine how middle-class families' economic decisions reflect and shape their identities. In addition to the inequalities within the middle class signaled above (rather than the well-known differences between the middle class and the poor), this chapter argues that middle-class identity investments reflect individuals' family origins and relationships, precarious privilege (their limited choices and often fragile foothold in the middle class), and broader ideological affinities. Once families settled in or near Ñuñoa or La Florida, this decision influenced the schools they selected, the composition of their social circles, and the local amenities available to them. Their area of residence thereby influenced their identity investments in schools, home decorations, and leisure activities.

In examining the neighborhoods families selected, we find that activists and moderate Catholics seek communities with "people like us" not only to avoid the poor, but also to mark their distance from elites. Similarly, they describe a desire for "manageable diversity"—they seek communities where members hail from different occupational groups within the middle class rather than cross-class diversity. These attitudes are similar to the "partial exit" strategy other scholars noticed among southern European managers that lived in central cities but sent their children to private schools, for example.[8] Finally, activists' rejection of "McMansions" and "showroom houses" signal their ascetic tastes, "symbolic mastery" (an emphasis on homes' unique aesthetic properties),[9] and rejection of neoliberal policies; while moderate Catholics' worries about violence near gated communities reflect their emphasis on morality. Finally, pragmatists' efforts to avoid high poverty neighborhoods respond to their upwardly mobile aspirations.

Before exploring these findings, I provide some context on Chile's housing market and the communities studied. In Chile, beginning in the mid-twentieth century, poor migrants to cities organized land takeovers and built informal housing, while middle-class people accessed housing via employers or through government-built social housing. Chile created its current mortgage system in the late 1970s and established subsidies that helped the poor and middle class purchase housing. The government also offers subsidies and tax benefits to large developers to spark renewal of inner-city communities that had experienced disinvestment and population loss. Nearly three-quarters of Chileans are homeowners, unlike affluent countries that host large rental markets.[10]

While Santiago had a wealthy area prior to the military coup (the so-called "high rent cone"), many of these communities included a mix of different income groups. The military and subsequent elected governments developed policies that increased class-based residential segregation. The dictatorship's slum clearance policies displaced poor families from affluent eastern Santiago communities to areas of concentrated poverty in the southern part of the metro area, and Concertación governments built social housing in remote locations with cheap land. The dictatorship's deregulation of land markets allowed large developers to build gated communities and malls on inexpensive land in the urban periphery.[11]

The two communities studied in this book were influenced by these broader processes. Ñuñoa is an older community founded in the late nineteenth century that historically was a mixed-class area with a middle-class image. The community hosts numerous higher education, cultural, and educational institutions, and ample green space. Between 2000 and 2010, Ñuñoa experienced a high-rise apartment construction boom that long-time residents believe threatened its quality of life. In 2007, massive protests (described in chapter 6) led to a moratorium on new apartment construction along the community's central artery, while displacing it to its southern boundary. The building boom led to a substantial increase in land values. Ñuñoa has a reputation as a desirable middle-class community with a good quality of life, whose residents are more politicized and progressive than their counterparts in the traditional wealthy suburbs.[12]

La Florida is a formerly rural community that linked Santiago with the colonial village (now suburb) of Puente Alto located to the south of the city. Its "pioneer" settlers were poor families that conducted land takeovers in the late 1960s. In the late 1970s, government and private firms developed housing for working- and lower-middle-class residents. In the late 1980s and 1990s, the area experienced a boom in gated community construction along its eastern edge in the Andes foothills, and two shopping malls built in its center near rapid transit spurred rapid retail development. Between 2000 and 2013, land values increased astronomically as affluent families arrived, leading to tensions with social housing residents. Finally, poor families living "doubled up" with extended family have mobilized to demand affordable housing in the community.[13]

In this context, the chapter proceeds by first examining how middle-class families in these two communities access housing and how they understand their housing decisions. Next, we explore the homes and communities families select, exploring how they manage cost constraints while seeking a sense of place in their communities. Finally, we examine how middle-class adults construct symbolic boundaries with other groups and communities as part and parcel of their identity investments.

Accessing a Home: Privilege, Family Support, and Precarity

Upper- and lower-middle-class couples entered the housing market under different financial circumstances that affected their ability to rent or buy homes or to use housing as an investment. Additionally, the uncertain labor market and marital separation or divorce could compel couples to temporarily return to the family home until their situation stabilized. Finally, some pragmatists never left their family home due to both financial restrictions and the desire to remain close to extended family.

Elsewhere, I have interpreted these financial and family circumstances through the concept of "housing pathways."[14] There, I argued that middle-class families follow three pathways. Claudia's discussion at this chapter's beginning describes a *linear pathway*, in which couples access housing according to an established plan. Víctor's comments exemplify a *chaotic-progressive pathway*, whereby couples move from precarious to more stable housing. Finally,

Nelly describes a *reproductive pathway,* in which she lacked the resources to access adequate housing.[15] Within the first two pathways, activists, moderate Catholics, and youngsters enjoy larger homes in higher status neighborhoods than do pragmatists. In contrast, with one exception (a college-educated activist), only pragmatists experienced reproductive pathways.

In this section, I focus on couples' interpretation of their housing pathways in light of their preexisting understandings of housing as a central component of middle-class identity. I found individuals that inherited property normalized this experience rather than understanding it as a form of privilege and advantage over other families.[16] Additionally, families saw ownership of multiple homes (used either for rental income or as a vacation residence) as legitimate. These families suggested that ownership of a second home reflected their financial sobriety, a core middle-class value.

Families that followed chaotic-progressive pathways were grateful for the support they received from extended family during times of financial difficulty, but did not consider family financial support as a form of privilege in relation to other families. These families constructed narratives that highlighted how they overcame adversity to arrive at their current housing arrangement. First time home buyers with modest incomes expressed considerable anxiety regarding the long-term debts they had incurred. Thus, some mortgage holders did not normalize their debts. Rather, they highlighted their condition of precarious privilege.

Finally, those who followed reproductive pathways had two competing interpretations of their housing situations. Those that remained in their childhood homes described themselves as staying true to their roots. In contrast, individuals that experienced downward mobility described a "fall from grace" and expressed nostalgia for their former financial circumstances. Here, precarious privilege moved to the forefront.

Each of these pathways highlights the centrality of extended family to homeownership in Chile. Like other studies of southern Europe[17] and Russia,[18] I found that middle-class Chileans rely heavily on extended family for capital and guidance to enter the housing market. With a relatively new mortgage system and a weak welfare state, these authors argue, young couples rely on family for capital and support with child-rearing. This close tie to extended family also illustrates middle-class identity investments. Whether they relied on family for capital, short-term assistance, or a shared dwelling, many middle-class families saw housing as an identity investment informed by their childhood experiences and kinship ties.

Housing as an Investment

Activists and moderate Catholics with high earnings or whose parents gifted them a home were able to purchase investment properties or vacation homes. They understood their purchases as normal, legitimate investments and highlighted their financial acumen. Ricardo, an activist, comments, "When we moved to Valdivia, that changed our life because before, we were earning much less. We were finally able to buy a home. When I got a better job in Santiago, we bought our current home. We bought both houses without a down payment and kept the second home as a rental dwelling to pay our current mortgage. The second home will serve as a nest egg for retirement because the pension plans aren't very reliable."[19] Like Claudia, whose remarks appear in this chapter's introduction, Ricardo highlights the couple's careful financial planning that allowed them to benefit financially from housing investments. Others also suggest that ownership of a second home reflects their careful financial management. Luis, an activist, comments, "We may not earn huge salaries but we've been very careful with money and are actually better off than some folks that earn more. We have a second home where we could possibly retire and volunteer to help the community." These accounts highlight individuals' financial discipline and foresight without considering their privileged position in relation to other Chileans.

Housing as a Gift or a Debt Burden

While the above families explained their purchase of more than one home as resulting from their financial acumen and disciplined savings, a second group had a more complex pathway toward stable housing. These individuals lacked the savings to purchase homes, or they faced personal or financial setbacks that forced them to leave their homes in the short term. These individuals received homes as gifts or benefited from access to parental housing when times were tough.

Clara, an activist, lived in a guest house after her marriage dissolved: "When I separated, I moved back to the guest house at my mom's home with my two kids. My brother had converted the garage into an apartment, and I had lived there prior to my marriage. I wasn't able to get a mortgage for my apartment until five years later." Clara describes the guest house as a kind of safety net that she used more than once when she was unable to live independently.

Like Clara, who describes her return to her mother's home as a normal occurrence, Jimena feels fortunate that her father gave her a house: "My dad did more than a father has to. If I can afford it, I'll do the same for my kids."[20] Víctor, whose comments appear at the beginning of this chapter, was initially uncomfortable with the idea that his father-in-law would buy a house for his family: "We wouldn't have been able to buy this house on our own." Víctor's father was a teacher and his mother was a factory worker. He intimates that receiving a home that he could not afford to purchase himself makes him uneasy given his modest origins and limited salary.

While those with more affluent families or in-laws could rely on family resources to build equity in a home or adapt to personal or financial difficulties, others relied on mortgages to purchase their homes. In contrast to Claudia and Ricardo, these individuals worried about the consequences of taking on a mortgage. Morgana, an activist, remarks, "I'll be in debt for the rest of my life. Teachers earn so little in this country. It was kind of crazy to take on a mortgage, so I don't even want to think about it." César, another activist, remarks, "I began a thirty-year sentence when we bought the apartment."[21] Morgana and César highlight their worries about holding a mortgage given their limited incomes and Chile's job instability.

These comments underscore the precarious privilege many middle-class families experience. While the most fortunate families enjoy financial or in-kind support from their extended kin, this support reflects their inability to purchase their own homes. Similarly, those that took out mortgages but did not have the start-up capital to use housing as an investment felt uncertain about their decision because they could not visualize how they would finally be debt-free. While these families lived in comfortable homes in pleasant communities, they had a fragile hold on their middle-class standing.

Housing as Shared Resource or Uncertain Shelter

Some pragmatists and activists were unable to secure independent housing. They understood these arrangements as reflecting their strong relationships with extended family. Aniluap, an activist, lives with her youngest daughter rent free in her aunt's apartment. Due to her sporadic income as a freelancer, she is unable to access independent housing. She gratefully acknowledges her aunt's in-kind support (providing housing) and that she helps pay her daughter's private school tuition. Alejandra, a pragmatist, lives with her mother and sister: "My sister, my mother, and I live here now. My parents bought the house after my brother was born, and we have lived here ever since." Iván lives in a home his mother inherited, though she lives in a separate house. Both Alejandra and Iván view their residence in family members' homes as normal and desirable.

In contrast, individuals that could not secure permanent housing felt greater uncertainty about their living circumstances. Nelly, whose comments appear at the chapter's beginning, describes a downward slide in her quality of life due to her job loss and marital separation. Dany, a moderate Catholic, opted to live in Ñuñoa, where housing is expensive, in order to be close to her children's school: "We rent this house. I'd like to buy a house, but it's very expensive here. We're trying! [*laughs*]. We offered to buy our home from the landlord, but he said he wouldn't know what to do with the money. I can't imagine being in that situation. The house was trashed when we moved in, and we've spruced it up and planted a garden. The owner has visited and likes how it looks." Thus, while Dany cannot purchase the home, she tries to put her "stamp" on it so that it feels more permanent.

While Aniluap, Alejandra, and Iván could count on family support, Nelly and Dany relied on their own income to rent their homes. However, none of these families can accumulate equity through home ownership. While those living in family homes were likely more protected, those dependent on landlords were in a more precarious circumstance.

We can see middle-class families' distinct assumptions regarding housing through these three patterns. Those that used housing as an investment highlighted their financial acumen. Families receiving housing as a gift expressed gratitude toward parents, while those that took out mortgages evidenced anxiety about the long time horizon of their debt. Individuals that lived with extended family found this situation normal, while tenants worried about the instability of their housing arrangements. The first pattern illustrates how the most advantaged families did not acknowledge their privilege. In contrast, the second and third patterns highlight the precarious privilege of many families because they depended on family, long-term mortgages, or landlords to access housing.

"Choosing" Neighborhoods and Homes: Cost, Community, and Place

Much of the international discussion on housing focuses on how middle-class settlement patterns harm poor people, either through their displacement when middle-class people move to poor urban neighborhoods, or through their exclusion from suburban gated communities that "privatize public space."[22]

Within that discussion, some scholars focus on middle-class home buyers' perspectives and attitudes and how they may lead to the symbolic exclusion of long-term residents in the communities where they settle.

Butler and Robson studied middle-class people in several gentrifying communities in London and coined the term *metropolitan habitus* to describe couples raised in the suburbs that prefer lower income urban communities for their connectivity and "buzz," although they have few interactions with local residents.[23] Savage et al. developed the related concept of "elective belonging" to describe middle-class residents that moved into preexisting communities in Manchester, United Kingdom.[24] These incoming residents constructed narratives about their choices based on these communities' aesthetic qualities, but like their London counterparts, had limited contact with long-term residents. In contrast, recent work on London drawing on these same ideas finds that middle-class residents may become more connected to their residential communities over time.[25]

Other scholars did not find patterns of gentrification and gated community settlement in Continental Europe. Research on Spanish, French, and Italian cities finds that many middle-class people choose to remain in or return to their childhood communities in central urban areas rather than seeking "adventure" or "buzz" in "edgy" neighborhoods or seclusion in suburban gated communities.[26] This impulse reflects these families' roots in central urban communities and the social support extended family can provide for child-rearing. Additionally, those that move to new cities or communities often follow a spouse that was raised there and extended family nearby. By remaining in their home communities, middle-class families do not influence land values and retail environments in poor communities, though they may contribute to rising housing prices in central neighborhoods.

These observations on Southern European middle classes bring us back to the concept of "identity investments." Many of the families I interviewed remained in or returned to their neighborhood of origin. When this was not possible because they were priced out of desirable communities (most notably Ñuñoa), or they were migrants to Santiago, they sought to develop a sense of place—sentimental attachments to specific communities—based on their childhood experiences or their growing attachment to the communities where they settled.[27] Families with a strong sense of place might settle in a community that has less desirable housing formats because of their sentimental attachments to that community.[28] Further, some families engaged in "place-making"[29] by migrating along with several family members to a new community—they created a sense of place by reconstructing their extended kin network in a new setting. Thus, the affordability of specific communities as well as families' sentimental attachments to community and family constrain middle-class housing choices. Their identity investments in the housing market build on their childhood experiences and efforts to settle close to extended family when this was possible. I begin this section by exploring how families are priced out of some communities and then go on to examine their motivations for selecting specific areas.

The Middle-Class Housing Squeeze in Santiago

In accord with this book's broader focus on precarious privilege, this section explores the financial constraints middle-class families faced when deciding where to live. Many families found Ñuñoa attractive due to its central location, transit access, and educational and cultural institutions. Numerous families had children enrolled in Ñuñoa schools and/or had grown up there. Nonetheless, those families were priced out of Ñuñoa and became what I call the *Ñuñoa diaspora*. Their displacement may reflect Ñuñoa's increasing land values in the mid-2000s as noted above.

Several families had been raised in Ñuñoa and their children attended its schools, but they could not afford to purchase housing there. Rodrigo, an activist and Ñuñoa native, comments, "Ñuñoa was our first choice, but it was very expensive. We applied for a housing subsidy and all of the homes in that community were too expensive given the mortgage we could obtain based on our savings, so we purchased this home in Peñalolén."[30] Claudia, whose children attended school in Ñuñoa, complained, "Ñuñoa was unaffordable."

In the context of our comparison of these two communities, it is notable that several Ñuñoa families settled in La Florida due to financial or other factors that pushed them out of the community. Luis comments, "We lived in an apartment in Ñuñoa, but one day someone tried to kidnap our daughter when the nanny was taking her for a walk, so we decided to move." At that time, Luis and family lived in Villa Olympica, an older apartment complex located in the more modest western section of the community. Mario describes another factor that precipitated his family's move to La Florida: "My dad had moved to a country house in La Florida, and for financial reasons, we needed to rent out the Ñuñoa house and live with him. Then, my mother sold our Ñuñoa home and used the money to buy one home for herself and another one for us in La Florida." Thus, crime victimization, and financial restrictions led some families to move to La Florida.

Those that left often expressed nostalgia for the community. Luis continues, "I really liked Ñuñoa—my grandmothers lived there. However, the types of homes that we would have liked there were just too expensive." Rossana, a pragmatist and La Florida resident, recalls her childhood there: "I'd like to move back to Ñuñoa. I spent most of my youth there. It's a quiet area with walkable streets. There's a park there where we used to play. It has small stores instead of a mall. I don't care for malls, especially since I work in one." Thus, members of the Ñuñoa diaspora adapted to life in La Florida, but missed key elements of their former community.

A smaller group of families whose children attended school in La Florida either could not afford to live in the community or had to live elsewhere for family reasons. Marcela, a pragmatist whose children attend school in La Florida, comments, "I had to buy in Peñalolén because Macul [next to La Florida] and La Florida were unaffordable." César, an activist whose children attend school in La Florida, comments, "We lived in La Florida for four years, but due to a personal situation related to my mother, we bought an apartment near her in Ñuñoa." Álvaro, a moderate Catholic whose children also study in La Florida, remarks, "My wife is from La Granja, and she had already purchased our house when we married. Our neighborhood has a lot of delinquency and drug use, so we'd like a quieter place. We're looking in La Florida and Peñalolén."[31] Thus, a few families were priced out of La Florida, or family circumstances led them to live elsewhere. These examples demonstrate that housing costs and family responsibilities prevented some upper- and lower-middle-class families from living in their preferred communities. Only the most affluent families among those interviewed had a "free hand" in selecting where to live.

Neighborhood Amenities

Middle-class families sought different kinds of amenities in the two communities explored in this book. Those settling in Ñuñoa emphasized its central location, neighborhood feel, and cultural activities. Given long, arduous commuting times in Santiago, living in a central location contributed to residents' quality of life. Lorena, an activist, describes the advantages of living in Ñuñoa: "I feel like Ñuñoa is close to everything. Any place you would want to go to is not very far away. My partner takes the bus to work downtown, so he doesn't need to drive."[32] Patricia, a moderate Catholic, makes a similar comment: "My husband works downtown, and it takes him one half hour to ride his bike to work. I drive to my job in Vitacura, and it only takes fifteen minutes. So, we have convenient routes to get to different places."

La Florida residents sought more spacious lots or homes that offered the opportunity for building additions to accommodate family needs. Thus, Mario comments, "The country house was ideal for my kids when they were young. They could run around and play. We had three or four dogs. Once they got bigger, we decided to buy our current house in a neighborhood." Tomás, an activist, remarks, "When we first bought the house, it was really small, but it had a big yard, which gave us the opportunity to build an addition. We've practically built a new house. Since we have six family members, the original house was too small."[33] Thus, in-migrants to La Florida found that the lot sizes and land values allowed them to accommodate larger families and pets.

Community, Sense of Place, and Place-Making

Selecting a home and neighborhood was not merely a question of identifying an affordable house or apartment in an area with the right amenities. Rather, middle-class families desired to be part of communities that provided them with a sense of place. Pragmatists that remained in their childhood homes and upper-middle-class families that stayed in or returned to their communities of origin experienced a sense of continuity with their childhoods. Those that moved to new communities sought to experience a familiar sense of community and place.

Some individuals preferred living in their childhood community. Pamela, a pragmatist who currently lives down the street from her parents in La Florida, comments, "When I first married, we moved to Las Condes [a wealthy eastern Santiago community]. Since my children's father worked so much, I became ill. So, I rented a house near my mother and got better [*laughs*]. I just missed my mother [*tenía mamitis*]." Marcelo, a moderate Catholic, remarks, "You always tend to return to the old neighborhood. We also moved here because my wife grew up here as well, and we needed a place close to our children's school." Marcelo and his wife both attended the school where their children study. Those that remained in their childhood communities expressed a strong sense of place attachment as well as a desire to live near extended kin, as observed among managers in southern Europe.[34]

Some pragmatists remained in their childhood homes and related their strong sense of rootedness to their communities of origin. Iván, a pragmatist who lives in his grandmother's former home, highlights his strong social connections to family and other long-term residents as well as the appeal of living near the Andes mountains: "If I ever moved, it would be near here but higher up in the mountains." Alejandra, who lives in the same community in her childhood home, relates fond memories from when the area was still rural. She describes outings with her father when they milked cows owned by local dairy farmers and collected grass to feed her pet rabbits: "I have beautiful childhood memories." In describing their sense of attachment to their homes, Iván and Alejandra highlight the local landscape, strong community ties, and nostalgic childhood memories. Their comments reflect the sense of rootedness as well as connection to kin and place others observe among working-class families.[35]

Other couples followed extended family members to a new community. While those that remained in their childhood communities drew on a pre-existing sense of place, families that followed extended kin engaged in place-making: they developed affective ties to these new settings in part through their family ties. Jimena, an activist and Ñuñoa resident, describes her decision to live in that community: "My mom has always lived in Ñuñoa and was close by, as were my sisters. We all wanted to live together." Similarly, Tamara and Luis migrated from Ñuñoa to La Florida after several family members moved there: "We liked the scent of country air and the trees here in addition to the fact that our relatives had moved here." By following extended family, Jimena, Tamara, Luis, and other couples could reconstruct their extended kin network in a new community.

Some families sought ties with neighbors. Rodrigo, who preferred to live in Ñuñoa, but ended up in Peñalolén, remarked, "We were looking for the neighborhood concept and we found it here. We both grew up in neighborhoods and have fond memories of our childhoods." Israel, who moved to La Florida from Maipú, was pleasantly surprised by his supportive neighbors: "We started to get together with the neighbors here. We were lucky that they were really friendly and cool. We moved into an established community, and it ended up being a blessing. We had lived in downtown Santiago, and no one greeted us. It's been marvelous here: we arrived in October and left our house keys with the neighbor in February when we went on vacation. That's a big advantage. We hang out with them and have barbecues together." Thus, residents tried to identify communities that approximated their childhood experiences and sought social ties with neighbors, in contrast to some of the analyses of belonging noted above. As outlined below, their willingness to engage with neighbors may result from their location in relatively homogeneous middle-class neighborhoods in contrast to the mixed-class communities gentrification scholars have analyzed.

In addition to building ties with extended kin and neighbors, families that moved to new communities sought to be part of a "community of peers" or in a setting with "manageable diversity." While others emphasize middle-class residents' avoidance of the poor in gentrifying neighborhoods, individuals I interviewed expressed a desire to avoid both poor and wealthy communities. Lorena comments, "The type of people that live in Ñuñoa are more or less like us. People aren't earning massive salaries [*no tantas millones*]."[36] Luis describes his La Florida community: "We first noticed that there were mostly homeowners here, because people take care of their gardens. Renters usually don't maintain their homes, and the area around them looks dirty. All these houses are homogeneous. You're not going to walk by a monstrous, ostentatious house. People don't compete over who has the fanciest house or car. My wife and I grew up next to parks. All the kids would play in the street. There's a plaza here, too, where our kids could play."

Lorena and Luis describe their preference to live in a community of peers that is neither too rich nor too poor and whose residents are not overly status-conscious. Much like the discussion of symbolic boundaries in the workplace in chapter 1, we again see activists' discomfort with unbridled competition among peers. Additionally, for Luis, both the design and social composition of his La Florida community evoked memories of his childhood. Thus, these families sought a sense of place that included familiar people as well as emblems of their childhood communities.

High-Quality Schools

Some upper-middle-class residents moved near high-quality schools that fit their values, as outlined in the next two chapters. Since students need to test into private and charter schools, and many high-performing schools are oversubscribed, adults whose children are admitted to a desirable school seek to support their children's success.[37] Thus, many interviewees secured their child's school admission before selecting a home, in contrast to the findings in other studies of more affluent families in Santiago.[38] Miguel, a moderate Catholic, describes how he and his wife selected a school before finding a home nearby: "My cousins attended Calasanz so I had a high opinion of the school. We picked the school and then found a home nearby."[39] Ernesto, whose children attend the same school, recalls leaving their apartment for a house located around the corner from the school. They wanted to live close enough so their children could eat lunch at home.[40] Tomás describes how he and his wife purchased their La Florida home after their children began attending their school because "the school ties us down." Lula, an activist, tried this strategy, but it backfired: "I wanted to pick the school first and then find a home. However, after I moved to Ñuñoa, the school changed its location to Peñalolén. I'm not moving there because it's too far away, too chilly, and I don't want to leave the kids alone while I work all day. My family is very tight-knit, and my home is very centrally located, so if the kids are home alone, I can always ask my sister-in-law or mother to pick them up. No one will drive to Peñalolén to get them."[41] Thus, schools could act like magnets drawing parents to particular communities.

To conclude this section, families' access to economic resources set basic constraints for the neighborhoods where they could afford to live. Beyond those initial "hard" constraints, families identified several aesthetic, social, and educational characteristics that guided their identity investments in homes and communities. Families sought specific amenities (like transit connectivity, housing formats, and schools) but also prioritized sentimental attachments to their communities of origin, extended families, or communities that felt familiar and welcoming. Unlike middle-class gentrifiers in London or Manchester, these Santiago middle-class residents sought familiarity and a connection (if imagined) to their roots. Much like southern Europeans, the people interviewed in this book selected homes and communities that reflected their identity investments in family, community, and a familiar peer group.

Housing Distaste and Symbolic Boundaries

The preceding section highlighted the housing formats and neighborhoods middle-class families actively choose. This final section explores the types of homes and communities middle-class families explicitly reject. This refusal illuminates how middle-class families construct symbolic boundaries with other groups to reinforce their individual and group identities.

Bourdieu highlighted the importance of "distaste" in understanding taste. He remarked, "In matters of taste . . . all determination is negation; and tastes are perhaps first and foremost distastes, disgust provoked by horror or visceral intolerance ('sick-making') of the tastes of others."[42] He here refers to artists' and intellectuals' intolerance of wealthy people's aesthetic tastes. While these comments focus on tastes in the visual arts and literature, he argues that individuals from specific classes and class fractions apply the same aesthetic principles to other domains. Hence, we could anticipate that members of different classes and class fractions would have conflicting aesthetic tastes and distastes for distinct types of homes and communities. Additionally, Lamont argues that some upper-middle-class men construct moral boundaries with others they view as excessively competitive.[43] We can extend her discussion to think about how homes and communities may symbolize a competitive spirit.

In this context, we find similar patterns regarding how each of the four groups studied in this book construct symbolic boundaries in the workplace and in the housing field. While members of all groups wanted to live in safe communities that included adequate amenities and transit connectivity, and many wished to recreate a semblance of their childhood communities, each group displayed a distinct pattern of distaste. Activists rejected opulent homes in affluent neighborhoods and standardized housing, which they perceived as cold and artificial. Both expressions of distaste align with their critique of neoliberalism and its promotion of economic success over social solidarity. In contrast, moderate Catholics rejected homes and communities rife with conflicts between neighbors or gated communities located near poor settlements. These distastes reflect their focus on morality and the display of pleasant manners in face-to-face interactions, qualities they believe a competitive society is eroding. Youngsters rarely expressed aversion to specific Santiago communities, perhaps because many had experienced upward mobility and thus had limited previous social contact with economic elites. Finally, pragmatists avoided neighborhoods where their children's exposure to poverty, delinquency, and drug abuse could undermine their goal of upward mobility. These expressions of distaste are critical illustrations of identity investments.

Activists and the Perils of the Market

Several activists were dumbfounded that their childhood friends had abandoned values of simplicity and humility learned in school to purchase opulent homes in remote, affluent communities. Conny, a psychologist and activist, comments, "I went to dinner a month ago at a former classmate's house . . . She lives in a big, gated community with a guard—it's private." She found it strange that her former classmate ended up in a remote, gated community: "I looked at this house filled with objects way out on the mountaintop where the condors fly, and I thought, 'It's horrible that she needs to drive forty-five minutes to our kids' school.'" She recalls Manuel de Salas, her alma mater (an alternative school in Ñuñoa analyzed in the next chapter) as a left-wing school with diverse students: "We respected the staff and did volunteer work. I still go to visit and greet the janitor with a kiss on the cheek. Some of my classmates work in the government, and they are very humane people."[44]

Conny's remarks highlight the *hysteresis effect*, which we have already observed in the workplace. Conny is confused that her friend has changed in ways she has not. Her friend's decision to live in an affluent, gated community far from her child's school is unthinkable given their shared childhood in a left-wing school that espoused egalitarian values.

Activists also rejected "showroom houses"—homes with standardized designs and decorations promoted by developers and magazines. Luis comments: "Showroom houses symbolically compensate for their residents' personal development that prevented them from acquiring tools needed to construct their own identities. [These houses] are for people who don't take their destiny in their own hands. They're born, they live, and they die. We have family members that live in showroom houses and they're great people, but the house is an expression of their unresolved relationship conflicts. We don't want to criticize them; we just like to live authentically."

Rodrigo makes a similar remark: "The percentage of children with flat feet has increased. They don't play. Parents get them from school, and they go to malls on the weekend. Everything is flat, and they are never on irregular surfaces. In more affluent areas, they take the elevator in their apartment to the car, and go from there to the mall." Here, Luis and Rodrigo implicitly argue that neoliberalism has produced people without self-awareness and matched them with standardized homes, schools, and malls devoid of feeling. They suggest that market values have produced physically, emotionally, and creatively stunted individuals that are unable to confront their lives, design their living spaces, or experience "natural" activities like outdoor play. They contrast this pattern with the authentic lives they seek to live. Their comments are reminiscent of Baudrillard's criticism of interior designers' efforts to market home decoration styles to different sociodemographic groups.[45] These comments also echo the argument that high cultural capital individuals prefer handmade and craft goods to standardized objects[46] as well as the concept of "homeyness"—the sense of warmth and authenticity middle-class adults associate with personalized home decor.[47]

Moderate Catholics and Neighboring

If activists think that neoliberalism has stunted competitive individuals' values of solidarity and capacity for genuine self-expression, moderate Catholics see new housing developments as undermining authentic neighborhoods and friendly interactions with neighbors. They, too, suffer from the hysteresis effect, but their focus is less on politics, wealth, and creativity than on the ability to enjoy personal relationships in one's community.

Marcelo describes difficulties in his sister-in-law's upper-income neighborhood: "My sister-in-law lives in one of those apartment buildings with about ninety units. The problem is that you run into all kinds of people with different habits, lifestyles, and levels of education. We visited her last weekend, and there were kids running around throwing rocks and damaging things. You know how parents are these days—they weren't watching them . . . Living with ninety families represents a violent demographic explosion. And my sister-in-law tells me, 'If it's not this neighbor then it's the other one. One was screaming and the other had a party until late at night.'" He contrasts his sister's building with the more human scale of his home: "In our much smaller building, if you go downstairs to barbecue with family, you are much more likely to see people, and it creates an agreeable family atmosphere. The developer gave the salesman instructions to be very selective about who could purchase a unit. He tried to make sure potential residents had good habits and certain characteristics. He was so charming that you would feel comfortable telling him your life story. He figured out right away what the applicants were like, and I think he was 80 percent successful."

Here, Marcelo argues that large developers have created unsustainable building designs that throw together younger families with different class and cultural backgrounds to create an explosive social cocktail. In contrast, his smaller apartment building allows him to enjoy a familiar, pleasant social environment among people who share his education, lifestyle, and values—a community of peers. In this vision, large-scale, high-density apartment development is destroying the social fabric by generating unwanted social encounters across class, cultural, and generational lines.[48]

Moderate Catholics also criticized newer gated communities located in poor neighborhoods. Claudio, a moderate Catholic and insurance salesman, comments: "I wasn't going to go live in Peñalolén City up in the hills in gated condominiums that don't fit my lifestyle. You live in a bubble there, but when you go to the bus stop, you get mugged. It doesn't have the neighborhood life we enjoy. We went for a walk around here in the evening, and we felt safe. We don't have an alarm system and don't need armed guards. We prefer our quality of life."[49]

Claudio's comment in some ways mirrors Conny's narrative above; but rather than focusing on materialism and social solidarity, he emphasizes the lack of neighborhood life in gated communities and the risk of crime in Peñalolén, which is much poorer than the area Conny describes. He humorously references New York City by calling the municipality "Peñalolén City," conjuring images of a menacing, crime-filled Gotham that finds its counterpart in the foothills of the Andes mountains in suburban Santiago, Chile. Like Marcelo, he states his preference for living in safety among his class peers rather than being exposed to the dangers of a poor community, even if he would be "safe" in his bubble. He references the externalities caused by Pinochet's liberalization of land markets that allowed developers to build large, gated communities on cheap land in Santiago's periphery.

A few activists and moderate Catholics did live in gated communities. Ricardo explains his family's selection of a gated community: "We wanted to live in a condominium so we did not need to secure our yard with a metal fence and metal bars on the windows." He and Gloria, his wife, continue:

> *Ricardo:* We don't have much in common with our neighbors.
> *Gloria:* We don't see the world the same way.
> *Ricardo:* We have ideological differences with some neighbors—the ones across the street are evangelicals. Others are social climbers and have big cars.
> *Gloria:* They're more conservative.

Thus, while Ricardo and Gloria live in a gated community, they express similar criticisms of their neighbors as other activists that refuse to live in those settings. Paula, a moderate Catholic, purchased a home in a gated community in Peñalolén: "We couldn't find many houses that were big enough and affordable in Providencia, Ñuñoa, and Las Condes. Many of the used houses were old, in bad shape, and expensive. We found a larger new home in a gated community in Peñalolén located next to a vineyard. It's large and safe."[50] Paula's motivations for purchasing her home were similar to those expressed by the Ñuñoa diaspora—she bought a house in a suburban location because it was more spacious and affordable than those in older urban communities.

It is important to note that several activists' and moderate Catholics' sharp criticisms of gated communities and showroom houses contrast with many of the discussions of gentrification and middle-class families' anti-urban bias. These testimonies demonstrate an important ideological division within the middle classes whereby some families view new housing formats as emblems of neoliberalism, while others value their features. This observation suggests that there are multiple middle-class tastes and distastes regarding housing that reflect each couple's identity investments.

Youngsters' Satisfaction with Their Communities

In contrast to activists and moderate Catholics, most youngsters demonstrated satisfaction with their homes and communities and did not express distaste for other areas. María, a librarian, speaks about the built environment but not about people: "I like the density level in Ñuñoa. It's not overpopulated. They are building apartments, but some areas have a lot of single-family homes, so it's not so many people. I lived in downtown Santiago for a few years and liked the connectivity, but after a while, the pollution was horrible. When my daughter was a baby, we needed an air purifier so she wouldn't get sick." Similarly, Lisette enjoys her gated community: "Now that we're living in a gated community, we developed a taste for it. I need a safe place for my son to play."[51] Hence, rather than reject the populations in other communities, youngsters value their own homes and neighborhoods. This may result from their modest or provincial origins: they do not have a point of comparison with other Santiago communities. Others have suggested that migrants to cities often make "safe" residential choices because they lack the knowledge of the city to know how to navigate mixed class environments.[52] Additionally, it may also reflect their practical approach to housing that was also apparent in their attitudes toward the workplace.

Pragmatists and the Fear of Contact with the Poor

Pragmatists also highlight security in relation to their housing choices, but their concerns differ from the other three groups. Rather than fearing crime or social disorder, pragmatists are afraid direct contact with poor people could expose their children to negative influences and derail their hopes for improved educational and professional opportunities for their children. Pamela comments: "My friends have had financial problems and needed to move to Puente Alto [a community near La Florida with a high poverty rate]. Their child is already speaking poorly because of who he hangs out with. I want my daughters to associate with the best people in La Florida." Pamela references poor people's linguistic style and her fear that her children would become like them. Long-term exposure to these children would harm their educational and job opportunities. She adds a second angle to her mobility aspirations—she wants her children to build friendships with higher income children—"to associate with the best people"—who could potentially aid them on the job market.

In addition to fear of social contamination through contact with poor children, pragmatists worry about their children's possible exposure to crime or substance abuse. Nelly comments, "You can tell it's not easy to get in my building. In the past, I lived in apartment buildings where people could sneak into the entryway. My son had to see alcoholics and drug addicts." Here, alcoholism and substance abuse are negative influences that could harm or misdirect children. Again, contact with poverty could potentially undermine these parents' plans for their children's ascent through dint of hard work and discipline.

In this section, we observed how members of each group construct symbolic boundaries with residents in other communities. Like their discussion of the workplace, many activists and moderate Catholics criticized the competitive spirit and materialism evident in exclusive gated communities, standardized showroom houses, and harsh conditions in slums near gated condominiums. In contrast, youngsters were pleased with their communities, while pragmatists avoided poor communities where they feared exposure to working-class speech patterns or the visible presence of alcoholism and substance abuse might harm their children. Members of each group avoided communities they found aesthetically abhorrent, morally depraved, or physically dangerous, highlighting similarities with their attitudes about the workplace and their desire to live in a community of peers.

Conclusion

In this chapter, I have argued that middle-class families articulate different understandings of housing access that draw on well-known narratives about what it means to be middle class, like ideas about disciplined financial planning. The importance of family economic and social support for housing access underscores the continued presence of the "intergenerational transmission of homeownership" in Chile, even though the mortgage market has expanded in recent decades. Chileans' use of family savings and inheritance to finance homeownership is similar to southern Europe[53] and post-Soviet Russia.[54]

The discussion of middle-class housing tastes revealed the financial constraints families face as well as the sentimental attachments that guide their decisions. Middle-class families have precarious privilege: their limited resources mean that many struggle to find affordable housing in their preferred neighborhood. Furthermore, their housing decisions are identity investments: they reflect sentimental attachments to childhood experiences they seek to reproduce in adulthood. The discussion of middle-class tastes in homes and neighborhoods revealed some pragmatists' decision to remain in the family home. In contrast, activists, moderate Catholics, and youngsters alternatively selected neighborhoods that provided desired amenities, helped them create or reinforce a sense of place, or facilitated the reproduction of cultural capital through schools. In contrast to many analyses of gentrification highlighting young adults' move away from bland suburbs to impoverished inner-city communities, this chapter highlights these adults' desire to remain in urban communities or to settle near family.[55]

The discussion of distaste for homes and neighborhoods demonstrates how the housing field is a platform for the construction of symbolic boundaries with other groups perceived as threatening or polluting. Activists and moderate Catholics avoid living in communities where affluent people display ostentatious lifestyles, youngsters express satisfaction with their preferences, and pragmatists seek to shield their children from the poor in nearby communities. As we saw in chapter 1, activists and moderate Catholics constructed similar symbolic boundaries with others in the workplace. Additionally, some middle-class families soundly reject the new housing formats of gated communities that many other scholars have studied.

The discussion of housing access, tastes, and distastes in Ñuñoa and La Florida highlights contrasts between these two communities that are further explored in the next two chapters. Ñuñoa was a much more desirable and expensive community due to its central location, cultural infrastructure, and reputation. This made housing in the community unaffordable for some families studied in this book, even if their children attended school there.

Additionally, the community's relatively affluent population meant it included more private schools than La Florida, and residents there were more exposed to the wealthy living in or near the community. Ñuñoa also has an urban, artistic character that appealed to those that grew up there as well as others seeking a walkable, lively community with good transit connectivity. Thus, Ñuñoa residents more often criticized their rich and competitive counterparts than did La Florida residents.

Due to its location in Santiago's southern periphery, more recent urbanization, and mixed-class population, La Florida offered housing prices that were accessible to most of the middle-class families in this book (though a few lower-middle-class families found it unaffordable). The community has a suburban feel and was hence more appealing to those upper-middle-class families that sought larger homes, a backyard, and a more relaxed lifestyle. While wealthy families do live in the Andes foothills on the community's eastern edge, La Florida has a "low key" middle-class feel that is less overtly competitive than Ñuñoa. Hence, as we learn in the next two chapters, upper-middle-class families in La Florida are more likely to criticize less educated, upwardly mobile families than the wealthy. Additionally, there were more lower-middle-class interviewees in this book's La Florida sample. Hence, through this chapter, we can begin to see the contours of distinct middle-class communities in these two areas. These differences come to the forefront when we consider schooling in the next two chapters.

3

School Choice
Neighborhoods, Values, and Concerted Cultivation

CLARA IS AN ACTIVIST and psychologist who grew up in Ñuñoa. She attended Manuel de Salas, a secular alternative school, as did her father and several members of her extended family. She sends her children there in part due to her traumatic family history: "My dad attended Manuel de Salas . . . He was disappeared, and I have been searching for him since I was eight years old. The sensation that he had studied there was so important." Elba, a moderate Catholic, grew up near downtown Santiago, but now lives in La Florida and sends her children to Rosario Concha, a Catholic charter school: "A friend recommended the school because many teachers' children attended there. The parents were middle-class Catholic people like us." Clara highlights how family, neighborhood, and political traditions influence many Ñuñoa families' educational decisions. In contrast, Elba, who has a similar background to Clara, notes how parents need to look for objective characteristics to select schools in La Florida due to the dearth of schools with established reputations there.[1]

This chapter explores how parents navigate the distinct educational markets in these two communities. More importantly, it illustrates how schools are a central site for middle-class parents' identity investments. Educational decisions reflect and reaffirm activists', Catholics', youngsters', and pragmatists' core identities. The chapter explores how local school choice markets differ in the two communities studied, how parents select schools based on their identities and a reflexive understanding of their own school experiences rather than based on academic performance or reputation alone, and the ways they use enrichment activities to overcome perceived deficiencies in their children's schools. The chapter thus offers an important corrective to most research arguing that middle-class parents seek to use schools primarily to promote their children's economic and social advantages.

A large international literature explores how parents and schools reproduce class inequality. Building on Bourdieu's and his colleagues' seminal analyses of how colleges provide advantages to upper-class students over their working-class counterparts,[2] scholars examine how middle-class parents select schools to benefit their children,[3] how these parents use extracurricular activities to enrich children's cultural capital,[4] and how those that place children in mixed-class schools still seek advantages for their own children while pursuing ostensibly altruistic goals.[5]

Most research on Chile echoes this work on Europe and North America by showing that charter schools exclude lower income students and those with learning disabilities,[6] middle-class parents send children to charter schools to avoid poor children,[7] and Chile's school choice model has not improved overall learning outcomes.[8] A small number of qualitative studies understand middle-class parents' motivations as more multifaceted and examine mixed-class interactions at schools.[9] However, most scholars assert that Chile has a class-segregated school system that does not effectively educate students in comparison with leading countries in Latin America and other member states of the Organisation for Economic Co-operation and Development (OECD), which includes the world's wealthiest countries.[10]

In the context of this broad pattern of educational inequality, this chapter explores two understudied dimensions of middle-class schooling in Chile that highlight this book's core concept of identity investments. The discussion is framed around the important differences between school markets in Ñuñoa and La Florida, drawing on the idea of local school "micro-climates" with distinct characteristics.[11] Fully private schools predominate in Ñuñoa, while more affordable charter schools prevail in La Florida. I first look at parents' motivations for selecting their children's schools in the two areas. Ñuñoa parents focus on their own family traditions and schools' reputations, while La Florida parents place a greater emphasis on schools' educational plans, cost, and performance. Additionally, Ñuñoa residents explicitly reject elite schools while La Florida residents distance themselves from high-cost private schools, public schools, and the poor. I argue that these differences reflect the distinct class composition and school markets in the two areas.

In both communities, school choices reflect parents' identity investments. Upper-middle-class parents prioritize schools' promotion of socioemotional, creative, and critical thinking skills over standardized test scores or school rankings. These values, in turn, reflect their political and religious identities that build on earlier life experiences in childhood and college. Surprisingly, upper-middle-class parents reject elite public and private schools, even though many of them graduated from similar schools. They reject the intense academic and social competition in these schools as well as their exclusionary practices. Pragmatists, in contrast, see schools' academic performance as offering their children the best chance for professional success.

Second, I explore how parents supplement the educations schools provide. While upper-middle-class parents reject the most academically competitive schools, they "hedge their bets" by engaging in "concerted cultivation": they offer their children enrichment activities to compensate for some of the academic deficiencies they see in the children's schools.[12] Thus, activists', moderate Catholics,' and youngsters' knowledge of the educational system and greater economic resources that can be marshalled to pay for enrichment activities provide them with the "luxury" of selecting "values" over "academic performance." However, as we learn in the following chapter, values reflect more than personal preferences—activists and moderate Catholics engage in political activism and volunteer work that express their core commitments to social equity. In contrast, pragmatists must rely on the knowledge and skills that schools provide.

Exploration of these two themes reveals a paradox: upper-middle-class parents harshly criticize elite schools' exclusionary practices and their hyper-competitive peers, but still try to use their cultural and economic capital to benefit their children through concerted cultivation. Lower-middle-class parents primarily rely on schools' academic programs to support their children's education. Both upper- and lower-middle-class parents experienced "precarious privilege" in that they could opt out of the public school system, but were excluded from the highest achieving, highest status schools due to cost and these schools' "hard mechanisms of exclusion" noted above. Their identity investments that built on their childhood habiti provided them with a rationale for rejecting the schools that rejected them. After providing a brief overview of how Chile's school choice market is structured, I take up the themes of educational choice, identity, and concerted cultivation. The discussion highlights contrasts between the two communities and among schools studied within each community.

Middle Classes and Schooling in Santiago, Chile

Under the Pinochet dictatorship, Chile shifted from a largely public school system to one in which private and privately-run charter schools predominate. While private elementary and high schools have maintained their historic share of 7–8 percent of the K–12 education market, a 1981 educational reform under the military regime created publicly subsidized charter schools and shifted school financing and oversight from the Education Ministry to municipal governments. A 1993 law under a democratically elected government allowed charter schools to charge tuition.[13] By 2010, charters represented over half of all educational institutions.[14] In spite of the market logic behind the reform that promised improvements in quality as "consumers" shifted demand toward efficient service providers, charters have not shown consistently better performance than public schools.[15]

Legal reforms in 2004, 2008, 2009, and 2015 sought to decrease socioeconomic segregation between public and charter schools, but because these laws were weakly enforced and some include voluntary opt-in mechanisms for schools, students in public and charter schools remain highly segregated by class.[16] Charters have historically used tuition fees or entrance exams to exclude poor students and those with learning disabilities or behavioral problems even though the law prohibits this practice for schools receiving public subsidies. The 2008 Preferential Educational Subvention law (SEP) offered an additional subsidy to schools that enrolled low-income students contingent upon improved standardized testing performance, but 40 percent of charters opted out of the subsidy. The following year, in response to the Penguin Revolution, the General Education Law (LGE) prohibited schools' selection of students based on academic performance or income before the sixth grade, but charters have continued to use these admissions criteria due to lax government oversight. The 2015 School Inclusion Law created a national application system for charter schools and banned the use of entrance exams to exclude students, but has not yet eliminated school fees. The law will be phased in over several years and its effects on segregation are still uncertain.[17]

Charter and fully private schools continue to use "hard mechanisms of exclusion" (tuition, entrance exams, and parental interviews) and "soft mechanisms of exclusion" like marketing a school by promoting characteristics that appeal to affluent parents or solely advertising in affluent neighborhoods.[18] Elite private schools select parents through high fees, income or stock purchase requirements, entrance exams, parental interviews, evidence of parents' religious affiliation and marriage/baptismal certificates, and recommendations from current parents.[19] These screens reinforce these schools' exclusivity and make them inaccessible to families that are low income, are not religious, are not part of school networks, and whose children have special needs.

Some argue that parents select schools based on the class makeup of students rather than their academic performance, and schools compete for higher income students rather than high-achieving children.[20] In contrast, others note that parents use a variety of criteria to select schools (values, discipline, safety, students' class background), but only affluent parents are willing to send children to schools outside their neighborhood.[21] Since poor parents are unwilling or unable to send children to schools outside of their residential areas and high-performing schools are clustered in affluent communities, poor families are at a disadvantage for accessing high quality schools.[22]

Choosing Schools

The research outlined above helps explain broad patterns of inequality in Chile's education system and offers a critique of its institutional design that I share. However, research seldom explores parents' motivations for selecting specific schools and how local school markets frame those decisions. In both Ñuñoa and La Florida, I found that Chile's religious- and class-based political cleavages with roots dating back to the nineteenth century profoundly shaped parents' choices.[23] Adults were not simply looking for high-performing schools or institutions where their children would build ties with affluent peers. Additionally, parents made reflexive choices based on their past school experiences—they often hoped their children would not face the same harsh experiences they endured in school. Thus, all parents in this sample sent their children to private and charter schools, which contributed to broader patterns of socioeconomic segregation. However, their motives for selecting schools built on their identity investments. The specific way this played out varied across the two communities based on the characteristics of local school markets.

In contrasting parents' school choice practices in Ñuñoa and La Florida, I draw on the concept of *micro-climates*. This term describes how middle-class families primarily use social networks as information channels to steer them toward specific neighborhoods (and hence school districts). They settle in neighborhoods or micro-climates whose residents, shops, and schools consist of people like them. These class-specific network mechanisms result in more affluent children attending higher performing schools even though they do not put more effort into seeking information than do working-class parents.[24] I examine parents' motivations for school selection in each community to discern differences across space. Table 3.1 highlights parents' attitudes in the five schools studied.

School	Location	Year Founded	School Type	Parents' Identity Investments in School	School Types Rejected
Manuel de Salas	Ñuñoa	1932	Private, secular	Secular identity, humanistic/experimental education, alumni status, diversity	Religious, elite
Calasanz	Ñuñoa	1951	Private, Catholic	Religious identity, alumni status, social justice, diversity, personalized attention, ethical training	Secular, elite
Raimapu	La Florida	1982	Charter, secular	Political identity, tradition of protecting political dissidents, humanistic education, diversity, special needs services	Religious, private, local public, elite
Raíces Altazor	La Florida	1985	Charter, secular	Charismatic principal, humanistic education, diversity, special needs services	Religious, private, local public, elite
Rosario Concha	La Florida	1913	Charter, religious	Academic excellence, religious training, drug/ alcohol prevention	Secular, local public, private

Table 3.1 Identity Investments in Schools

Ñuñoa Schools

As noted in the introduction, Ñuñoa is an established upper-middle-class community with an array of well-known private and public schools and a rich cultural infrastructure. At the time when research was conducted, it was home to 20,886 children and had twenty-two private schools, eleven public schools, and fifteen charter schools.[25] A plurality of schools in the community were fully private, and this characteristic had an important influence on the parents I studied.[26] In Ñuñoa, I focused on two fully private schools—Manuel de Salas Experimental School (LMS) and Calasanz School—both of which are well known in the community and in Santiago.

Manuel de Salas

Amanda Labarca was LMS's founder and first principal. Labarca was the Director of Secondary Education during the Alessandri administration (1932–1938), played a crucial role in the development of public education, was a feminist activist, and conducted pioneering research on Chile's middle class.[27] The school partnered with the Ministry of Education and University of Chile Teacher's College to develop innovative curricula and policies that would later be disseminated to other public high schools. After the 1981 educational reform that separated the Teacher's College from the University of Chile and renamed it the Metropolitan University for Educational Sciences (UMCE), LMS was placed under this newly autonomous entity and converted into a private school. The UMCE skimmed resources from the school, and in 2002, parents (some of whom I interviewed) successfully lobbied Congress for its return to the University of Chile.[28]

At the time of my 2008–2010 fieldwork, LMS included a devoted group of parents that strongly valued its history, promotion of the arts, diversity, and high levels of democratic participation among parents and students. The school, however, faced several challenges. First, a large percentage of parents were in arrears, and hence the school established more strict payment terms that would lead to the expulsion of students whose parents did not clear a portion of their debts. A new parent-teacher association leadership team collaborated with school officials to improve the school, raise money, and organize cultural activities. An unpopular principal had been replaced and the new principal, while well liked, was finding his footing. High school students staged takeovers of the school two years in a row in support of the Penguin

Revolution leading to the departure of some families, particularly parents of elementary school students.[29] Finally, some parents of elementary school students complained that high school students bullied their children, and the school's alternative conflict resolution disciplinary policy did not have adequate sanctions to protect young children. I explore these last two points in detail in the next chapter.

Activists and youngsters at LMS faced the challenge of finding a secular private school because the vast majority of offerings were Catholic schools. Their desire to educate their children in secular schools in some cases reflected their political beliefs as leftists, and in others their criticisms of religious proselytism present in Catholic schools. José grew up in Ñuñoa but rejected religious schools out of hand: "I'm uncomfortable with religious schools. I had a great time as a student at a religious school—the priests were fantastic—but I think the church has changed over the last thirty-five or forty years. I didn't want my kids to have religious training as I am an absolutely secular person."[30] José's comments underscore the Catholic Church's dedication to liberation theology as an outgrowth of Vatican II and the Medellin, Colombia, Episcopal Conference in 1968, as well as its conservative shift in the 1980s under Pope John Paul II.[31] Thus, while he admired the progressive church, he felt alienated from today's more conservative church.

Additionally, he highlights the enduring religious/secular divide that dates back to the nineteenth century and has filtered its way into Chileans' enduring political preferences.[32] As a leftist architect, José strongly identifies with the civic and cultural vocation of secular parties dating back to the mid-nineteenth century. He connects Manuel de Salas with the rise of a learned middle class (*una clase media ilustrada*) formed through mid-twentieth-century policies that promoted public education: "You can't understand Chile's artistic and cultural development linked to the University of Chile [which includes a campus adjacent to Ñuñoa] without considering the Chilean government's policies under Radical Party governments. I remember a conversation I had with José Balmes, a painter that won the National Art Prize. He told me, 'Look—we were college professors and we also painted. Our university jobs gave us the space to do our creative work.' The same was true for theater: my father founded one of the university theater companies, and it was absolutely tied to the government." Here, José ties LMS (because it was affiliated with the University of Chile) with the mid-twentieth-century rise of government policies promoting secular public education and artistic production. It also shows his family's and friends' roles as artistic innovators that contributed to Chile's cultural life.

So, for parents like José, sending children to LMS carries the torch of secular public education. It is an identity investment that builds on family history and a legacy of public policies that contributed to his identity and enacts his values. It also highlights how some members of the upper-middle class see themselves as part of a cultural elite that shaped aspects of public policy prior to the coup and that is now increasingly marginalized in the face of a dominant private business sector. This theme has already surfaced in discussions of activists' discomfort in the workplace and criticisms of "McMansions" and gated communities. Their sense of a lost dominance is central to their condition of precarious privilege and their identity investments in the school market.

Youngsters whose children attend LMS also bristled at the idea of selecting a religious school. Mickey, a history teacher, comments, "We looked at one Catholic school run by nuns, and my daughter is totally opposed to religion. Even though we are believers, we don't go to church often. She didn't like the atmosphere the nuns created. We like the fact that LMS is economically and intellectually diverse. It's more like the real world—it opened her mind." While Mickey does not express principled opposition to religious education, she notes that Catholic schools clashed with her daughter's values and also that LMS provides a diverse environment that prepares her well for adult life.

The choice of a secular school required negotiation in interfaith couples. In some cases, one partner preferred a religious school, but the other persuaded them to select LMS. Jimena, an LMS alumna, comments: "We applied to Saint George [an elite Catholic school], which offered similar values to LMS. My daughter did well on the test, but the school prioritized children of alumni. In reality, we wanted a secular school because I'm Catholic and my husband is agnostic, so we hoped to compromise. My husband had no intention of attending a religious ceremony [laughs]. We didn't want our daughters to complain that we wouldn't attend their school activities." In this scenario, one parent "put their foot down" and insisted that their children attend a secular school even though their spouse was open to providing their children with a religious education. Notably, an elite school rejected their daughter's application because it prioritized children of alumni, illustrating a "hard" mechanism of exclusion.

Other interviewees who were alumni sought to build on valued childhood experiences. Rodrigo, an activist and alumnus that could not afford to live in

Ñuñoa, still decided to send his children to LMS: "My classmates' children and my kids attended a daycare center together where the staff were former teachers at Manuel de Salas. Everyone moves in the same social circle." Rodrigo trusted the former teachers employed at his children's daycare center, and sending his children to LMS allows him to retain his friendship connections to his former classmates.

Clara, whose story is discussed at the chapter's beginning, notes her entire family's connections to LMS and the fact that her children's attendance there allows her to honor her father. "My whole family studied at Manuel de Salas. My uncle, an engineer, did the construction work on the current building. My extended family was part of the intellectual vanguard and involved in the school." Clara's comments point to her nostalgia for a great educational and family tradition at the school. Like José, telling her family story is a way to signal both accumulated cultural capital across generations (the intellectuals and artists in her family) and to underscore how her family contributed to Chile's cultural development. It also underscores how her choice of LMS for her children helps her cope with the trauma of having lost her father (as noted in the chapter's beginning) due to the dictatorship's repression of left-wing party militants.

Some activists expressed concerns about the school's administrative decisions and academic performance. However, they rationalized their decision to stay based on the school's affordability (relative to better options), the difficulty of moving high school children, or the social and civic training students receive there. Carola, a freelance physical education teacher and practitioner of alternative healing arts, comments: "I think it's a good school, in spite of all its crises. The system worked for my kids, if not academically, at least in terms of their ability to develop relationships. One of my kids struggled academically, but he graduated and is starting his life path [laughs]." Rodrigo and Lenka remark:

> Lenka: They fired several veteran teachers that had a "mystique," and I have no idea why.
> Rodrigo: Our oldest has one year left, and the middle child has two years left.
> Lenka: Our daughter is younger and I would have loved to change her, but few other schools are affordable. Even if we found a school we liked, we know every school has its dramas [en todos lados cuecen habas].

Thus, some activists that criticized the school recognized that they had "sunk costs" there and felt attached to its history. Rodrigo and Carola are alumni, and Lenka speaks highly of the school's "veteran teachers." Thus, in addition to concerns about cost and the unknowns associated with a new school, these parents retained strong emotional attachments to the school in spite of their criticisms.

While most studies see private school parents as primarily focused on academic achievement and/or building their own and their children's pools of social and cultural capital,[33] the upper-middle-class parents I interviewed almost universally rejected elite private and public schools because of their perceived promotion of unbridled competition. LMS parents counterposed their choices to those of parents who sent children to highly selective, elite schools. Jimena comments, "That's what happens with schools like Andrée [an elite private Catholic school]. You say to yourself, 'Gosh, they give no training in personal and emotional development, but the students get into the best universities and develop lots of connections that help them get jobs.' But those students' hearts are small. If I wanted my daughters to be success-oriented, I wouldn't have sent them to Manuel de Salas." Here, Jimena rejects elite schools' exclusive focus on students' success to the detriment of their social and moral development.

María, a youngster, describes why she discarded an elite private school: "We were considering Kent School because it is bilingual, has small class sizes, and is supposed to be really good. However, I met a Peruvian couple at my daughter's daycare center. They are pharmacists and have a dark complexion. The mother went to Kent School and they told her they didn't have any openings for new children, but I knew they had spaces available . . . So, I said to myself, 'This is terrible. I don't want my daughter to discriminate against others,' so we discarded this option." María highlights youngsters' sensitivity to discriminatory practices toward immigrants at elite schools.

José takes aim at the lack of class diversity within elite private schools: "I think LMS is more diverse than Grange and Saint George [two of the top-performing, highest status private schools], but it's probably less diverse than public schools in Ñuñoa. The community has a rich and an impoverished middle class, both of which are present at LMS. That should be the middle class people refer to when they talk about the middle class that built this country." Here, José again sees LMS as the guardian of a secular, socioeconomically diverse civic educational tradition that is missing in elite private schools.

Parents who studied in elite public schools also rejected these options due to their negative experiences as students and concerns about safety in the communities where these schools are located. Rafael, a youngster, and National Institute alumnus, comments: "At the National Institute, students are not allowed to express their opinion. The teachers were detached and promoted competition between students in different classes. Students are encouraged to express their opinions at LMS. The National Institute is extremely rigorous academically but offers students zero support to develop their values." Again, Rafael rejects the singular focus on academic success that Jimena noted above.

Tamara, an activist, is a graduate of Liceo #1 de Niñas, the top public girls high school in Chile. She remarks, "We could have sent our daughters to Liceo #1 but public education has declined since I attended, and I don't feel that downtown is as safe as it used to be for our girls to walk around. The school's quality has declined and it has less resources, so it wasn't an option." Here, Tamara pinpoints an issue that some scholarly critics of middle-class parents miss. One consequence of the Pinochet regime's educational reforms is that private charter and fully private schools receive six times the funding of public schools.[34] Middle-class parents that seek quality schools have limited choices because of the massive defunding of public schools. Thus, their selection of charter or private schools cannot be interpreted as solely motivated by a desire to avoid the poor in public schools; rather, it reflects their critique of elite schools' sole focus on academic results and their concerns about the funding of public schools.

Calasanz

Calasanz, founded in 1951, is located a few blocks from LMS and is a high-functioning school operated by the Piarist religious order.[35] Charging similar fees to LMS and waiving a registration fee (which often makes private schools prohibitively expensive), the school had expanded in the years immediately prior to my 2008–2009 research there due to high demand. Calasanz had a wide array of religious and secular activities for children and families, and parents appreciated the fact that it was an "open" school, meaning that they could come and go as they pleased and families participated in activities during weekday evenings and weekends. The school had an official policy to accept the children of separated and divorced parents as well as non-Catholics, which both parents and school officials emphasized as a stark contrast to most private Catholic schools. Parents and school officials agreed that the school was academically challenging but tried to minimize student stress and to educate the "whole child" through sports, the arts, second language education, and religious activity.[36]

While LMS parents emphasize their school's roots in secular, public education and cultural policies, Calasanz parents highlight their role as alumni as well as the school's religious mission, which also focuses on social justice. Marcelo comments: "We chose Calasanz because my wife and I both studied there, and all of our children attended as well." Claudio sketches the contributions and tribulations of Saint Joseph Calasanz, the Piarist Order's founder: "Calasanz created the first public schools in the world. He and Father Hurtado[37] provide the school's vision. Obviously, the foolish church [*la iglesia huevón*] excommunicated him for his beliefs. He was whipped, dragged through the streets, and thrown in the dungeon for providing public education."[38] Claudio's narrative highlights the themes of religious sacrifice, solidarity with the poor, and persecution by the pre-Enlightenment Catholic Church. Thus, in contrast with LMS parents who locate the school within the history of Chile's public policy, Calasanz parents anchor the school's identity in the history of the Piarist Order, Saint Calasanz's earlier contributions to public education, and the image of religious sacrifice.

While parents at LMS sought freedom, diversity, and creativity, parents at Calasanz expressed distinct preferences. Claudia comments: "We wanted a Catholic school that had a personalized style. We wanted our children to learn to be caring and humble. Academic training came second: if the school didn't give them all the necessary skills, I could provide them." Claudio makes a similar comment: "We wanted the school to reinforce our family's values promoting social equity and solidarity." Like LMS parents, Calasanz parents deemphasized academic excellence as their priority. However, they focused more on their children's *moral development* than their exposure to a diverse student body with a wide range of ideas and attitudes or a school with an overtly political identity.

Calasanz parents also feared their children would face ostracism at elite schools. Sofia, a moderate Catholic and physical therapist whose children attended school after living abroad, comments: "I felt like Calasanz had a group of families that were similar to us, so that my children would not be looked down upon and they would not look down on others." Sofia went on to explain that when her children began at Calasanz after living in Ecuador for a few years, other children bullied them because of their foreign accents. Thus,

she was particularly sensitive to her children's ostracism at school. Professionals in this community are exposed to members of the elite, but due to their
middle-class backgrounds, they reject the values of competition and success
in favor of a focus on individual expression.[39]

Calasanz parents also rejected the excessive academic focus at elite secular schools. Marcelo comments, "My wife is an educational psychologist,
and she was treating our family friends' children that attended Kent School [a
secular bilingual school]. I'll never forget that there was a child under severe
stress because he got a B in language arts class. When my son attended there,
we 'put up our antennas' and realized there were several kids suffering from
depression." These parents also sought to avoid the exclusionary practices
of elite Catholic schools. Gonzalo, who is married to Dany and works in his
family business, remarks, "The school doesn't marginalize the children of
single mothers, of a different religious creed, or who struggle academically."
Here, these parents highlight the effects of intense academic competition on
children's mental health as well as elite Catholic schools' exclusion of nontra-
ditional families. These comments highlight Calasanz parents' concerns that
their children would face ostracism or exclusion for their academic performance in elite schools, and that these schools only include a narrow group of
culturally homogeneous families. Those families that considered elite schools
determined that their costs were prohibitive.[40]

On the other hand, Calasanz parents also avoided what they saw as the other
extreme of alternative schools. Carmen, a computer programmer and moderate Catholic, comments, "My husband doesn't like alternative schools because
their graduates become artists or musicians. He has cousins that are artists,
and they are more laid back than we are."[41] Claudio had been an active parent
volunteer at San Juan del Evangelio, an alternative Catholic school. However,
he became disenchanted with the school's financial mismanagement, teachers'
excessive bargaining power, and the principal's refusal to assert his authority:
"The students supported the principal because he treated them like peers. If he
had smoked a joint with them, they would think it was fantastic. So, I left the
school." Carmen expresses concerns that at an alternative school, her children
would pursue studies leading to unprofitable careers. In contrast, Claudio
removed his children from an alternative school because of the absence of
sufficient order and hierarchy at the school. Thus, Calasanz parents wanted
a diverse environment for their children within limits so that they received a
high-quality education and maintained good job prospects.

Given the large affluent population in Ñuñoa and the many private schools with established reputations there, most parents in the sample did not even consider public or charter schools. They expressed their religious and secular values through their school selection and contrasted themselves with the elite, but made no reference to the poor in their decision-making or everyday life in schools. These choices reflect their precarious privilege: they were geographically close to wealthy families and schools, but their identities and limited resources led them to reject those schools.

La Florida Schools

La Florida is an up-and-coming suburban community that experienced explosive housing, population, and retail growth beginning in the late 1970s. When I conducted research, La Florida was home to 73,449 children and had ten private schools, twenty-five public schools, and ninety-four charter schools.[42] In contrast to Ñuñoa, charter schools predominate in La Florida.

I focused on three schools in La Florida: Raimapu, Raíces Altazor, and Rosario Concha. All schools had originated as private schools and transitioned to charters in recent years to gain public subsidies and expand their student base to remain solvent. This was a pattern, I learned, in many La Florida schools, which likely reflected economic changes (the late 1990s Asian financial crisis) as well as many residents' more modest incomes.

While upper-middle-class families in La Florida earned similar incomes to their Ñuñoa counterparts, they did not consider elite private schools as hypothetical options for their children and rarely even mentioned them. I argue that this reflects several differences between the two communities. First, as noted above, a plurality of schools in Ñuñoa are private, while most schools are charters in La Florida. Second, Ñuñoa had an affluent urban population dating back to the nineteenth century, and hence elite private schools were established there earlier. In contrast, La Florida's development as a suburb only occurred in the 1970s, and it has a much larger low-income population than Ñuñoa. Hence, there is a smaller group of parents that could support expensive private schools. This smaller market for private schools is evident from the fact that all three schools I studied in La Florida had begun as small private schools and became charters in the late 1990s and early 2000s. Interviewees also mentioned other schools that made the same transition.

Finally, Ñuñoa families (or those with children in that community's schools) have social contacts (based in family, work, voluntary associations, and neighborhoods) with others attending elite private schools due to the community's higher average incomes and location close to wealthier communities like Providencia and Las Condes. Consequently, these private schools are part of the "micro-climate" in which Ñuñoa families participate. In contrast, as detailed below, upper-middle-class families in the La Florida sample saw most local private schools as academically deficient, overpriced, or both. They were not concerned about these schools excluding their children; rather, they did not see them as appealing options.

Raimapu

Raimapu was founded in 1982 to serve the children of left-wing party members, many of whom had returned from exile as the dictatorship slowly relaxed restrictions on its political opponents. It began as a fully private school, but it was cooperatively owned by parents and educators. In 2001, the school governing board decided to convert it to a charter, leading to a split among parents. Some feared the end of the school's cooperative structure could lead to the principal or board members' private appropriation of school resources and that the school's educational mission might be compromised with the entry of new parents that did not share founders' political commitments. Thirty families left the school to form a new alternative school, Andares de La Florida.

The school has doubled in size since the transition, and its strong test scores make it appealing to a broad range of parents. Raimapu's educational mission and parental profiles are similar to LMS, though the latter school is more politically diverse. Raimapu seemed somewhat more stable and less conflictive than LMS, though when I conducted research, tense contract negotiations between teachers and the administration spilled over into parental discussions and loyalties. Camila Vallejo, a Raimapu graduate, was the face of the 2011 college student movement, served in Congress representing the Communist Party, and is currently a cabinet official in President Gabriel Boric's administration.[43] I revisit the school's political life and involvement in the Penguin Revolution in the next chapter.

There is a similar religious-secular split in La Florida to that we observed in Ñuñoa. In some cases, Raimapu parents had attended Catholic schools in an earlier progressive era but rejected that option today. César, a teacher and Raimapu parent who works for a local branch of the Education Ministry, comments, "We looked at a Catholic school in Macul [community next to La Florida]. I rang the doorbell, and I had to enter a cell—I don't know exactly

what it was—and they kind of stared at me and told me I had to come a specific day with the appropriate paperwork. It was like a jail cell. No way was I
sending my child there! I attended Patrocinio San José, a Catholic school, but
it was a center-left school. The principal was the head of Radio Chilena, one of
the two stations opposed to the dictatorship. So, they had a different teaching
style." Much like José, César had attended a progressive Catholic school and
the telltale signs of authoritarianism in the "jail cell" he entered scared him
away from the Catholic school in Macul. While the church hierarchy became
more conservative in the 1980s, activists that experienced its progressive phase
during the 1960s and 1970s still carry those values.

The parents in the three La Florida schools I studied were almost entirely in-migrants to La Florida and thus were not alumni of their children's
schools. Indeed, some Raimapu parents were part of the "Ñuñoa diaspora" I
described in the last chapter, while others were raised elsewhere in Santiago or
in provincial cities like Valparaíso. Nonetheless, some activists were founding
parents at Raimapu and valued its origins and identity developed under the
dictatorship. Mario recalls: "We got to know Raimapu a long time ago. We had
a lot of friends. At that time, your life depended on your friendship network
and their ability to protect you. In those days, we harshly criticized public
education because it was too militarized. So, Raimapu was a natural option.
It's an enjoyable space that offers greater freedom and more open-mindedness
[than other schools]." Ricardo and Gloria recall:

> *Ricardo:* That's an old story about how we arrived at Raimapu. My wife's
> cousin's children attended.
> *Gloria:* Her dad is my uncle, the artist, who was exiled. She was returning
> from exile in Nicaragua and chose Raimapu because it welcomed former
> exiles.
> *Ricardo:* It was a left-wing school, like Latinoamericano and Francisco de
> Miranda.[44] I also taught classes there one year when our first child was
> born, so we decided to send her there. We're both teachers, so we knew
> what we were looking for.

Both these comments demonstrate that several Raimapu families selected the
school because of their immediate needs for safety and a welcoming environment under the dictatorship as well as their embeddedness within left-wing
subcultures. Like LMS families, some of these individuals had experienced

intergenerational trauma due to their parents' repression (as was the case with Mario) and sought an educational community that respected diversity of thought.

Youngsters at Raimapu selected the school for different reasons. Gladys, a graphic designer, comments, "My oldest daughter is deaf, and she attended a Catholic school administered by nuns using the oralist teaching method. The problem is that the oralist method is very challenging for deaf children and families. Working parents can't keep up with all of the assignments. I met my partner and he had a child at Raimapu. We asked if they would admit my daughter with my commitment to provide additional support via an educational psychologist. They were kind and had good intentions, but they could not meet her needs." Her older daughter later had to shift to another school that specialized in educating children with hearing impairments. However, "My partner and I started attending events at Raimapu when my older daughter went there. My younger daughter said, 'I want to go to Raimapu. I don't care anymore about the Olympic size swimming pool at my school.' My partner's younger son also decided to go there."[45] Here, we see how Raimapu's social activities and sense of community attracted parents and their children that have a different profile from the "founding parents."

Like their Ñuñoa counterparts, activists in La Florida rejected elite public schools. Ricardo, who attended the National Institute, comments, "We wanted a space that was not authoritarian or success-oriented but was still academically demanding. I taught at the National Institute [he is also an alumnus]. A good teacher there gave students an 800-page study guide. And I thought, 'You've gotta be kidding me!'" Raimapu parents also rejected neighborhood-based public schools due to their poor academic performance and difficult social environments. Mario remarks, "Sometimes we wish our kids were in public schools, but there weren't any good ones in 1992. Recently, our son wanted to try a public school. We sent him to a public trade school, and he felt like a fish out of water. He lasted about two weeks. He had a couple of bad experiences and quickly returned to Raimapu." Like Ñuñoa activists, these Raimapu parents were products of the public education system or valued it, but determined that its reduced funding and warehousing of poor children made it untenable for their children. I discuss activists' rejection of local private schools below.

Raíces Altazor

Raíces Altazor, unlike the other schools in this study, solely serves elementary school students. Founded in 1985 by former Raimapu teachers as a private school, Raíces is currently a charter school. While Raíces shares with both Raimapu and LMS a focus on developing students' socioemotional skills as well as fostering their artistic and creative capacities, its orientation and the types of families it serves are somewhat different from these two other alternative schools. Raíces is less overtly political, and the parents I interviewed did not see the school as an expression of their political identities. The school also explicitly sought to build a socioeconomically diverse student body.[46] When I met one of the two directors, she told me that "most of the Raimapu parents share similar outlooks. Here, you will find a diverse group of families with distinct perspectives."[47] Perhaps because of this more muted political identity, Raíces appeared less riven by conflict than LMS and Raimapu, as we explore in the next chapter.

Most Raíces parents I interviewed were averse to sending their children to a religious school, like their counterparts at LMS or Raimapu. For example, Israel, an activist and Raíces parent, comments: "I love what the Jesuits do with education. I think it's extraordinary, but I'm not Catholic, so I'm not going to enroll my child in a Catholic school, dude [*yo no voy a meter a mi hijo a un colegio católico, po' huevón*] [*laughs*]. I don't go to mass, so I would tell them that it's all a bunch of nonsense." Tomás comments, "Even though I grew up Catholic and my dad was very religious, I think Catholicism and most religions educate based on fear: 'If you do this, something bad will happen to you.' None of my three kids are baptized. Those schools don't interest me." Israel and Tomás display their strong secular identities that prevent them from sending their children to a Catholic school, even though Israel respects Jesuit education and Tomás attended a Catholic school.

While activists at Raimapu emphasized its political identity and youngsters arrive at the school because it integrated children with learning disabilities, Raíces parents emphasized the school's pedagogical approach and the charisma of the school's founders and principals (two sisters who were former teachers). Tomás continues, "The kids that graduate from that school are critical thinkers, autonomous, and have very healthy judgments and opinions. They break out of established canons because they have the spirit of discovery, innovation, and the desire to search for new things." Others expressed a deep devotion to the school's principals. Ingrid comments: "After my child's first teacher, he had Paz [one of the principals] and she is one of a kind . . . If she asks us to volunteer at the school we can't say 'no' because she's so committed to the kids." These descriptions echo some of the above discussions of LMS and Raimapu with regard to the schools' emphasis on creativity, discovery, and free thought. However, Raíces parents did not discuss the school's political identity, and their devotion to the school centered more on its leadership than was the case in other schools. Perhaps because the school is smaller than the others and does not have a high school, parents felt their volunteer activities gave them greater influence over the school's administration.

Much like Raimapu, youngsters found Raíces attractive because they believed the school served children with learning disabilities or behavioral issues. Lisette comments: "Sending our son to Raíces has been stress free. Since we recently moved from Talca [a few hours south of Santiago], I didn't want to stress him out given the transition and his being far from extended family. I liked the fact that the school was relaxed because that's what my son needs right now. He doesn't need someone scolding him all the time, and he's a restless kid, too." Like youngsters that selected Manuel de Salas, and Raimapu, Lisette's decision was also informed by her criticisms of discriminatory behavior: "Where I attended school, the custodian's child was classmates with the child of Talca's richest man. The school had zero tolerance for discrimination. In fact, only students expressing racist and classist attitudes faced discrimination." Thus, Lisette sought a safe space for her son given his behavioral challenges, but her criticisms of discrimination also informed this choice.

The two pragmatists I interviewed at Raíces were teachers. Their perspective on the school bore some similarities to those expressed by activist parents, though they had more modest backgrounds and incomes than the activists. They drew on their work experiences in selecting the school. Alejandra, who also was a part-time administrative employee at Raíces, remarks: "My ex-husband and I wanted a school that wasn't so rigidly structured. We wanted a small school with direct and close human relationships that valued diversity . . . We liked the artistic activities they developed in kindergarten." Alejandra went on to recount the harsh experiences she had at a public school where teachers did not recognize her and she did not develop friendships. She also noted that her son had some behavioral issues, so like Lisette, she wanted teachers to offer him personalized attention and a nurturing environment.

Iván, a pragmatist, also appreciated the school's artistic focus: "When I was looking for schools, Raíces and one other school had appealing educational projects. They don't require uniforms and let the kids wear long hair. They respect children's identities and treat them as individuals rather than numbers. The National Institute may be an excellent school, but you are a number there, not a person. As a teacher, I wanted to find the best school for my kids." Alejandra and Iván note similar themes to those activists mentioned—diversity, individuality, creativity—without referencing the more abstract concepts of educational canons, critical thinking, and innovation that Tomás emphasized. This difference likely reflects their more modest family origins and graduation from second-tier universities.

Raíces parents also rejected elite public or charter schools. Israel comments, "We looked at a charter school with the highest test scores in the area but it was like the National Institute. My daughter took the entrance exam for first grade, but it included everything students should know after having completed first grade. So, we realized it was the 'meat grinder.' We were like Forrest Gump in the scene where the mother sleeps with the principal so Forrest can be admitted. My daughter didn't pass the test, but the secretary said we could talk to the principal to ask for an exception. I said, 'If she's not good enough for the school, the school isn't good enough for her.'" He continues, "We rejected local public schools because of their poor performance and also because my daughter is a little precious. She is timid, and we couldn't imagine her in a class of forty or forty-five students." Here, we see echoes of César's experience applying to a Catholic school. If parents faced humiliation or rejection when applying for their children's admission, they pursued other options. Israel, like other activist parents, sought an alternative to the harsh competition present at the National Institute and the perceived shortcomings of local public schools.

Like their Raimapu counterparts, activists at Raíces also rejected La Florida's private schools because they perceived them as academically inadequate and viewed the parents at these schools as buffoons. José Miguel, a chemistry teacher, comments, "Here at the British American School, the children don't speak English [laughs]. They think the name gives it a higher status. It's as if it were the Grange School [one of the highest ranked bilingual schools in Chile]."[48] This is an important contrast with the discussion in Ñuñoa. Parents in that community found elite private schools academically challenging and potentially beneficial to their children's learning and career opportunities, but saw them as excessively exclusive, expensive, and homogeneous. In contrast, activists at Raimapu and Raíces made fun of the private schools in their community because they aspired to be like elite private schools in upper-class communities, but these aspirations were unrealistic. Again, La Florida's more recent settlement and mixed-class character meant it had few high-performing private schools with appealing reputations.

Rosario Concha

Finally, Colegio Rosario Concha, founded in 1913, was originally a private school located in the wealthy community of Providencia and later moved to La Florida.[49] It is the oldest of the schools studied and subsequently became a charter school. The most socioeconomically diverse of all five schools, Rosario Concha focused on academic excellence as well as religious instruction. When I first met the principal, she commented, "Perhaps your study will help us understand why some of the parents inflate their income declarations. They are poor and if they stated their real incomes, we would receive a larger subsidy under the SEP, which would benefit all students."[50] Her comment highlights the shame poor parents likely felt due to their low incomes. While Rosario was unpretentious, school authorities made the most consistent effort to educate both poor and middle-class students. At the same time, cross-class parental tensions did not permit the development of a strong school identity, and hence social relationships in the school were distant, fractious, and at times, hostile, as I explore in the next chapter.[51]

Many parents that sent children to Rosario had attended Catholic schools themselves, so this seemed like an obvious choice for their children. Nelson, a youngster, comments, "I attended a Salesian Catholic school located about a kilometer from our home." However, like parents at Manuel de Salas in Ñuñoa, some Rosario parents were interfaith couples and thus had to reach a compromise about sending children to a religious school. Elba comments, "I'm not that interested in religion, but my husband is because he attended a Catholic school. He's more interested in values. I'm interested in values that contribute to my kids' development, but I'm more of a free thinker. My daughter is a true believer, which is fine with me—it's her choice." Thus, like Jimena, the LMS parent, Elba's agreement to send her children to Rosario was a compromise with her husband although it was not necessarily her first choice.

Moderate Catholics at Rosario Concha believed the school protected their children from violence and drugs. Ana, a housewife and former secretary, comments: "A coworker at the bank had their child at Rosario. It was a small Catholic school. The kids there are still well-balanced and studious, and there aren't big disciplinary issues. You see cases of bullying, drugs, and aggressive behavior on the news. School officials know each student, and they keep things under control."[52] Similarly, as noted in this chapter's introduction, Elba appreciated the school's academic performance and the fact that many other parents are middle class like her. Ana and Elba thus emphasize the academic training and moral guidance the school provides children as well as its class composition.

Nelson emphasizes the school's academic performance: "It's one of the best schools in the area. It has a Western Christian orientation because it is run by priests, so it offers students culture, education, and ethics. I like the teachers my kids have had because they are academically demanding. We did a little research and found out which teachers were the most challenging." Janneth, a physician who immigrated from Ecuador, comments, "The school has a lot of positive features. It's easier for my son to make friends there than at his school in Ecuador. I also appreciate the religious instruction. I'm currently attending workshops to prepare for my son's first communion." Janneth's concern about her son's social integration at school in part reflects her negative experiences applying for his admission to other schools. "I looked at the American British School and Shirayuri, but they require too much documentation. My son had to take a test and participate in a play session. I was required to supply my marriage license [she is a single mother] and his baptismal certificate, which was back in Ecuador. At Shirayuri, they wanted to know who recommended the school, and the woman at the American British School was brusque with me. I thought, 'If I'm the mother and they treat me this way, how will they treat my son?'"[53] Both these schools are secular, suggesting that their request for marriage and baptismal certificates was a ruse designed to exclude an immigrant child. Nelson and Janneth emphasize Rosario's academic performance, its focus on religious and moral instruction, and its inclusion of immigrant children.

While activists and moderate Catholics sought schools that expressed their intellectual and ethical values, and youngsters pursued academically sound schools, pragmatists at Rosario Concha used cost, safety, and schools' proximity to their homes as the main criteria for selecting schools. Paulina comments: "I started identifying the schools that we could afford and that were neither too cheap nor too expensive—that's how we arrived at Rosario

Concha." Pragmatists also sought to protect their children from exposure to poverty. Nelly comments: "If my son didn't have a scholarship here, he would have been stuck attending a public school far from home."

Cost and distance were perceived barriers that deterred moderate Catholics in La Florida from sending children to high-performing private schools. Elba comments, "I thought about sending my son to Paul the Apostle School, where I am a bus driver. I brought him to take an entrance exam. It costs about three times as much as Rosario Concha. He passed the test, but I came down to reality after talking to my husband. I might be able to send my son to a high-achieving school, but couldn't afford to send all three kids there." Parents interested in treating all their children equally had to determine the maximum tuition they could pay for all of them. Like Calasanz parents, they considered elite private schools but determined they were too costly.

Tania, a youngster who is married to Nelson, emphasizes distance as a barrier to exploring other schools: "We think the kids are too little to go to a school that is far away because of the transit times, the rain during the winter, and so on. My in-laws who live near school can pick them up when my husband and I are working. We'd like to send them to a better school when they can get around on their own." For dual-career families, school proximity was a priority for their elementary school children.

However, while activists at alternative schools rejected elite schools, Rosario parents—especially pragmatists—sought to avoid local public schools at all costs, as Nelly intimated above. Paulina comments, "The other schools in the area are public, and they offer a poor education and a bad environment." Elba remarks, "If I put my kids side-by-side with a child attending a public school, the difference in their knowledge base would be enormous." In contrast, some pragmatists saw elite public schools as an excellent option for their children. Marcela comments, "My daughter went to Liceo #1 de Niñas and continued on to college. She's now a professional." Other pragmatists explored this option for their children. Thus, the specter of neighborhood public schools as a "worst case scenario" loomed large for Rosario parents. Additionally, pragmatists saw elite public schools as an attractive choice for their children, in contrast to activists who had painful memories of their childhoods in these schools.

To summarize, La Florida's heterogeneous class structure and the preponderance of charter schools create distinct choices for parents. Activists, moderate Catholics, and youngsters avoid public and private schools due to their poor academic performance or excessive cost. Additionally, activists avoid elite public schools for similar reasons as their LMS counterparts. In contrast, pragmatists avoid local public schools due to their perceived low-quality instruction and to shield their children from poverty, but view elite public schools as potential options to prepare their children for college. The clustering of different types of schools in specific communities shapes parents' options in the educational market.

Concerted Cultivation as a Hedge against Schools' Academic Limitations

In both communities, activists and moderate Catholics consciously chose to opt out of elite private and public schools due to their pedagogical and ideological critiques of these educational formats. Youngsters shared many of these two groups' educational goals, but did not seek strong partisan or ideological identities in schools. However, most parents in these groups still retained hopes for their children's academic and professional success. Thus, they took steps to counteract their schools' academic shortcomings by engaging in concerted cultivation and intensive mothering.[54] Pragmatists, too, partook of these activities to the extent that their resources permitted them to do so, but they looked primarily to schools to provide children with necessary skills. This paradoxical focus on concerted cultivation highlights upper-middle-class parents' precarious privilege: they are unwilling (due to identity investments) or unable (due to cost) to send their children to elite schools, so they use their economic and cultural capital to supplement what their children's schools do not provide.

While activists, moderate Catholics, and youngsters at all three alternative schools and Calasanz criticized the excessive competition at elite schools and standardized test scores' limited capacity to measure student learning, they acknowledged that their children still needed to compete to gain college admission. As Luis, an LMS parent, put it, "I think most LMS parents hope their children will go to college. If someone told me, 'My daughter wants to be a nanny,' I doubt any of the parents would say, 'That's fantastic!'" Here, Luís offers a somewhat outlandish hypothetical example to underscore a larger point—while LMS parents were committed to social justice and criticized upper-class elitism, they still were committed to the middle-class value of educating their children to become professionals. They would thus be disappointed if their children went on to toil in low-status, working-class jobs. This quote thus captures activists' paradoxical position: they rejected the markers of high academic performance (like standardized test scores) but still attempted to ensure their children's college admission and professional success.

Parents thus used extracurricular activities and lessons to cultivate their children's talents and skills. As Alicia, an activist, comments, "My son is studying piano because they encouraged it at LMS. They discovered his talent. We know it's not one of the best schools educationally, but the kids are happy." Dany, a Calasanz parent, sends her children to speed-reading and other classes designed to improve study skills. Tamara remarks, "LMS is not a bilingual school, but if you want your kid to learn English, you have to pony up the money to send them to the Chilean-British Institute. If you want them to study art, you need to send them to classes." Ledda, a Calasanz parent, comments, "We wanted to level up our children's English, so our daughter has been taking classes in the Chile-British Institute for five years." Other authors note upper-middle-class parents' focus on second language acquisition as a desirable skill.[55] These parents take their privilege for granted: they assume their peers can afford extracurricular activities that many parents would find too expensive.

Some parents whose children attend alternative schools provided them with unconventional classes. Tomás, a Raíces parent, comments, "We set up that acrobatics rope in our backyard because our son would like to work in a circus. He hopes to study acrobatics in France. He's in several after-school juggling and circus classes. We bought tickets—which were really expensive—for the two boys to see Cirque du Soleil last year." While developing a career in the circus is unconventional, supporting this interest fits with Tomás's desire that his children explore their creativity and illustrates the broader idea of "symbolic mastery"[56] that upper-middle-class children gain through the family and in school. For Bourdieu, symbolic mastery is an interpretive template focused on aesthetic judgment that includes a set of transposable skills. Adults can use these skills to effectively navigate distinct fields (like cultural consumption or professions) to accumulate resources and status. Others argue that apparently impractical leisure pursuits (like language study or travel) provide participants with discipline, social skills, and artistic abilities they could apply to other domains, such as child-rearing or job interviews in prestigious fields.[57]

Parents of high school students had particular apprehensions about their children's college admission possibilities. Carmen, a Calasanz parent, comments, "I have to constantly monitor my kids' progress in school and make sure they do their homework because the future is going to be more difficult for them." Miguel, a doctor and Calasanz parent, remarks, "When we went to college, we were able to get student loans due to our parents' economic situation, but because of our higher incomes, we will have more difficulty getting loans for our daughters' college education."[58] Several parents counted on a "second chance" if their children did poorly on the college entrance exam. Alicia comments: "I hope the kids do well and are able to study in their preferred majors, but if it doesn't work out the first time, we'll support them so they can take the test again or take a college prep course. It's not something we're losing sleep over." Given the significant increase in college attendance rates during the 2000s, these parents are logically concerned that their children will likely face intense competition for admission to selective colleges.[59]

Youngsters also sought to supplement their children's formal education with extracurricular activities and one-on-one study support. Nelson comments, "The children's grandfather takes them to the La Moneda Cultural Center and the Quinta Normal Museum. He brings them to historic sites and tells them about the history of different areas. I provide them with a tour of the different museums during summer vacation." Rafael, an LMS parent, comments, "I read to the kids every night. If I miss a night, I owe them more stories the following night. My wife [who is a teacher] helps them with homework and exams. She reinforces their study habits; my support is more all-encompassing." Thus, youngsters also utilized concerted cultivation with their children, though they relied less on formal, extracurricular activities.

Pragmatists availed themselves of extracurricular courses to the extent that their more limited budgets allowed, and sometimes their children took the initiative to access resources. Nelly comments, "My son applied to attend summer school in engineering at the University of Chile and was accepted. One of his friends has a math tutor, and he tags along in the math classes." In contrast to activists, moderate Catholics, and youngsters, pragmatists attempted to send their children to elite public high schools. Nelly comments, "I tried to send him to the National Institute in eighth grade but he deliberately failed the entrance exam because he wanted to stay with his friends at school." As noted above, Marcela's oldest daughter attended an elite public school. Thus, pragmatists were resourceful in seeking learning support for their children but had less cultural or economic capital to provide them with individual support or invest in extracurricular activities.

Conclusion

The idea that middle-class parents select schools and engage in concerted cultivation to benefit their children to the disadvantage of working-class and poor children has become something of a truism. If we take a superficial glance at this chapter's findings, this truism seems to apply to the middle-class parents in these two communities. Middle-class parents select private or charter schools that are unaffordable to poor families, and these same parents avoid public schools that primarily serve poor children. Consequently, these parents' private market decisions contribute to the socioeconomic segregation of Santiago's schools.

However, I have argued that when we take a closer look at parents' motivations, we find a more complex story that cannot be reduced to the truism that middle-class parents seek advantage for their children with negative consequences for the poor. It became clear that the middle-class parents studied here go through a complex, multifaceted decision-making process of school selection that reflects their deeply held values and a careful evaluation of an education market that is different from the one they experienced as children. In short, schools are an important site for identity investments that reveals these parents' precarious privilege.

These identity investments reveal individuals' reflexive interpretation of their childhood experiences as well as their positioning in two geographically distinct submarkets in Santiago. Hence, parents with very similar educational and professional backgrounds in the two communities made different choices because of the distinct types of schools present there as well as their different social networks. In Ñuñoa, activists, moderate Catholics, and youngsters selected private schools based on the assumption that they were their only acceptable option even though public and charter schools were present there. Additionally, they explicitly rejected public and private elite schools based on their own experiences in these institutions or their exposure to them through family, friends, coworkers, and neighbors. They disliked elite private schools' exclusionary practices, found them unaffordable, and believed the competitive environments in elite public and private schools were unacceptable.

In La Florida, the absence of well-known private schools with storied histories and interviewees' in-migration to the community led these same groups to select charter schools and reject both elite public schools and local private schools. While activists' reasons for rejecting elite public schools were similar to those articulated by their Ñuñoa counterparts, they provided different reasons for avoiding private schools in La Florida: they found them educationally deficient and poked fun at the upwardly mobile families that attended there.

Pragmatists, who primarily resided in La Florida, had a quite different attitude toward schools. They selected charters to avoid the poor at public schools, permitting their children to gain an academically sound education in a safe environment.[60] Additionally, pragmatists saw elite public schools as attractive options for their children due to their high performance.

Thus, parents' decisions were both place-based (they reflected the class composition and school characteristics in their local community) and class-based—upper-middle-class parents had broader options than their lower-middle-class counterparts. More importantly, all parents' decisions reflected their identity investments. Activists sent their children to secular alternative schools based on their political and secular identities and educational experiences; moderate Catholics selected Catholic schools based on their religious training; youngsters looked to schools' educational profiles and the tailored services they provided; and pragmatists sought an environment that was safe, orderly, and academically sound to provide their children with the best opportunities they could afford.

Each of these decisions reflects middle-class parents' condition of precarious privilege. Upper-middle-class Ñuñoa parents could not afford to send children to elite private schools, were denied admission to these schools, or simply rejected them as discriminatory institutions that offered a toxic and exclusionary learning environment. However, while they were part of a social world in which attendance at these schools was commonplace, *they rejected the schools that rejected them*, revealing their precarious privilege. Elite public school graduates in both communities had painful memories of their school experiences and also lamented declining funding for public schools. Hence, they perceived that route as closed to them. Even pragmatists who had the least economic resources in this sample saw their ability to send their children to charter schools as an achievement, although they were not fully satisfied with their options. Members of each group could look up to the next rung in Chile's unequal class structure and observe their children's exclusion.

Parents found different ways to compensate for their experience of precarious privilege. Upper-middle-class parents engaged in identity investments in religious and alternative schools. They believed their decisions made them morally superior to parents in elite schools that excluded them or which they found unacceptable. They also saw these decisions as staying true to their educational and family origins. Pragmatist parents sent children to affordable charter schools they believed shielded their children from poverty, drugs, and violence, while providing them with a leg up in the academic competition. Activists and moderate Catholics also "hedged their bets" through concerted cultivation. If they could not or would not send their children to elite schools, they could supplement their education with in-home academic support and extracurricular activities.

This chapter primarily explored parents' entry into schools. The next chapter examines how parents seek community with their peers, construct symbolic boundaries in relation to other parents, and exercise citizenship through their children's schools. The analysis will reveal how these parents' profound identity commitments materialize through their membership in school communities and how their activism and volunteerism reflected the 2006 inflection point in Chilean politics that ushered in a wave of social conflict beginning in Michelle Bachelet's first presidential administration.

4

Community, Conflict, and Citizenship at Schools

CLAUDIO SENDS HIS CHILDREN to Calasanz. He expresses concerns about how the school's expansion has affected social relations among parents and students: "They started a third class for each grade and our daughter was in one of the expanded classes. The problem is that those classes don't have a history together, and people enter them from all over the place." Javiera, his spouse, adds, "The classes just didn't gel." She continues, "There's a girl in my daughter's class that has perfect scores, but she really ruins the class and the school because her behavior goes against its values. In contrast, our daughter has struggled academically, but she's a good kid. They've suggested maybe she should consider another school. That's what bothers me about the school."[1]

Susana, a housewife and former teacher, worries about the changing profile of parents and students at Raimapu: "I'm concerned about my younger daughters. When I served as a substitute teacher at Raimapu last year, 80 percent of the kids' parents had emotionally abandoned them. The parents were around thirty-five years old, a little younger than I, and nannies were raising the kids. The nannies had no idea about child-rearing or what the kids should watch on TV. This happens with my youngest daughter's class—the other parents don't provide them with emotional support."[2]

Claudio, Javiera, and Susana describe similar concerns about the arrival of newcomers in two very different schools located in distinct communities. Their distress regarding the arrival of a new group of parents and children whose attitudes and behaviors diverge from the norm in their schools illustrates one of this chapter's core foci. In the last chapter, we explored parents' selection of secular or religious schools and decisions to avoid elite and local public schools. In this chapter, we examine parents' and children's relationships inside their schools, and what they tell us about schools as communities, settings for interpersonal conflicts, and sites for activism and volunteer work.

Analyses of school choice and school interactions in other settings present a portrait of some middle-class parents that espouse egalitarian values by sending children to racially diverse public schools, but who ultimately focus on accumulating privilege for their children. White middle- and upper-class parents either avoid public schools due to a fear of racial others[3] or because they believe their children are gifted.[4] Parents that select urban public schools wrestle with the dilemma between "being good parents and good citizens,"[5] expose their children to poverty but do not mobilize for systemic change,[6] or remain open to "opting out" of public schools at the high school level.[7] While much research on Chile reviewed in the previous chapter focuses on broader structural patterns of socioeconomic segregation that harm working-class children, the few studies focused on middle-class parents' in-school practices argue that they are concerned about the potential for poor children's misbehavior.[8] The key finding in this literature is that while middle-class parents may espouse egalitarian rhetoric, they mainly act to support their own children rather than mobilizing for more equitable education policies that would benefit all families.

This chapter offers an important departure from this literature. First, I found that even in schools that displayed limited class differences among families, parents that had spent more time at the schools asserted "symbolic ownership"[9] over the school: they criticized newcomers that did not reflect their perceived educational and cultural goals. As discussed in previous chapters, however, activists and moderate Catholics contrasted their educational and moral identities with newer parents' competitive behaviors. Youngsters, in contrast, criticized the lack of order and academic rigor at schools, highlighting their desires for upward mobility. Finally, pragmatists (primarily at Rosario Concha) criticized upper-middle-class parents' microaggressions against them. In sum, even in schools that were relatively homogeneous in class terms, parents erected symbolic boundaries with "others" they viewed as educationally or morally deficient.

Why would parents criticize their counterparts with similar backgrounds? One answer comes from Elias and Scotson's classic study of community conflict.[10] They found that the "established" residents criticized the "outsiders" for causing juvenile delinquency even though the two groups were quite similar. While this analysis suggests that superficial differences between groups can generate community conflict, I argue that parents at the schools studied here responded to changes in how schools recruited students. Both LMS and Calasanz had experienced an influx of new students in the years immediately prior to this research, and by all appearances, these parents had more upwardly mobile aspirations than established parents. A similar process occurred in La Florida, where all three schools had transitioned from private to charter schools, thus making them more affordable and/or increasing their size. Hence, the pool of students had expanded, and many long-term parents believed that these younger parents (and their children) were too competitive, academically deficient, or both.

A more substantial departure from the scholarship described above relates to how parents and children exercised their citizenship through schools. While much of the international discussion and analyses in Chile argue that middle-class parents primarily focus on their children's academic success or social status, parents at Manuel de Salas, Raimapu, and Calasanz engaged in political activism and social action alongside their children. This exercise of citizenship built on their political and religious identities as well as their prior organizational experiences. Their social and political activity contributed to broader social movements in Chile that ushered in a major transformation of political institutions over the next decade. However, youngsters and pragmatists opposed these protests and the disorder they believed they had unleashed. Hence, school-based activism both contributed to broader social movements and provoked opposition within schools. At Calasanz, the school encouraged parents' and children's less controversial volunteer action supporting the poor. I take up the themes of community, symbolic boundaries, and citizenship in turn.

Community and Symbolic Boundaries

Activists, moderate Catholics, youngsters, and pragmatists responded to conflicts in schools differently with implications for the construction of symbolic boundaries within the middle class.[11] The first two groups see schools as a principal setting for friendship and family life. Thus, as schools expand or the composition of parents changes, they express discomfort that their community is eroding. This process pitting "old timers" against "newcomers" is reminiscent of Elias and Scotson's study[12] insofar as long-time parents resent the arrival of younger parents even though the two groups have similar incomes and levels of education. Youngsters less often seek out community in schools than the first two groups, so their concerns center around their children's academic success and emotional well-being. Most pragmatists see school as an oasis amidst dangers linked to poverty. However, their multiclass schools offer little basis for the construction of community and therefore provide them with limited opportunities for sociability. A small minority of pragmatists enroll children at one of the alternative schools (Raíces) and feel included by their school community.

Because all of the schools studied included families that varied by class, occupation, and/or age cohort, school life was rife with tensions and symbolic conflicts. These tensions emerged in part because many long-term parents developed much of their social life in connection with the families in their children's classrooms. Since many students in Chile remain with the same classmates from kindergarten until twelfth grade, parents and children often develop close friendships; and parents, especially mothers, are sensitive to disruptions to these friendly relations. This pattern of close friendships was evident in all the schools except Raíces and Rosario Concha, where relationships were more distant.

In the best of cases, parents felt strongly identified with and attached to their schools as well as other families. Thus, Mario, a Raimapu parent, comments, "We hang out more with other parents at Raimapu than with our neighbors. They're our friend group. We see one of the families at least once a week outside school because our kids are in the same class. We meet at our respective homes, at parties, or at one of the many school activities." Marcelo, a Calasanz parent, comments, "I spend a lot of time at the school. My daughter sometimes tells me, 'You spend more time at school than at home' because I'm involved in sports activities, the catechism class, and lead a marriage counseling group."

If "friendship" is a keyword for parents at Raimapu and Calasanz, "diversity" is an oft-repeated term at LMS and Raíces Altazor. Luis and Tamara, both leftists, tell a story that others repeated:

> *Luis:* We have the meetings for our parent leadership council in a very right-wing man's home. So, he says, "My house is full of communists!"

Tamara: But we have a great time. I love him so much. The school gives you that opportunity—you hug, you laugh, and you have a great time.
Luis: He's very lovable.
Tamara: You cross all those boundaries.

Raíces parents also emphasized the healthy debates at parents' meetings. José Miguel comments: "At the last parent meeting, the teacher scolded the parents because the children often make excuses for not completing their homework. The good thing about Raíces is that we deal with the problem of the moment rather than avoiding or hiding it. It's very enriching for children and parents. We discuss sexuality and conflict resolution. We have heated debates and address actual problems so the kids will develop necessary life skills." While parents appreciated the open atmosphere at Raíces meetings, they had more distant ties to other parents than those at LMS, Calasanz, and Raimapu, as we will explore in chapter 6. Thus, in three of the five schools, parents and children had very strong affective ties to their schools and other families. These strong social ties echo other authors' focus on parents' efforts to accumulate social capital through schools.[13]

Regular parent meetings, as well as periodic religious, cultural, or fundraising events reinforced this strong sense of community. I attended a flea market (*kermesse*) at LMS that included food and recorded live music, concerts by famed folk rock group Inti-Illimani at both LMS and Raimapu, and a book sale at Calasanz. Parents—especially activists and moderate Catholics—saw these events as demanding time and energy, but also as expressions of their connection to the school and its families. Thus, Gloria, a Raimapu parent, comments, "The parent association was inactive for a while, but recently we created a 'Getting to Know You' [*Encontrarte*] event in October. The activity attracts tons of people, and parents make and display really interesting creative work. There are singers and painters. It's been very successful." Deyda, a Calasanz parent, comments, "There is a family singing activity in November in which parents spend a month preparing a song with their children's class and then they compete with other classes. It's a chance for the family to share an activity."[14] These activities provide the "glue" that connects the most active families to one another and the school.

While three of the five schools had an active formal and informal social life and Raíces parents appreciated the school's parent meetings, parents that had spent years at these schools often clashed with newcomers who they felt lacked a commitment to the school's identity or displayed odious preferences and disrespectful behaviors. In addition to their long-term participation at the schools, many of the activists and moderate Catholics I interviewed in all five schools held elected positions in the parent association in their children's classes or the school-wide parent association. They thus had a greater degree of power and influence over school life than did other parents. Thus, youngsters and pragmatists sometimes felt subject to or marginalized by parent association decisions. Activists' and moderate Catholics' criticisms of newcomers thus carried some weight in school decision-making and had moral influence over school culture.

In spite of long-term parents' criticisms of youngsters, some activists were friends with youngsters: members of the older cohort did not reject *all* of their younger peers. Rosario Concha, due to its mixed-class makeup, had distinct dynamics from the other schools. There, moderate Catholics and youngsters shared criticisms of poor or less educated parents, while pragmatists found themselves wedged between upper-middle-class parents (whom they resented) and the poor (whom they feared). We revisit each of the five schools separately to examine common themes as well as different patterns across schools and communities. Table 4.1 summarizes the different types of parental conflict across schools.

School	Location	Primary Conflict
Manuel de Salas	Ñuñoa	Activists emphasize political identity; youngsters prefer academic excellence, criticize bullying.
Calasanz	Ñuñoa	Moderate Catholics criticize youngsters' and their parents' aggressive behavior.
Raimapu	La Florida	Activists criticize youngsters' consumerist attitudes; youngsters prefer academic excellence and are uncomfortable with students' alternative lifestyles.
Raíces Altazor	La Florida	Activists criticize youngsters' consumerism and lack of academic focus although cross-cohort relationships are positive.
Rosario Concha	La Florida	Moderate Catholics and youngsters criticize pragmatists' and poor parents' lack of academic focus and moral judgment; pragmatists criticize moderate Catholics' and youngsters' privileged mindset as well as poor parents' moral character.

Table 4.1 Parental Conflicts in Schools

Ñuñoa Schools

Manuel de Salas

At Manuel de Salas, the main conflicts pitted activists committed to the school's political identity (discussed in detail below) with youngsters seeking an orderly, academically demanding environment. Activists viewed youngsters as more conservative, materialistic, and lacking in intellectual curiosity. Alicia, an LMS parent, comments, "A lot of parents at meetings complain that the teachers are not completing course objectives or preparing students for college entrance exams. When high school students took over the school [discussed below] it was like the last straw for parents concerned about academics, and many left. The high school students took over the school and the elementary school parents paid the price." Luis comments, "Manuel de Salas has an important history as an experimental school. The younger parents that enroll their children in the school have no idea about that history." These parents emphasize a shift across age cohorts whereby youngsters' emphasis on academic achievement challenges activists' focus on the school's political identity and history.

To wit, youngsters appreciated the school's holistic learning models, but expressed concerns about its administrative disorganization or lack of academic rigor. Mickey, a history teacher who worked as a student teacher at Manuel de Salas, comments, "The students think they are self-sufficient and aggressively assert their rights. I think schools need to have certain rules. The children don't see teachers as authority figures. They arrive late to class and don't pay attention. Since there is a self-discipline system at LMS, they do whatever they want."

Youngsters at LMS also worried about bullying. María comments, "Since the school has an alternative conflict resolution system, there is no adult supervision during recess. They need more control. There's bullying, there are accidents. The bathrooms are a 'no man's land.' My daughter's friends have been victims of abuse of power when big kids have grabbed them and stuck their heads in the toilet. It's terrible for a first grader." When I asked Mauricio, a school administrator, about this issue, he minimized it: "The small kids get upset when someone steals their lunch money. We find the perpetrators, discuss it with them, and persuade them to do an act of solidarity for the whole class to resolve the problem."[15]

What underlies these conflicts? As noted in chapter 3, activists' identity investments focused on the school's political orientation and its historical legacy.

This vision was based on either their status as alumni or their belief that LMS carried on Chile's historic tradition of public education. Additionally, activists' professional positions and educational backgrounds made them confident that they could "hedge their bets" through concerted cultivation strategies if the school was academically deficient. They also interpreted youngsters' interest in academic performance as symbolizing a competitive mindset. In contrast, youngsters did not have strong emotional ties to the school and hence believed student political mobilization and misbehavior undermined their educational goals. As Alicia noted above, some of these parents simply left the school.

Calasanz

At Calasanz, parents with a longer tenure at the school bemoaned its declining academic demands and/or younger parents' more competitive attitudes, as Javiera indicated at this chapter's beginning. Ledda recalls, "We think the school was less selective when it expanded. When our kids applied, not everyone was accepted. Now, there are a lot of aggressive people. I've seen parents fighting, cutting off children walking by with their cars, and fighting at sports games, when that's not the idea. I was playing basketball and got fouled. I was running and someone tripped me. I tore a ligament in my knee, and had to get surgery." Ledda implies that newer families at Calasanz are more hostile than their predecessors, highlighting conflicts across cohorts. Several other interviewees complained about parents' "road rage" when they drop off or pick up their children. Dany raises a similar concern: "What really burns me up is that in some cases, a new kid will enter the class but they are 'bad down to the roots.' You're stuck for two years with this girl who is a disaster that messes up the whole class . . . You can tell she started out bad at home, so there's no changing her." Dany, Ledda, and Javiera highlight perceived differences in parental values and child-rearing styles across cohorts that generate hostile relations in the classroom and among parents.

Calasanz witnessed a similar transition as LMS since the school's expansion meant that arriving youngsters had different cultural orientations than moderate Catholics. Carlos, the school official I interviewed, explained that the school moved from 1,200 to 1,600 students in 2002. He commented, "The change in scale was significant, but I don't think there's been a major change in the parent profile. I have noticed that parents are busier and have less time to participate in school."[16] However, the school's "old guard" framed these differences in moral terms: newer parents were disrespectful or violent toward their peers and other children, and newer children misbehaved and disrupted an ideal social harmony among children and parents in each class. Some moderate Catholics saw newer families as less academically inclined, while others complained that they were high achieving but poorly behaved. However, they shared the view that newer families disrupted parents' and children's peaceful coexistence through their immoral and ugly behavior. Like LMS, moderate Catholics at Calasanz criticized youngsters' competitive, antisocial behaviors. I have little evidence of youngsters' responses to these criticisms given limits in the sample at the school, but the parents I interviewed frequently noted the conflicts outlined here.

La Florida Schools

Raimapu

Activists at Raimapu, like their LMS counterparts, felt a strong sense of symbolic ownership of the school based on their entry in its early years and contributions to its ethos. Also, like LMS, activists noted some youngsters' concerns about the school's disorganization. However, rather than the intense politicization or alleged bullying that were key sources of division at LMS, youngsters at Raimapu were uncomfortable with many children's participation in alternative youth subcultures.

Alejandro, a former teacher that conducts trainings for the national teacher's union, remarks, "There are a bunch of families that are consumerist, competitive, success-oriented, and that prioritize cognitive growth over the social and emotional dimension."[17] Like LMS, these activists criticize younger parents' competitive mindset as antithetical to the school's identity.

Other parents highlight the clash between more conventional youngsters and many Raimapu children's alternative dress styles and behaviors. Gladys, a youngster who has several activist friends, highlights Raimapu's "deviant" appearance: "My partner's son had attended a Catholic boys' school, and then when he was a high school junior, he asked to go to Raimapu. My partner almost died! The boys at the Catholic school arrive with their hair perfectly combed, but the kids at Raimapu belong to all the urban tribes you can imagine. It was a drastic change for my partner—his son used to have nicely combed hair, but then he ironed it so it was stuck to his scalp and wore earrings." In this amusing comment, Gladys highlights Raimapu students' membership in well-known urban youth subcultures that model their appearance after Japanese anime cartoon characters, Gothic rock bands, and "emo" styles.[18] When these subcultures emerged in the 1990s, journalists and citizens expressed shock at these "deviant" forms of youth social expression.

Mario offers another amusing story about younger parents' discomfort with Raimapu's informal style: "The teachers are really stubborn and say, 'We don't give any homework because we think all the learning should happen at school [*laughs*].' Some friends left the school because they couldn't believe this. I worked with a woman who lives in La Florida and sent her son to Raimapu because I guess they thought it was nice and the people were friendly and cool [*gente simpática y buena onda*]—I don't know. So, they were freaked out about this. They decided to show up unannounced at 11 a.m. when they noticed that half the kids were on the playground, and the teachers were all over the place. It's very disorganized. Teachers discourage parents from coming for that reason [*laughs*]. When they tried to take this little boy home, he threw a huge temper tantrum and said, 'This is *my* school! I want to stay!' It's a very unique situation because the parents are worried, and the kids have a great time. In spite of this, the kids do well on standardized tests with little preparation." Mario's comment that children "love their school" echoed activists' remarks at LMS, who often stated that their children "adored their school and their classmates." His remarks illustrate the sharp divide between activists that feel at home with the school's antiauthoritarian, experimental ethos and youngsters that seek an orderly, academically rigorous school.

While Calasanz had deliberately expanded due to parental demand and LMS had also grown,[19] Raimapu and the other two La Florida schools had been converted to charters in recent years. This meant that their tuition fees declined, and class sizes expanded (at Raimapu). Consequently, "founding" parents, whose children entered the school during the 1980s and 1990s and who had built a community based on their shared political loyalties, were confronted with parents that were markedly different. Apart from being younger, these parents were also more conventional and committed to academic achievement. Thus, activists criticized youngsters' "success mindset" although some youngsters, like Gladys, befriended activists. Additionally, activists attempted to recruit younger parents to the school's parent association, indicating that the boundaries between age cohorts were "softer" than at LMS.

Raíces Altazor
Raíces lacked Raimapu's storied past, but activists at the school had similar educational profiles and attitudes as their Raimapu counterparts. Again, activists highlighted the contrast between intellectual and competitive parents. Israel, a Raíces parent, remarks, "At the third grade parents' meeting the other day, four mothers told the teacher they had asked their child several

times to do their homework and they wouldn't listen, so they didn't know what to do. It's because they're working like crazy to buy things, and they don't even know why. It's probably to compensate for their bad marriages. They don't confront their relationship problems head on. Then you have the separated parents that put each other down in front of their kids, and each has a different parenting style. The parent meetings generate enough raw material to write a book."

After remarking on his admiration for the school's teachers, Tomás recounts a similar issue: "There was an English teacher from Cuba who taught my kids very well. Parents sent an email complaining about his teaching, and I responded that my kids did great with him and that to learn English, going to class wasn't enough—the kids need to be motivated. The conversation sputtered out after that." Israel's remarks indicate he believes some (presumably younger) parents have not found a healthy work-life balance because they lack essential interpersonal and child-rearing skills. Their dysfunctional coping skills have negative effects on their children's behavior and learning. Tomás also implies that other parents blame an effective teacher rather than promoting their children's study habits. These two men are highly educated professionals—Israel is a former teacher with an MA and Tomás is an engineer. They take their educational privilege for granted when they construct cultural boundaries with less educated, more materialistic parents.[20]

In spite of these activists' criticisms of youngsters' parenting styles, overall, Raíces displayed more amicable relations between activists, youngsters, and pragmatists than the other schools studied. Relationships among parents were cordial, and some parents developed friendships at school, although parents did not see the school as their main social setting. Still, parents universally applauded teachers' personalistic approach and problem-solving skills, and saw parent meetings as opportunities to confront and amicably solve problems. Youngsters and pragmatists felt respected and included. Lisette, a youngster, comments, "Last year one of the principals encouraged us to have an end of the year outing, which we repeated in March. That generated some new connections between parents, who are all really nice and just like us." Alejandra, a pragmatist, comments, "I have respectful and cordial relationships with other parents. I'm very close with two or three. Sometimes people cross your path and they're different from you, but you need to accept them because it's like a gift." Iván, another pragmatist, remarks, "We have good relationships. We may disagree at parent meetings, but we're all on the same page. Our kids visit each other's homes, and I sometimes receive invitations to birthday parties.

The relationships here are much friendlier than those I observed as a teacher."
Lisette, Alejandra, and Iván feel that other parents include, respect, and appreciate them, helping ameliorate the clashes across age cohorts and class
fractions observed at the other schools.

Why were parents able to establish ties across boundaries at Raíces unlike
the other schools studied? Several factors were at play. Raíces was the smallest
of all the schools studied with only 200 students. This made it one-third the
size of Raimapu (600 students) and less than one-quarter the size of Rosario (900 students). The La Florida schools were all smaller than their Ñuñoa
counterparts, each of which had about 1,500 students. Thus, parents were part
of the same small group and hence may have felt the need to remain on good
terms with others. The school's leadership also encouraged parents to social-
ize (as Lisette noted) and recruited a diverse student body (as mentioned in
chapter 3). Teachers and principals also developed close ties to parents so they
could anticipate and neutralize potential conflicts. The pragmatists I interviewed, though they received modest incomes, had teaching degrees, so they
had both the linguistic skills and professional socialization that allowed them
to see activist parents as peers. Additionally, since the school only went to
eighth grade, some of the pressures and anxieties parents experience regarding college admission exams were not top of mind, and this may have eased
social relationships. Finally, activists endorsed academic performance (as evident in Israel's and Tomás's remarks), and hence they were "on the same page"
with youngsters and pragmatists. Thus, although parents often disagreed and
some erected symbolic boundaries with others, Raíces did not display the parental conflicts observed in the other schools.

Rosario Concha

Rosario witnessed the most stark conflicts and displayed the weakest sense
of community among parents. This likely reflects two factors. First, it was
the only school among those studied that included parents ranging from the
upper-middle class to the poor. Second, the school did not have a strong overarching identity, in contrast to the other schools studied. While it included religious activities and emphasized academic excellence, it did not have a strong
ethos that parents could identify with. Unlike LMS, Calasanz, and Raimapu,
moderate Catholics and youngsters were united in their criticisms of pragmatists they perceived as materialistic, morally suspect, or unconcerned with
their children's education. In contrast, these other schools witnessed divisions

across age cohorts rather than those based on differences between the upper- and lower-middle classes.

For example, Nelson, a youngster, comments: "We think that if our kids fall down, we need to encourage them to get back up themselves. A lot of the mothers at the school do their children's homework for them. If a child doesn't complete their homework, it's their problem. It needs to be their work. We can try to motivate and pressure our kids, but the results are up to them." Elba, a moderate Catholic, comments, "Sometimes I feel like a chicken that's lost in the wrong coop [*como pollo en corral ajeno*]. Some parents are well educated and cultured, but others don't care about their kids' education. For example, when my daughter graduated from eighth grade, the parent that hosted the class party asked if my daughter had permission to drink alcohol. I raised a ruckus. I said, 'I beg your pardon, but my daughter has a good reason why she doesn't want to go.' Some kids drink and smoke at age fourteen. I told her it's the parents' responsibility to prevent that." Nelson and Elba criticize parents for not supporting their children's learning and for encouraging dangerous habits. They express strong moral judgments about poor and less educated parents.

Pragmatists noticed similar dynamics in parent meetings. Paulina, comments, "Some people complain that the school has started to admit poorer students. I don't mean to be discriminatory, but I studied and worked, while other women chose to be housewives, and they isolate themselves because they feel like they have no conversation topics to share. They can also be mean with each other, making indirect comments that other children's clothes aren't very nice. I have no issues with having poor parents here—you could be rich and still be a low-life [*ser una rota*]. I want my kids to get to know different kinds of people."[21] Here, Paulina expresses ambivalent attitudes about the school's class mixture. On one hand, she notes that other parents complain about the arrival of poor families. On the other hand, she suggests poor parents are at fault for withdrawing from conversation. She goes on to insist that she tolerates poor families and wants her children to interact across class lines. This attitude echoes other scholars' observations that some middle-class families see their children's exposure to poor families as enriching although they do not anticipate their children will form friendships with them.[22]

Other pragmatists felt ostracized in parent meetings. They argued that upper-middle-class parents engaged in microaggressions toward them, displayed attitudes they could not relate to, or they simply preferred to withdraw from interactions with these parents, as Paulina observed about poor parents. Marcela comments: "The parents at Rosario Concha are too big for their britches [*son muy agrandadas*], so I really don't like it. They compete over who has the most money. In Catholic schools, people think they're economically superior; they are not spiritual at all." She continues, "At parent meetings, all they care about is whether or not people are up to date with their fundraising contributions, and if you ask a question, they get mad." Marcela continued that she had to divide herself between three classes (for her two children and one grandchild) during parent meetings, so it was hard to participate. Nelly complained that the school had little understanding of single parents' difficulties: "At parent meetings, they always complain that parents don't help their children with their homework. I want to reiterate that not all families are the same. I'm out working all day. My child raised himself. The teachers assume every child has two parents." Marcela and Nelly feel that affluent parents and teachers judge them and explain their difficulties participating in meetings as well as supporting their children's learning. They believe that other parents and school authorities do not understand their plight, and thus they feel alienated from the school.

Thus, at Rosario, moderate Catholics and youngsters had conflicts with pragmatists. All three groups criticized the poor, although pragmatists felt the brunt of affluent parents' criticisms. Rosario thus represented a fractured community in which parents' sharply contrasting class positions left little room for common ground. Some parents enjoyed friendships with others in their children's class, but few strongly identified with the school. These findings echo other analyses demonstrating that schools favor middle-class children and are often blind to the challenges working-class children face.[23]

To conclude this section, we can see important fissures within these middle-class schools that reflect their changing student populations as well as the sense of "symbolic ownership" that activists, moderate Catholics, and youngsters (at Rosario) feel in relation to their school. In contrast to other studies in Chile arguing that parents tend to sort themselves into class homogeneous schools,[24] or that note class-based divisions among parents within charter schools that opted-in to new policies promoting class integration,[25] I found important differences within largely middle-class schools that reflected the contrasting mindsets of distinct age cohorts with different identity investments. With the exception of Rosario Concha, which did have considerable class diversity, the symbolic boundaries among parents in the other schools were analogous to the kinds of boundaries constructed at work, in neighborhoods, and when selecting schools. Activists' and moderate Catholics' strong political and moral identities contrasted with youngsters' more achievement-oriented mindset and pragmatists' fear of the poor. We now turn to parents' activism and volunteer activities as part of broader political changes in Chile.

Collective Action at Schools

In this last section, we explore how parents and schools were enmeshed in national public debates and social conflicts centering on class inequality. While other studies of schools in Chile emphasize parents' pragmatic efforts to seek advantages for their children rather than to push for policy changes that benefit all children, the evidence presented here shows how some private and charter schools became highly politicized battlefields in the late 2000s. The first Bachelet administration (2006–2010) ushered in a period of social ferment that sharply contrasted with a prevailing consensus during the first fifteen years of democratic rule. Beginning in 2006, students, workers, transit riders, environmentalists, and native people engaged in bold and consequential mobilizations, sparking a protest wave that culminated with Chile's successful late 2020 constitutional referendum and Gabriel Boric's 2021 election to the presidency.[26] In addition to protests' effects on the policy process, as noted in our chapter 1 discussion of *las universidades cota mil*, these protests generated a public debate initiated by Chile's archbishop, who called for the establishment of an "ethical wage" after a wave of strikes.[27]

The student movement was at the forefront of these protests. Middle and high school students began the Penguin Revolution in 2006, and students reemerged as leaders of broader, multi-issue movements in 2011 and 2019. The protests initially focused on the price of student bus passes, but students' demands quickly escalated to question public subsidies issued to for-profit charter schools and the unequal funding of public and charter schools. While public school students began the protests, students at private schools quickly followed.[28] Students demobilized in 2007 after the government set up a roundtable dialogue, but protests reemerged in 2008 when students expressed disappointment that the new General Law of Education excluded their main demands.[29]

Growing social movement activism challenging Chile's free-market model and religious officials' denunciations of class inequality influenced social and political processes in the schools I studied. Additionally, student leaders from these schools became active in national protests. The conflicts were most apparent at LMS and to a lesser extent at Raimapu. Some youngsters, moderate Catholics, and pragmatists opposed student activism inside and outside their schools. Thus, student activism was a lightning rod that divided parents. In contrast, parents and high school students at Calasanz addressed social inequality through a volunteer program supporting homeless people.

Parents' and children's protests and volunteer work in schools demonstrate that an important group of activist and religious parents do not view schools primarily as a vehicle to maximize economic and symbolic profits for their children. Rather, activists and moderate Catholics (as well as their children) took aim at class inequality through their participation in schools in support of public protests and in concert with religious leaders' statements. In contrast, some moderate Catholics, youngsters, and pragmatists criticized student protests, reflecting more conservative or meritocratic beliefs. Thus, middle-class parents' identity investments in schools reflected their core beliefs, extended beyond their immediate setting to national social and political conflicts, and contributed to broader processes of social change.

Activism and Polarization at Manuel de Salas and Raimapu

At LMS and Raimapu, parents were long-term party members and activists. They selected their schools in part because of their progressive political orientation. For example, as Alicia reflects on her son's participation in a school takeover at LMS, she remembers observing and participating in protests at the same school when she was a student during Allende's socialist administration: "That's why the recent takeover didn't scare me very much. When I was a kid, I'd arrive to classes. One week the leftists took over, and the next week the rightists took over. The following week the 'half-and-halfs' took over. I asked someone who they were. They responded, 'Oh, they're neither on the right nor the left.' My parents have always been leftists. One time the parents took over the central office to protect the principal from right-wing people that wanted to take over the school." Alicia thus locates her son's contemporary activism in relation to her childhood experience and the school's activist history. As her memory implies, there is an entire political history of schools that is missing from analyses that mainly focus on schools as engines of social class reproduction. In fact, this tradition of protest and student volunteer work at LMS dates back to the 1950s.[30]

This history is essential for understanding conflicts in LMS and Raimapu. In 2002, before the Penguin Revolution, LMS parents organized to remove the school from the Metropolitan University of Educational Sciences (UMCE) and restore its affiliation with the University of Chile. Morgana, a freelance physical education instructor, comments, "The UMCE didn't invest in the school. At a critical moment, parents decided it was necessary to return the school to the University of Chile to improve its academic performance. The struggle lasted for several years, and we finally succeeded. Unfortunately, the change has not helped the school define its educational plan." Other parents that participated in the movement agreed that while it had been a noble struggle, the changes they hoped for had not been realized. Nonetheless, the important point for our purposes is that just as Alicia recalled her classmates and their parents mobilizing during the 1970s, parents again organized in the early 2000s: the school has an enduring tradition of student and parental activism.

High school students took over LMS repeatedly in support of the 2006 Penguin Revolution. As Mauricio, a school administrator comments, "Our graduates have become college student leaders, and one was elected mayor. They were very active in the Penguin Revolution. The sixth graders even created a web page explaining why they supported the high school protests. Our students are aware of what is going on nationally and globally." Mauricio's comments indicate that school officials support student activism. Student political participation continues into college and can be the stepping-stone into election to public office.

Parents like Alicia happily supported their children's activism. Alicia comments, "When my son called to tell me students were going to take over LMS, I called my husband [Víctor, a long-time activist with ties to the Communist Party] and told him he wanted to participate. He replied, 'Obviously he can participate!' [laughs]. So, I said, 'Obviously!' I told my son it was fine."

However, elementary school parents worried the strike would take away from their children's education. Aniluap, an officer in the parents' association, described the conflict: "Some parents supported the student takeover, while some opposed it and wanted classes to resume. Some parents removed their children from the school after fighting with others. High school students made the decision to take over the school, so some parents of elementary school kids felt like they were steamrolled [pasados a llevar]." At a focus group I held with parents from several schools, Tamara criticized these younger parents: "The parents in their forties shared childcare duties during the takeover so they could support the movement. The parents in their thirties don't know where they stand politically so they refused to collaborate."[31]

Youngsters were uncomfortable when they learned their high-school-aged children had participated in the takeover. Mickey comments, "At the public protests, they typically arrest a group of kids from Manuel de Salas—the police have identified them. My daughter was arrested at a protest downtown. Manuel de Salas [students] are the 'ringleaders' [*se la lleva*] in the community." Thus, while activists strongly identified with the takeover, some youngsters opposed it. These protests both contributed to the broader student movement and led to polarization in the school, leading some parents to remove their children.

Protests continue at LMS up to the present day. In 2016, students took over the school for twenty days to influence legislative discussions on education reform until the police arrived to remove them. Parents and school officials supported the protest and bore witness to the police action to protect the students.[32] An eleven-day takeover in 2018 built on a national feminist mobilization. In that protest, students demanded a nonsexist curriculum a year after school officials had promised a curricular change. An LMS student leader during that protest was also a spokesperson for the National High School Students Association.[33] During Chile's 2019 to 2020 social explosion (*estallido social*), Víctor Chanfreau, an LMS student, became a national spokesperson for the high school students' association.[34] Thus LMS students, with the support of their parents and the school administration, have continued to participate in broader social movements that were decisive in Chile's recent political transformation.

Raimapu parents mobilized in 2001 when the school leadership decided to transform it into a charter. Ricardo recalls: "Some parents wanted to know how many students per class were needed to keep the school afloat. We were a small school with twenty-five students per class, which the parents liked, but charters usually need forty-five students in a class to remain solvent." He continues, "We were concerned that there was no space to expand. We organized a parallel board of directors, but we were still short sixty students in order to break even. Miraculously, a whole class left another school due to a conflict, and they all came to Raimapu. Some parents paid more than they owed, we held raffles, and we raised a lot of money. That first year was a community-wide effort." Due to Raimapu's conversion into a charter school, thirty families left the school to form another alternative school. Tamara, who later moved her children to LMS, was one such parent: "It was one of the most beautiful experiences of my life to have created a school, and I'm proud to have done it."

Although the conflict reflected parents' strong commitment to the school's identity and its survival, it left scars among parents. Alejandro recalls, "The school's transition really divided parents. I was in favor of converting to a charter because it opened it up to families that could not afford a private school, but it also meant new families didn't always see things the way we did." Ricardo continues, "In the process, things got all mixed up. Instead of making arguments, people would put each other down, saying things like, 'I'm a communist but you're not a true communist because you left the school.'" Thus, while the parents that remained managed to save the school, many friendships ended due to the split. Tamara comments, "The best thing Raimapu had was our human relationships. When the college split and turned into a business, we left and got really depressed because the one good thing about the school was destroyed." Thus, the conflict was painful for all those that participated.

However, this earlier conflict as well as the school's leftist origins acted as a seedbed for later student mobilization. Mario remarks, "During the Penguin Revolution, my son joined the Communist Youth organization. He goes to meetings and protests and is involved there." More importantly, Camila Vallejo, a Raimapu alumna, became the face of the college student movement in 2011, was later elected to Congress, and is now (in 2022) a cabinet secretary in Gabriel Boric's progressive administration. Nicolás Grau had been an elected student leader at the University of Chile a few years prior. During the 2011 college student mobilization, Raimapu students staged a several-month-long school takeover supporting the protests.[35] Thus, Raimapu had an important history of parent and student activism that reverberated in national politics.

LMS and Raimapu also had similar exchange programs with Mapuche communities in southern Chile that are relevant for understanding the 2019 social explosion and 2021–2022 constitutional convention. Students and teachers from the schools would spend a short time with host families and attend school in these communities, and indigenous children would come to Santiago to study.[36] These exchanges speak to growing interest in and awareness of indigenous issues at these two schools. This interest was also evident in school fundraisers at LMS, as discussed in chapter 6.

Indigenous rights became important to the iconography of the 2019 protests. Additionally, the election of the Constitutional Convention guaranteed seats to indigenous representatives, and in 2022, the convention delegates voted to make Chile a plurinational state providing autonomy to indigenous communities. Thus, these exchange programs prefigure growing alliances between indigenous Chileans and other groups that may become institutionalized if voters approve Chile's new charter in September 2022.

Social Action at Calasanz

LMS and Raimapu are schools where student and parent activism held sway. In contrast, several Calasanz parents and their children were committed participants in social action with homeless persons. Dany and her daughter remark:

> *Dany:* I'm part of the school's social action committee. We collect canned goods and clothing to donate to the poor.
> *Laura:* I joined the street pastoral.
> *Dany:* That's very intense.
> *Laura:* You see everything under the sun. The poor in the US must be different.
> *Dany:* No, Laura, the poor are the same everywhere—they smell the same. We're all human beings.
> *Laura:* Did you know that housing is a human right? I swear—they just taught me that in class!

This discussion is interesting because it demonstrates linkages between the Piarist Order's mission to serve the poor, classroom discussions, and social action. Claudia, another Calasanz parent, also observes, "The school has a lot of social action around poverty, so our kids realize they are privileged to have a family, food, and a comfortable home. They learn that they can never forget that some people don't have anything, and they need our help and support. The kids don't live in an economic bubble; they see other realities." Other authors suggest that this mentality benefits affluent children by enriching their perspectives but does little to help their poor counterparts.[37] However, in this case, parents and students were not merely exposed to poverty; they committed to provide direct aid to poor people on a weekly basis. This commitment reflects parents' Catholic faith.

When I participated in the street pastoral, I found a large group of parents and teens preparing food, collecting used clothing, and delivering these items to homeless persons following a brief sermon by a deacon. The parents appeared highly motivated, described similar activities they had participated in at their children's previous schools, and asked about others that were missing and normally attend the pastoral. The group was highly cohesive and appeared very committed to the project.[38] Other parents volunteered outside of school. Claudio and Javiera did volunteer work with blind and hospitalized persons.

Some Calasanz parents expressed critical political perspectives, although they were not party members. Ledda comments: "We have political opinions about what is going on in the country, but we're not party members. At Calasanz, we could discuss this in an intimate setting, but never at a parent meeting . . . The people who know us at school see us as 'reds' [*laughs*]. They think we're communists. But that's because they're Pinochet supporters. We're friends and accept each other." Here, Ledda points out that at a school like Calasanz that includes conservative parents, she avoided expressing her political opinions. In contrast, Claudio criticizes the school for not living up to its commitment to support the poor: "I'm most critical of the fact that the school and congregation have not stayed true to their founding principles directed toward helping kids with less resources. Obviously, if they followed through on this 100 percent, my kids couldn't attend." Ledda's and Claudio's remarks demonstrate that even parents that did not actively participate in school-based volunteer activities demonstrated a deep commitment to the school's social justice mission.

Critiques of Student Activism at Calasanz and Rosario Concha

While many LMS and Raimapu parents participated in activism alongside their children, and several Calasanz parents did volunteer work, some moderate Catholics and pragmatists sharply criticized student activism outside their own school. Marcelo, a Calasanz parent, remarks, "My older children attend private universities because they are well known for the subjects they are studying. Also, if you send your kids to the University of Chile, the Catholic University, or other universities, [you will say to yourself] 'Oh, no! The protests mean you'll miss three months of classes. What a mess—the rock throwing, the police!' So, thank God we can afford to send them to private universities because college is so expensive now." In addition to his discomfort with student protests, Marcelo also alludes to the fact that many private universities did not have student governments during this period, so many observers assumed that students would not protest there.[39] Ironically, students at the private Universidad Central initiated the 2011 college protests.[40]

Paulina and Guillermo, parents at Rosario Concha, criticized the Penguin Revolution:

> *Paulina:* When I went to the Liceo # 1, it really gave me a lot of study skills that could help me academically in the future. I didn't go there to waste my time.
>
> *Guillermo:* In the past, students used to study. Now, you watch the news, and the students at the National Institute are on strike. You didn't used to see that. There's lots of violence in the schools now, too.
>
> *Paulina:* They say there aren't enough opportunities for kids, but I think the opportunities are there; they just don't take advantage of them. Or maybe they want it served to them on a platter. You've got to work hard to succeed.

While Marcelo emphasizes how protests disrupt students' ability to learn in college and potentially threaten them with bodily harm, Paulina and Guillermo criticize protesting students' laziness. Their criticisms demonstrate that student protests did not only lead to political polarization within schools like LMS, but provoked others outside schools where protests occurred. This reaction against protests may have led some middle-class voters to support conservative Sebastián Piñera's successful presidential bid in 2010.[41]

This last section illustrates how some private schools became hotbeds of political activism before and during the Penguin Revolution; others were sites for volunteer activities supporting the poor, but some parents at these schools criticized student activism. These findings suggest that many middle-class parents do not see their children's schools only as means for upward mobility; rather, they also see them as organizations that can lead to social change. Further, it shows how parents and children at private schools were part of the social ferment beginning during the Bachelet administration rather than sitting on the sidelines. Finally, it shows the connections between activists' and moderate Catholics' identity investments centered on their political and moral identities, and their willingness to engage in and support activism and volunteer work in their schools. Their criticisms of competition and neoliberal policies were not merely self-serving platitudes—they did not just "talk the talk"; rather, these parents "walked the walk" because their participation in schools built on their long-term membership in activist and religious subcultures. Simultaneously, youngsters,' pragmatists,' and some moderate Catholics' identity investments in their children's upward mobility through education help explain their opposition to student activism.

Conclusion

This chapter has explored schools as communities, the construction of symbolic boundaries within schools, as well as activism and volunteer work in three of the schools. The chapter offers an important contrast to much scholarship in Chile and elsewhere that sees middle-class parents as segregated into class-homogeneous schools and/or as primarily focused on using schools to accumulate economic and social advantages for their children. In contrast, I found important fissures among parents in both class-homogeneous and class-diverse schools. In four of the five schools, activists and moderate Catholics clashed with youngsters regarding their schools' overall academic and social goals (though these conflicts were more muted at Raíces). Activists' and moderate Catholics' identity investments centered around their political and moral loyalties led them to criticize younger parents. They believed youngsters did not subscribe to their school's larger political or moral purpose and corroded its identity through their emphasis on academic performance and competition.[42] In contrast, at Rosario Concha, the most class-diverse school, moderate Catholics and youngsters teamed up against pragmatists, who felt wedged between the poor people they feared and upper-middle-class parents that disrespected them.

Established parents responded to a changing student body resulting from the Ñuñoa schools' expansion and the La Florida schools' transformation from private to charter schools. Following Max Weber, we might see activists' and moderate Catholics' actions as efforts to exclude lower status groups via social closure.[43] However, our analysis reveals a relational dynamic in which established parents criticize newcomers and pragmatists, but these latter groups "push back" with critiques of ostensibly dominant parent groups: conflict intensifies group identities.[44] Each school operated as a field in which groups with different capital portfolios vied for power and influence.[45] Additionally, activists' and moderate Catholics' critiques of the other two groups are broadly similar to their criticisms of elitism, competition, and ostentation in the workplace, housing market, and elite schools.

Activists' and moderate Catholics' participation in and support of student activism and volunteering at schools also contrasts with the view that
liberal or progressive middle-class parents "talk a good game," but their selection of public or progressive schools is primarily centered around supporting their children's education rather than pushing for policy changes that
would improve social equity. This chapter shows that schools are not solely
or always "engines of social reproduction"[46] but also platforms for social
change. Students and parents at LMS and Raimapu engaged in several waves
of activism in recent years, the second of which was part of the Penguin
Revolution. Parents' experiences as activists and party militants led them to
support their children's activism. Here, too, activism at LMS led to criticisms
from youngsters who thought student protests undermined their identity
investments focused on academic performance and social mobility. Likewise,
student movements reverberated into parents' discussions at schools where
protests did not occur. Some Calasanz and Rosario parents criticized student
strikes. Thus, student activists contributed to broader political changes
under the first Bachelet administration, and some parents supported the
"countermobilization" against student activists by leaving LMS or criticizing
student protests.

Calasanz parents' participation in social action with the homeless and
other volunteer activities were less controversial. Nonetheless, these actions
were rooted in their Catholic faith, the school's mission, and broader public
debates led by clergy that called for greater social equity. Here, too, middle-
class parents did not seem solely focused on their children's social advancement; rather, they saw their own and their children's volunteer activities as
addressing a real need and helping their children become moral individuals.

Why did some parents support and participate in social justice activism
while other studies show middle-class parents as largely focused on family
needs and aspirations? I argue that parents' activism and social action reflect
the persistence of social cleavages based on religion and class that are present
in Chileans' political allegiances but also form part of their cultural orientations.[47] Many middle-class parents are not solely engaged in opportunity
hoarding or social exclusion of the poor. Rather, their identity investments
reflect their long-term immersion in deeply rooted political and religious
subcultures. Furthermore, their precarious privilege (social interaction
with elites in the case of the upper-middle class) intensifies their critiques of
market society. Activists' and moderate Catholics' public action reveals their

embeddedness in ideologically-based subcultures and their participation in broader social movements that resurfaced in the mid-2000s.

In our next chapter, we consider how members of each group engage in identity investments in the intimate space of their homes, and how these aesthetic choices reflect the broader social and ideological divisions between segments of the middle class that we have observed thus far.

5

Home Decorations as Representations
of Family, Taste, and Identity

MORGANA IS A FREELANCE physical education teacher and activist whose teenagers attend Manuel de Salas. She frequently goes to gallery openings, and her living room includes several reproductions of paintings by European masters like Matisse and Dalí. She also has a set of colored bottles similar to those found in Nobel Laureate poet Pablo Neruda's three homes, all of which now function as museums that provide guided tours. She recalls, "When I was ten years old, they had closed Neruda's Isla Negra home [located in a small community on Chile's central coast] after 1973 [when the military took power]. We entered the property—it's a huge plot of land on the coast. I looked through gaps in the boarded-up windows and saw all the colored bottles. I loved the way they reflected the light." She continues, "At some point, a friend gifted me a colored bottle. It's not like I'm a big collector. Then another friend saw I had three bottles and she said, 'I brought you this bottle because I see you like them.' So, that whole area filled up with bottles" (see Figure 5.1).

Marcelo, a Calasanz parent, explains his attachment to heirlooms and their connection to his family's rural past: "We have a cuckoo clock with a pendulum, and there is a receipt inside indicating its cost in 1932. There is also a letter that I treasure inside from the Ministry of Foreign Relations. It is written to my wife's great-grandfather recruiting him to join the War of the Pacific [against Perú, 1879–1882]." He continues, "I love my wife's family heirlooms more than she does, so my mother-in-law gives them to me to take care of. During my childhood, I would spend summer vacations on my grandmother's rural estate. We each had a horse, and I used to compete in the rodeo. I'm fascinated with horses, so you'll see images of horses all over this apartment" (see Figure 5.2).

The preceding chapters have explored middle-class identity investments in the workplace, housing market, and children's schools. This chapter and the following one examine investments with greater symbolic resonance. In this chapter, we explore the meanings families attribute to artworks and decorations in their homes. Chapter 6 examines families' public cultural consumption and leisure activities. Morgana's and Marcelo's comments reveal the powerful imprint of their childhood experiences on the ways they represent themselves and their families in their living rooms. Morgana connects the well-known image of colored bottles in Neruda's home to her own biogra-

Figure 5.1 Morgana's Collection of Colored Bottles. Source: photo taken by author.

Figure 5.2 Images of Horses in Marcelo's Apartment. Source: photo taken by author.

phy. Neruda is something of a national hero because his poetry is taught in schools, his homes are frequently visited by Chileans and tourists, and he was awarded the Nobel Prize for Literature in 1971. Additionally, Neruda was a long-term member of the Communist Party who served as a senator and in several diplomatic posts, and who escaped Chile to Europe during Chile's anti-communist period from 1948 to 1958.[1] The colored bottles, present in several activist homes, illustrate their strong connection to Neruda's literary production and political commitments. Along with the other artworks and decorations present in activists' living rooms, these colored bottles serve to connect their individual biographies to a powerful national cultural symbol.

Marcelo's recollections illustrate his aristocratic roots. His reference to his wife's and his own family lines through the images of the cuckoo clock and the horses as well as his nostalgic narrative about his childhood summers spent on his grandmother's estate reveal his strong identification with his extended family's "historic greatness" as well as yearning for an enchanted childhood that is no more. The War of the Pacific is a milestone in Chile's official history as the country's victory meant that Perú and Bolivia ceded territory containing nitrate and copper riches that bankrolled Chile's twentieth-century economic development.[2] Thus, the letter inside Marcelo's clock links his family to that war victory and all it signifies within the country's patriotic national story. Both these interview extracts provide clues to how identity investments in the home give meaning to individual biographies while connecting them to broader narratives about creativity, politics, and bloodlines. These examples highlight how home decorations link families to the broader cultural and political themes that anchor their identities.

In addition to providing an important new dimension to our analysis of Chile's middle classes, this chapter engages with a robust international discussion of taste in artwork and home furnishings. While much of Bourdieu's analysis of class-based tastes in *Distinction* is based on survey data, he also provides detailed analyses of different occupational groups based on qualitative interviews and photographs of individuals' homes.[3] In these interviews, he finds important differences in taste in home furnishings across families with different quantities and distinct types of capital (primarily economic versus cultural capital). In contrast, other analyses argue that there are no relevant class-based differences in artistic taste,[4] taste differences across families reflect symbolic boundaries based on moral and aesthetic rather than class differences,[5] or that home furnishings are primarily part of a gift economy through which families receive meaningful objects via inheritance and as gifts.[6]

The findings in this chapter build upon and extend insights from these studies. First, unlike some of the earlier chapters, there are some shared decorative themes among activists, moderate Catholics, youngsters, and pragmatists, suggesting that there is a common "middle-class aesthetic." Most interviewees displayed inherited items and gifts from family and friends, supporting analyses that view living rooms as part of a gift economy. Additionally, many families used custom-made wood furniture, reflecting middle-class preferences for craft or handmade goods.[7] Finally, several families described their decorations as practical—they did not purchase fragile or easily damaged items because they wanted their children to have free run of the house.

Second, variations in aesthetic taste between members of the four groups studied in this book broadly reflect Bourdieu's division between intellectuals' taste focused on symbolic mastery, business owners' focus on luxury, and working-class families' "taste for necessity." However, like earlier chapters, we find these differences between class fractions are deeply integrated into the political, religious, and meritocratic ideologies each group espoused. Activists displayed a progressive, cosmopolitan aesthetic; moderate Catholics evidenced traditional, religious tastes; youngsters' tastes spanned the boundaries between fine and commercial art; and pragmatists had a do-it-yourself (DIY) aesthetic. While some scholars observe an overlap between political/ideological affiliations and aesthetic tastes,[8] few examine how these two separate realms are in fact *unified* in the objects displayed in the home. I also found that these expressions of taste varied across the two communities, with more subdued home decorations in suburban La Florida, where I hypothesize that adults felt less pressure to conform to or distinguish themselves from established wealthy families. In contrast, Ñuñoa's location near wealthy communities made families more eager to differentiate themselves from the rich, highlighting the concept of precarious privilege.

Third, as in earlier chapters, we also explore the relationship between taste and the construction of symbolic boundaries. This section highlights the construction of moral boundaries *within* the middle class that are not coterminous with specific class fractions,[9] in contrast to the previous section. Here, women from different upper-middle-class groups sharply reject standardized decoration as exemplified by minimalist styles and the showroom houses discussed in chapter 2. In contrast, men (and one woman) from the same groups preferred minimalism to "gawdy" decorations. Interestingly, some individuals with contrasting tastes for different decorative styles shared an "anti-consumption" discourse that criticized materialism and social climbers.

The chapter begins with a review of common themes that straddle the four groups studied in this book. Next, I explore each group's distinct aesthetic preferences that reflect different identity investments. Finally, I examine the construction of symbolic boundaries related to home decoration and what they reveal about individuals' competing aesthetic and moral judgments.

Common Themes in Home Decoration

While there were important differences in the ways activists, moderate Catholics, youngsters, and pragmatists decorated and thought about their homes, there were also some common decorative themes that these groups shared. Many individuals expressed a preference for custom-made hardwood furniture. This attraction to organic materials and handmade goods mirrors other studies finding that middle-class adults associate craft goods with authenticity.[10] Moreover, many individuals described their living rooms as "practical."

Here, middle-class adults preferred adopting simple decorations so that children could have free rein in the home without adults worrying that they might damage expensive decorations or furniture. The preference for practical decorations fulfills the moral imperative in middle-class families to prioritize and safeguard children's healthy personal development as well as the family's needs over outsiders' impressions of the home. Finally, almost all respondents' homes included inherited and gifted items, illustrating how the living room reflects extended family and friendship networks.[11]

Many families enjoyed custom-made hardwood furniture, evincing a strong preference for simple, durable, and organic materials. Mickey, a youngster and history teacher, comments, "We love noble woods. My husband spent his childhood in the country because his grandmother has a home there, so he has always felt close to the land and wood. He has an interest in history, and since I'm a historian, I provide background on certain objects. That barrel belonged to his father" (see Figure 5.3). Mickey's and her husband's preference for hardwood objects reflects his nostalgia for his rural childhood and connects him to his family of origin. For this couple, hardwoods symbolize their ties to nature, rural life, and the family line.

Figure 5.3 Mickey's Wooden Barrel. Source: photo taken by author.

In addition to signaling durability and simplicity, the term *rustic* also implies a warm, informal, and welcoming environment. Several families went to great lengths to find rustic furniture, for example, by purchasing custom-made pieces in small towns while on vacation. They emphasized their design and affordability in contrast to standardized objects available in Santiago. Patricia, a moderate Catholic, remarks, "I had my furniture custom made because they don't sell rustic furniture at department stores." For Patricia, acquiring custom-made furniture allows her to provide a distinctive style to her home.

Some pragmatists saw rustic decorations as a way to reclaim unused materials. Alejandra comments, "My ex-husband built that liquor cabinet with surplus wood my father had kept. My dad enjoyed doing carpentry projects, and when my parents separated, he left a lot of wood in the yard. My mom kept it for years, but didn't realize it was hardwood. My ex-husband knew about different types of wood, so he cleaned and salvaged some of it to build the cabinet. It has strong affective meaning for us." Here, Alejandra implies that her ex-husband was able to "rescue" the hardwood that had been abandoned to pay homage to her absent father and his carpentry hobby. Hardwoods symbolize memories of a former spouse and a parent that are no longer present.

Several adults emphasized the practicality of their furnishings. Paulina, a pragmatist, remarks: "There's no point in buying expensive furniture with little kids who will damage it. I have a little furry thing, too—my dog—so he can damage it as well." Ledda, a moderate Catholic, comments, "There isn't anything here that can break, and we have protective covers on the sofas, so the girls can use them without a problem." Sofia, also a moderate Catholic, remarks, "I wanted our furniture to be practical so I could clean it easily and so that our kids would be comfortable. The house is for us and our close relations, not to show off to other people" (see Figure 5.4). This focus on practicality reflects both a child-centered model of the family and home as well as a desire to serve the needs of family members rather than to display the home to outsiders to maintain or increase the family's social status. Several studies associate this orientation with working-class or lower-middle-class homes,[12] yet I found this mindset in both upper- and lower-middle-class families.

Additionally, for most interviewees, the living room houses an array of objects inherited or gifted by parents, relatives, or close friends. For some, gifted furniture reflects financial limitations and the transfer of objects within extended families as older or more affluent relatives replace their furnishings.

Figure 5.4 Sofia's Practical Furnishings. Source: photo taken by author.

For others, decorations have important affective and symbolic meanings because they represent valued relationships.

These affective and symbolic attachments are particularly evident in the case of decorative items. As Jimena, an activist, comments, "All of the things in my living room were gifts from friends and family. I put everything here because I don't want someone to come over and think, 'Oh, she didn't like my gift.' Sometimes I think I have too much stuff here." Jimena displays these items out of a sense of obligation toward gift givers.[13] Inherited goods also reflect individuals' attachments to the deceased. Ana, a moderate Catholic, comments, "A very special friend who died of cancer painted those pictures for me, so they are priceless." The paintings in Ana's living room serve as a living memory of her friend and their special bond. Consequently, they hold an intense emotional meaning for her.

To conclude this section, many of those interviewed tried to create an authentic, wholesome family environment in their home that included hardwood furniture, adapted the home to children's needs, and connected the family to valued relatives and friends. These common themes and practices underscore a shared framework through which individuals engaged in identity investments in the home that prioritized simplicity and authenticity over ostentation, emphasized children's needs over the watchful eyes of visitors, and highlighted emotionally meaningful connections to the family's inner circle. These common themes echo other studies of middle-class preferences for authentic and distinctive crafts,[14] and the cross-class pattern through which homes function within gift economies that display valued relationships and cross-generational family continuity.[15] However, each group also displayed distinctive styles that reflected contrasting identity investments.

Contrasting Aesthetic Tastes across Middle-Class Groups

This section explores distinct decorative styles across activists, moderate Catholics, youngsters, and pragmatists. In contrast to the shared preferences noted above, I here identify unique aesthetic tastes within each group. Moderate Catholics developed a traditional, religious aesthetic evident in gifted original artworks, family heirlooms, and religious objects. These styles were more explicit among Ñuñoa families; La Florida families were less explicit in articulating their tastes. Activists displayed progressive cosmopolitan tastes focused on reproductions of celebrated artists, political artwork, and Latin American crafts. These tastes were also more subdued in La Florida. In contrast, youngsters expressed preferences for boundary-spanning decorative objects that included established and commercial art forms. Some youngsters in both communities expressed more explicit aesthetic tastes, but there was no clear geographic division within this group. Finally, pragmatists displayed a preference for do-it-yourself (DIY) artworks and decorative items that they or their children produced. All of the pragmatists interviewed in this book lived in or near La Florida.

How can we interpret these differences across groups? First, Bourdieu argued that intellectuals and public employees emphasize symbolic mastery in their aesthetic tastes, while business owners prefer mass market styles and private sector professionals display tastes in between the first two groups.[16] Further, he argued that working-class people favor function over form in their aesthetic tastes based on their more limited artistic exposure as children. Thus, in contrast to Halle, who found no class-based differences in aesthetic taste,[17]

I argue that the differences between moderate Catholics (who were primarily private employees or worked in business), activists (who were educators, artists, and public employees), and pragmatists (who worked in lower status clerical and sales jobs) follow the pattern Bourdieu identified.[18]

However, this argument does not offer a persuasive interpretation of the different taste patterns of moderate Catholics, activists, and youngsters. Here, I argue that activists' and moderate Catholics' roots in partisan and religious subcultures gave them different aesthetic orientations from youngsters, who came of age in the 1990s when these organizations' grassroots networks experienced a period of decline. While some authors have identified an *overlap* between political preferences and aesthetic tastes,[19] few researchers have shown how aesthetic and political preferences are *inextricably bound together*. The integration of political/religious and aesthetic taste offers further support for the concept of identity investments deployed throughout this book: aesthetic choices reflect deeply rooted, ideologically informed identities grounded in experiences in childhood and young adulthood.

I also found differences in aesthetic styles displayed by each group in the two communities studied. Activists and moderate Catholics living in or near Ñuñoa articulated more elaborate aesthetic preferences than did their La Florida counterparts with similar class and educational backgrounds. I argue that these differences reflect Ñuñoa families' proximity to elite groups that stimulated a desire to *articulate* an aesthetic style that *differentiated* them from elites, as I have argued in previous chapters. Ñuñoa families' precarious privilege was particularly notable in their tastes, distastes, and anxieties, as they were exposed to elites but excluded from those groups. La Florida families did not perceive such pressures as they were not regularly exposed to elite families. Consequently, they displayed patterns of "ordinary consumption"[20] highlighted in previous chapters and further developed in the next chapter. As noted above, there was no strong geographical difference between youngsters in the two communities; almost all the pragmatists interviewed lived in or near La Florida. I explore each of these aesthetic preferences and their meanings below.

Moderate Catholics

Moderate Catholics displayed a traditional religious aesthetic focused on the continuity of the family line, expressions of religious faith, and a taste for antiques and traditional items, as indicated in the introductory discussion of

Marcelo's living room. Many of the items displayed were family heirlooms, gifted original artworks, or religious icons and objects. Their identity investments signaled a connection to family forbears, a desire to preserve the prized possessions of previous generations (what others call "patina based consumption"),[21] and to assert their religious faith.

Individuals displayed gifted original artworks to foreground their connections to extended kin. Members of this group emphasized their family ties to well-known artists rather than their artistic knowledge. Miguel mentions that his mother gave him several paintings produced by a relative: "He was a sculptor who won the national art prize. People who know about art recognize him and his work." Miguel also displays a painting he produced. Here, he emphasizes his relative's fame rather than locating his work within an artistic genre or commenting on specific formal aspects of the painting (see Figure 5.5).[22]

Dany says, "My husband's uncle is American and is a painter. He told me to select one of his paintings and I said I wanted to pick one I understood because I didn't understand some of them. Otherwise, I wouldn't display it." Thus, Dany underscores her limited knowledge of contemporary art. However, importantly, she displayed numerous reproductions of paintings de-

Figure 5.5 Miguel's Painting by a Well-Known Relative.
Source: photo taken by author.

picting religious themes throughout her house, commenting on where the originals are housed: she *did* have knowledge about religious art. Additionally, she commented on how religious icons can protect family members: "One Christmas, my mother gave images of the Virgin of Schönstatt[23] to me and all my siblings to protect our families . . . I had these images in my bedroom when I was single. The originals are housed in the Sistine Chapel." Thus, while Dany articulates limited knowledge of contemporary art, many items displayed in her house signal her religious faith, knowledge of religious artworks, and the religious experience she shares with her parents.

Miguel and Ledda had several crosses in their home (as displayed in the introductory chapter). Ledda comments that they have numerous crosses because Calasanz school gifts them to each family every year. Miguel responds, "No, it's actually my fault. I like crosses, and we purchased some of them when we traveled to Brazil and Argentina. I like to see the different images of Christ." Earlier in the conversation, when I asked Ledda if any objects in their home had sentimental value, she remarked: "This has more symbolic value. When you enter the house, there is an altar that welcomes visitors with a Bible, the Virgin, and Padre Hurtado." Here, Ledda likens her home to a house of worship with an altar on its threshold. Also, it is notable that she includes an image of Padre Hurtado on the altar. Hurtado was a Chilean priest who participated in antipoverty efforts and was recently beatified. The selection of this priest highlights the family's commitment to Calasanz school's social justice mission (see Figure I.2 in the introduction).

Several moderate Catholics described their living rooms as traditional or implied as much through stories about how their furnishings came from their childhood homes. Most of these individuals hailed from provincial business or landowning families and felt these styles reflected those they had been exposed to as children. Patricia comments that, "Our style is very traditional." She goes on to describe paintings and other objects received from family members, historical prints from colonial Chile, and keepsakes from her spouse's family: "We like antiques. Those lighters belonged to my husband's grandfather, who was a diplomat. He had lighters and pipes he would take with him when he traveled." Here, Patricia highlights the important political role of her husband's relative, much like Marcelo's comments at the beginning of the chapter, while also asserting their preference for antiques (see Figure 5.6).

Moderate Catholics living in La Florida highlighted similar themes but came from more modest backgrounds than their Ñuñoa counterparts: they

Figure 5.6 Patricia's Original Artwork and Keepsakes. Source: photo taken by author.

could not speak of their ancestors' prominent roles in government or the arts. Ana, who came from a modest provincial family, comments, "I like to collect antiques. If you notice, I have collections of old irons, stoves, telephones, and small wooden boxes. I have a more traditional style." At first glance, these preferences seem similar to Patricia's. However, Ana does not mention that a famous relative owned these items, and she does not own any prize-winning artists' paintings. Elba, whose father was a "self-made" businessman, illustrates this difference: "A friend of mine is a painter and National Art Prize winner. I've given her a thousand hints that I'd like one of her paintings. She always tells me she'll bring one, but never does." Thus, Elba is weakly connected to a well-known painter—she does not have the family ties that would make her worthy of a gifted painting, in contrast to Patricia, Miguel, and Dany.

Activists

While moderate Catholics displayed a pattern of patina-based consumption focused on family heirlooms, religious symbols, and gifted original artworks; activists articulated *progressive cosmopolitan* tastes that represented their political identities, artistic knowledge, global mindset, and appreciation for artisan skills and objects. Like other groups, activists displayed family heirlooms, but with few exceptions, these objects did not take center stage in their narratives regarding their household possessions. Two exceptions to this general point bear reflection for what they reveal about activists' and moderate Catholics' different family origins. Morgana, whose story began this chapter, commented, "Those two chairs belonged to my great-great-grandmother, Isabel Le Brun de Pinochet, once of the first teachers in Chile." Le Brun was a teacher who advocated for secular education and greater public recognition of educated women's professional status. A statue in downtown Santiago commemorates her contributions to education in Chile.[24]

Additionally, Clara explained that her ancestors were political activists that pushed for secular, democratic rule in the mid-nineteenth century: "People on my dad's side of the family were widely recognized. My grandfather was president of the University of Chile, and earlier generations were positivists. This branch of the family was from France and was related to Auguste Comte [widely regarded as the founder of sociology]. They weren't very religious—they believed in science for science's sake."

These references to renowned family members certainly evince Morgana's and Clara's pride in their lineage, but they highlight important differences with Marcelo's and Patricia's comments above. Rather than focusing on their roles in government (although Clara later mentioned that one of her relatives was a cabinet official), both women emphasize their relatives' identities as educators, intellectuals, and advocates for secular public institutions. Additionally, the objects themselves are of secondary importance (Clara did not even mention heirlooms from these relatives) to their accomplishments as public servants. Finally, as we shall observe below, activists focused on their political identities (implicit in Clara's remarks), cosmopolitan artistic knowledge, and collections of Latin American crafts acquired through travel. These identity investments reflect their self-image as progressive intellectuals.

Unlike moderate Catholics, who displayed original artworks gifted by family members, most activists displayed original artworks they had purchased or reproductions of well-known European and Latin American modernist painters. Two individuals in this group had purchased or received original artworks as gifts but had an entirely different view of art than moderate Catholics.[25] Ricardo comments, "Gloria's uncle created that sculpture of the blindfolded person. It represents his wife, who was held captive at Villa

Grimaldi. They were actually both held prisoner in the dictatorship's torture center."

Tamara, a pharmacist, displays her artistic knowledge when describing her purchase of a painting. "The only art that is worth anything in this house is that painting. I didn't buy it because it was a Carreño [Cuban-Chilean painter who won the National Art Prize]; I bought it because it portrays an indigenous woman, and I am a big supporter of indigenous rights."[26] Tamara continued that they purchased the painting at an auction to support a museum employee who suffered from cancer.

Both these interviews highlight activists' political allegiances and family stories. Ricardo indicates that a sculpture in their home represents the imprisonment and torture of Gloria's aunt and uncle at the hands of the dictatorship. Hence, this artwork highlights the intergenerational trauma and political commitment at the core of activists' identities. Tamara differentiates herself from elites by commenting that she did not purchase the painting because its producer was famous, making an implicit jab at wealthy art collectors. She goes on to explain that the painting's focus on a Mapuche woman aligns with her political commitments, and the purchase also aided an ailing employee.[27] As noted in the last chapter, LMS and Raimapu highlighted indigenous issues, an issue of relevance for Chile's recent political and institutional changes. Hence, while they own original artworks, Ricardo, Gloria, and Tamara express their political commitments through the art they display as well as their knowledge of the art world. This political story sharply contrasts with moderate Catholics' display of religious images, landscapes, and still life paintings.

Other activists displayed reproductions of European modernist and Latin American artists and articulated an interest in and knowledge of art and art history. Morgana owns numerous reproductions and a copy of a famous Klimt painting: "I like Klimt and Van Gogh a lot. I don't care much for Velázquez—his work is too dark—or Rembrandt. It's not that I don't like them, but I wouldn't buy a magazine with Rembrandt prints. I like Picasso, Roberto Matta [Chilean surrealist painter who spent much of his career in Paris], and Dalí. It's not that I've studied art history, but I follow painters that I like." Rodrigo and Lenka also displayed Matta and Van Gogh reproductions. Activists' preferences for European and Latin American modernist art contrasts with moderate Catholics' display of artworks by Chilean painters who are family members. These activists demonstrate knowledge of dominant international artistic styles and forms that reflects their cosmopolitan worldview. Their artistic choices reveal the importance of symbolic mastery to their identities and tastes in contrast to moderate Catholics' focus on their social capital—their personal connections to well-known Chilean artists.

Several activists also displayed overtly political art, like the sculpture and Carreño noted above. Many living rooms featured reproductions of the Ecuadorean painter Oswaldo Guayasamín's work. Much of his artwork depicts images of poverty, human suffering, and indigenist themes.[28] Víctor remarks: "That painting is by Guayasamín and is titled, *The New Quixote*. It represents both Ernesto "Ché" Guevara [Argentine/Cuban revolutionary] and Christ. My father-in-law gave it to us." While Guayasamín's work is not well known in the US, he is widely respected and venerated in Latin America. The presence of his works in several households speaks to their admiration for Latin American art that fuses aesthetic and political principles. Víctor's interpretation of the painting juxtaposes the suffering of Christ, Quixote, and Ché [whom the CIA and Bolivian military assassinated during his effort to catalyze a rural uprising in Bolivia].[29] Several activists' display of Guayasamín reproductions reflects their social conscience, political commitment, and knowledge of international artistic figures and trends (see Figure 5.7).[30]

Figure 5.7 Reproduction of Guayasamín's *The New Quixote* in Víctor's Living Room. Source: photo taken by author.

Many activists display Latin American crafts in their homes. They acquired these objects during work-related travel or received them from family members that had traveled or lived outside Chile. Víctor remarks, "My in-laws have the means to travel abroad. We play a game with them: every time they travel, they bring us back a key chain and we hang it on the bar my wife bought with her severance payment" (see Figure 5.8). Family members who were exiled during the Pinochet dictatorship often provide gifts from abroad. Clara comments, "My uncle was exiled in Angola and married a woman he met there. We have some African crafts and goods that he gave us." This archive of travel also reflects the affluence of many in the sample in that their own or their parents' incomes afford them opportunities for international travel. More importantly, it confirms their cosmopolitan identities and social connections with remote places and cultures.

Tamara's living room is full of Latin American crafts. She comments, "My job requires me to travel a lot. When I am abroad, I try to bring a little piece of each country back with me—crafts, books, music. I want my daughters to know that there is a whole world out there for them to learn about" (see Figure 5.9). Here, Tamara engages in concerted cultivation to provide her children with a cosmopolitan knowledge base that both reflects the family's internationalist orientation and could serve to "broaden their horizons" as they consider educational opportunities, occupations, and travel in the future. However, it is notable that in this context, she seeks to educate them with

Figure 5.8 Key Chains Symbolizing Travel in Víctor's
Living Room. Source: photo taken by author.

Figure 5.9 Crafts from Tamara's Travels. Source: photo taken by author.

crafts rather than examples of fine art (though the home does include art-works), alluding to the populist ethos she noted above.

Crafts did not only symbolize travel; they also reflected activists' reverence for the skills and "authenticity" of artisans. Lenka remarks that she and her husband do most of their home repairs and remodeling: "I've always valued the ability to do things on your own instead of buying things. I don't like stan-dardized objects. I found a unique object and no one in the world has it." They continue by linking this orientation to their love of Neruda's homes. Rodrigo continues, "It's like Neruda says. You collect things . . . you find meaning in something that maybe no one else pays attention to." Lenka continues, "Our lifestyle is wholesome [*es sana nuestra onda*]." This discussion connects with Morgana's opening description of her colored bottles [also present in Lenka and Rodrigo's as well as other activists' homes], but also reflects the idea of the aestheticization of everyday objects. For Lenka and Rodrigo, seeking beauty in craft and everyday objects allows them to create an authentic and wholesome domestic space.

Others detail their reverence for artisan skills. Tamara comments, "We like handmade goods. Everything has a special meaning or essence, some representing other peoples." Luís continues, "What I like about crafts and handmade goods is that we take something lifeless and give it life." Thus, while Rodrigo and Lenka seek beauty in everyday objects, like colored bottles, Tamara and Luis highlight artisans' skills, the symbolism present in crafts, and artisans' capacities to imbue objects with meaning. They highlight the idea that vernacular cultures are more authentic than modern ones.[31]

The aesthetic tastes described above were more widespread among Ñuñoa families than those in La Florida.[32] Other activists in La Florida displayed more subdued styles, much like the discussion of La Florida families above. Even though their homes were less ornately decorated than those of their Ñuñoa counterparts, some of the same aesthetic principles were present. For example, Mario, a Raimapu parent, has a collection of postcards with images of European masterpieces, which his wife assembled. He remarks, "We try to be more creative than consumerist." Alejandro and Susana, also Raimapu parents, had the most austere dwelling I observed because they built their home. While they did not have reproductions on the wall, they did display Latin American crafts: "I inherited those crafts from a friend who lived in Ecuador. They are very traditional objects there." Israel, a Raíces parent, commented that he and his wife were not very attached to things. Nonetheless, he displayed a Picasso reproduction and an original artwork he had purchased in his living room: "I bought that piece at a gallery somewhere, but I don't know who painted it." Thus, La Florida activists felt less inclined to decorate their homes with numerous paintings, reproductions, and crafts. I hypothesize that because they lived in an environment with few established, wealthy families, there was little pressure to distinguish themselves from those families.[33] Nonetheless, the works and reproductions they did display fit with the general themes adopted by Ñuñoa activists (and members of the Ñuñoa diaspora).

Youngsters

Youngsters displayed diverse styles of formal and mass-produced artwork as well as decorative items that stretched beyond the boundaries of consecrated genres. Gladys, a youngster, described this mix of artworks: "The advertising firm where I work commissions young artists to produce signed prints based on the company's logo. They give reproductions to staff as an end of the year gift. I have two in my home that are signed by the artist. I also framed a Miró reproduction. My partner made a sculpture dedicated to democracy that's very meaningful to him." Gladys is a graphic designer in a large multinational advertising firm and displays a mix of corporate art (prints), consecrated art (Miró), and political art (the sculpture) reminiscent of other research showing that younger artistic practitioners and cultural intermediaries are more open to commercial art than older art connoisseurs.[34]

Lisette, a former social worker, also displays a taste for fine, commercial, and decorative arts. She comments, "We bought that artwork from some craftsmen selling their work on the street. We loved it and thought the colors fit the house well. I feel like you need to give the house a little love so you feel comfortable. You need to spend a little money and decorate it tastefully" (see Figure 5.10). Lisette went on to describe several decorative objects (vitraux lamps and mirrors with mosaic borders) gifted by family members. The lines between art and decoration are blurred. María, an LMS parent, articulates similar preferences: "I like simple designs with a modern touch. Things that are too modern are cold, so decorations need to have some warmth as well— the feeling of home." Here, the individual objects are less important than the "warmth" they convey, much like Lisette's comment that "you need to give the

Figure 5.10 Lisette's Wall Hanging. Source: photo taken by author.

house a little love." The feeling generated by the ensemble of objects is more meaningful to these youngsters than the religious, political, or personal significance of specific objects.

This sense of eclecticism is also evident in Tania and Nelson's home. Tania describes a drawing gifted by a friend, a postcard another friend sent from Norway, a painting she made and gave to Nelson, gifted furniture, small antique items purchased at flea markets, and a photo of her hometown. Nelson summarizes the meaning of these items by saying, "All of these things are personal." Thus, for Tania and Nelson, individual items do not have special importance, but the objects as a whole reflect both their tastes for antiques and their close personal relationships.

Mickey shares with her husband a taste for antique items that reflect their interest in history. She remarks: "He has a tea set upstairs that we brought back from the northern nitrate mining zone we visited. Since he is a pharmacist, he keeps containers that were used to store chemicals years ago. One of these days, we'll display them." While this couple prefers antiques to contemporary objects, they express greater interest in decorative objects than artworks, much like other youngsters.

I did not observe differences in aesthetic styles between youngsters in Ñuñoa and La Florida. This may reflect the fact that the youngsters I interviewed in each location either came from working-class backgrounds or attended technical schools and/or mid-tier universities. Thus, they may have had less exposure to fine art that would have provided them knowledge and a taste for specific artistic genres.[35] They also did not have prominent ancestors whom they could commemorate, unlike moderate Catholics and a few activists. Finally, their relative youth may have made them less nostalgic than the older groups.

Pragmatists

Pragmatists articulated a do-it-yourself style that highlighted using family members' skills and ingenuity to decorate homes. One example of this approach is Alejandra's discussion in the previous section of her ex-husband's reuse of hardwood to create her dining room furniture. In this context, she remarked, "The coffee table has sentimental meaning for us. When my dad lived with us, he built it with our help. We repair it periodically, and we'll keep it until it falls apart because my mom loves it." Iván makes a similar comment: "I'm traditional, so I've kept this dining room table that belonged to my grandmother. Even if someone offered me one that was more beautiful, I wouldn't give it away. It will stay here until it falls apart." Alejandra and Iván preserve and repair prized possessions because of their strong affective meanings. In contrast to moderate Catholics and one activist who kept heirlooms that symbolized their relatives' accomplishments, pragmatists keep and maintain everyday objects and furniture because they belonged to beloved relatives, not because of those relatives' achievements.

Others emphasize their own artistic skills. Paulina comments, "There's no point in buying a picture. I'd rather paint it myself because everything in my house needs to be meaningful. I studied art for two years" (see Figure 5.11). Similarly, Pamela remarks, "We're all artists in this family. I painted that canvas and my daughters paint, too. I studied oil painting, decoration, and artistic painting." Here, we see a DIY ethos through which individuals display decorative objects they have created themselves, but the emphasis is not on the professionalism or stature of the creator. These individuals focus on these objects' decorative qualities rather than their position within a hierarchy of artistic goods.

In a different vein, Nelly displays a collection of objects and posters with Egyptian motifs. She comments, "I had a dream of visiting Egypt. I would

Figure 5.11 Paulina's Still Life Paintings. Source: photo taken by author.

have liked to go there. I've always been interested in Egyptian culture. I did a major research project in elementary school on Egyptian culture, including the principal pharaohs, the pyramids, the social strata, and Cleopatra. The project had a big effect on me, and I have been interested in Egyptian culture ever since" (see Figure 5.12). Here, Nelly describes how an elementary school research project sparked a dream of visiting Egypt. While she implies that she thinks the dream will never be realized by commenting that "I would have liked to go there," she pays homage to her dream through her living room decorations.[36] Because Nelly buys and sells items in street markets to make ends meet, she can fill her home with reminders of her childhood dream. Notably, her interest is neither in highlighting particular artworks, displaying heirlooms, or constructing a decorative theme, in contrast to members of the other three groups. Rather, her living room commemorates her as yet unrealized childhood dream.

To conclude this section, we have seen important differences in aesthetic tastes across the four groups that key into the identity investments observed in professional, housing, and educational fields. Moderate Catholics use living

Figure 5.12 Nelly's Egyptian Decorations. Source: photo taken by author.

rooms to represent the family line, their connections to prominent artists, and their religious faith. In contrast, activists articulate their progressive cosmopolitan tastes by displaying reproductions of European and Latin American masterworks, political artwork, and Latin American crafts. Youngsters, in contrast, focus on decorative themes that take shape in the ensemble of objects in their homes and that straddle fine art and decorative genres. Finally, pragmatists display a DIY ethos that highlights their ties to family members, their commitment to restore valued items, family members' artistic skills, and their childhood dreams. These contrasts reflect activists' and moderate Catholics' strong and contrasting ideological orientations as well as their substantial cultural and social capital; youngsters' comfort with less traditional, boundary-spanning decorative items; and pragmatists' resourcefulness in making and maintaining valued objects. The economic differences between the two communities were reflected in activists' and moderate Catholics' more ornate Ñuñoa living rooms and the relatively subdued decorations in La Florida homes. Identity investments in the home are a declaration of household members' core values to visitors. Furthermore, living rooms are intimate settings for embedding tastes, relationships, and traditions in families' daily lives.

Symbolic Boundaries

The preceding sections focused on shared middle-class aesthetic styles and taste variations across middle-class groups, respectively. This final section focuses on anxieties, disavowals, and expressions of distaste toward specific decorative styles and the people who choose them. If, as I have argued, shared styles among middle-class groups coincide with important variations across those groups, the construction of symbolic boundaries highlights a distinct pattern. Many individuals interviewed in this study sharply contrasted their own tastes with those of others, but these attitudes were not consistent among members of any one group. Rather, I will argue that middle-class individuals erect symbolic boundaries with others based on aesthetic and moral ideas that are not exclusive to a single class fraction or age cohort.[37] These boundaries drew upon discourses that criticize consumerism, the lack of taste expressed through gawdy and tacky styles, and the "coldness" of modern design styles.[38] Most men interviewed expressed confidence in their positions, while women felt that others negatively judged their decorative preferences. Critiques of materialism and elitism observed in other chapters are apparent in some of these judgments and disavowals. I begin with critiques of standardization, minimalism, and gawdy styles before exploring shared "anti-consumption" discourses.

Critiques of Standardization and Minimalist Design

Several individuals contrasted their homes' warmth and informality with "showroom houses," introduced in chapter 2. Here, they refer both to the "showrooms" used to sell newly manufactured houses to home buyers with their highly studied forms of decoration, and homes that are decorated for display. Lenka comments, "They say the showroom houses all have smaller furniture, so that's not very realistic . . . They sell you a concept that's not real; it's aspirational." Here, Lenka complains about the artificiality of show-room houses as well as their goal to sell a model of upward mobility.[39] The use of smaller furniture makes the houses look larger than their real size, which could trap unwitting home buyers. Lenka's rejection of artifice fits with the tendency of high cultural capital families to select "unique" and handmade goods and experiences in contrast to what they perceive as bland, mass-produced commodities.[40]

Some women express discomfort with minimalism. Claudia remarks: "My house is minimalist but with some warmth. I have friends with a more elegant sense of style whose houses are minimalist. They are beautiful, but they are too cold. I don't feel like I can sit in a comfortable position on their couches because I might stain or wrinkle them." Lisette has a similar criticism: "I don't like living rooms where you look at them and say, 'Can I sit down?' Everything is so neat that you feel like you are in a museum." The discomfort Claudia and Lisette express reflects the sense that their peers' elegant homes imply a criticism of their preference for vernacular tastes. Additionally, they contrast the "cold" feeling of these uncomfortable, elegant, and formal houses with the sense of ease they feel in their own homes. Walking into these minimalist homes is like a "trial by fire" in which these women risk humiliation if they do not follow unspoken behavioral codes.[41]

This trial by fire in minimalist homes is connected to some women's feel-ing that others judge their homes. This is a sensitive topic due to the dominant view that women are responsible for creating an attractive environment for family members and guests. Tamara, referring to the many craft objects in her home, says, "People have called this an Arab bazaar; they've called it all kinds of names." However, she does not buckle under the pressure. She continues, "We don't live in a showroom house. We don't want people to arrive and say, 'Oh, your house is so beautiful!'" Claudia similarly remarks, "My decorative objects all have sentimental value because they are gifts. I have a shelf unit in the dining room with lots of decorations and many people say it's—what's the word?—kitsch. But I don't care because they all evoke memories." Lorena makes a similar comment: "Everything in the house is hand-me-downs or gifts. It would be nice to have a precious, beautiful house like the ones in the magazines, but you need to spend a lot of money to do that and it's just not our priority." Tamara, Claudia, and Lorena offer counterdiscourses in response to the pressures from others to adopt a modern style in their homes. They prefer to keep meaningful objects and maintain an informal style, even though others criticize their choices.

Critiques of Gawdy Tastes and the Embrace of Minimalism

A second group criticized homes with "loud" or "tacky" decorations. This view is likely what the above women mention regarding others' criticisms of their tastes. This second group, who were mostly men in this sample, reject homes filled with ornamentation or decorative styles they perceive as garish. Claudio remarks, "We like our house to be as natural as possible; not cluttered with things. For example, you see this rug—it doesn't have green crescents all over it; it's simple, rustic. When I grew up, even if the furniture was simple and inexpensive, there wasn't anything in a rococo style." Claudio uses his austere aesthetic to criticize those whose homes are excessively or garishly decorated.

Others explicitly embraced "minimalist" or "modern" styles. For some, minimalist simply means "sparse" rather than referring to modern design styles, reflecting their disinterest in decorations. Israel comments, "We're not very fetishistic about things" (see Figure 5.13). Rafael says, "I've always prioritized having a lot of space over having things. My wife says she would like to have more decorations in the home, but she has never followed through on her desire."

Ricardo sees minimalism as a decorative style. He comments, "We prefer things with straight lines. We looked at a lot of chairs, but we don't want to buy these rococo styles with pink flowers painted on the fabric." Paula, a moderate Catholic with training in interior design, remarks: "We have gone for rectangular shapes and straight lines that people use now. My husband and I don't like old things, even though they can sometimes be pretty and deco-

Figure 5.13 Israel's Sparsely Decorated Dining Room. Source: photo taken by author.

rative, so we've gone for modern furniture. My husband's friend and former classmate has a furniture boutique and made our furniture." Paula's comment suggests that a connection to a design-oriented social and professional circle may make minimalism more appealing to some women.[42] These critics of gawdy styles reject "loud" colors, clutter, and ornate or outdated decorative motifs. They prefer open spaces, simplicity, and subdued colors. In contrast to those interviewed in the previous subsection, they do not feel that others judge them.

Anti-consumption Discourses

Interestingly, while different individuals expressed strong preferences for vernacular or minimalist styles, many individuals with contrasting preferences shared a critique of "consumerism" and "status-seeking consumption," a theme we explore in the next chapter. Luis, who prefers craft styles, comments, "We see a human value, not a commercial value, in our things. We could hypothetically have an art collection, which is an economic investment." Tamara continued, as noted above, that their original artwork was not

purchased with collecting in mind. Interestingly, Ricardo, who favors minimalist design, remarks, "We [Chileans] like to differentiate ourselves from
those below us. People buy big plasma TVs and ostentatious furniture. We're
not like that. We've always been hippies and we'll stay that way, even though
our earnings have increased." Nelson comments, "We have a plasma TV in the
kitchen. That's an example of consumerism. It's probably the only thing in this
house we would sell." Luis, Tamara, Ricardo, and Nelson, despite their different decorative tastes, share a common enemy—consumerism. They reject
the determination of objects' value through their price, the use of artistic and
consumer objects as investments, and status-seeking consumption. These
criticisms ignore other ways they assert their status through display of "authentic" crafts, artworks, and other items they find meaningful. Nonetheless,
their anti-consumption attitudes signal the strong moral opprobrium middle-
class people direct toward "social climbers."[43]

To conclude this section, middle-class adults constructed symbolic
boundaries with others based on decorative styles they rejected. We can observe a discursive opposition between craft-based, vernacular styles, and austere, modern, minimalist styles. Women who are exposed to minimalist styles
but do not adopt them feel judged by others, but construct counterdiscourses
highlighting their sentimental attachments to goods. Interestingly, while individuals articulate contrasting styles, they also share critiques of consumerism, understood as status-seeking, ostentatious consumer behavior. This
discussion of the construction of symbolic boundaries in home decoration
provides support for the argument that middle-class people construct moral
boundaries with others in the middle class rather than solely articulating distinction with other social classes.[44]

Conclusion

This chapter has examined the important phenomenon of aesthetic tastes in
home decorations. While previous chapters described explicitly economic
investments and phenomena in the labor, housing, and education markets,
household aesthetics offer a more intimate view of how families construct
their everyday lives and symbolically represent themselves to others. Unlike
other accounts that seek a unifying principle to interpret aesthetic tastes in the
home, I found three distinct principles of aesthetic display that revealed these
objects' underlying meanings.

First, middle-class families have a shared aesthetic centered around preferences for hardwood furniture, practical furnishings that prioritize children's
needs, and the display of inherited and gifted goods. This first approach aligns
with relational studies arguing that homes are embedded in gift economies,[45]
as well as research identifying crafts as symbols of middle-class authenticity.[46]

However, because these relational studies seek to identify a unifying principle that motivates families to select specific decorative items, they overlook
different middle-class groups' distinct identity investments. I found differences based on capital composition between activists' progressive cosmopolitan and moderate Catholics' traditional, religious styles; distinct aesthetics
based on capital volume that separate these two groups from pragmatists' DIY
style; and cohort differences between upper-middle-class groups revealed in
youngsters' genre-spanning preferences.[47] These findings contrast with Halle's
argument that there are no meaningful class-based differences in aesthetic
tastes.[48] This distinct interpretation likely reflects the fact that Halle did not
examine differences in capital composition or age cohort in his study, both of
which proved crucial in this analysis.

While some authors have extended Bourdieu's insights to identify a homology between aesthetic tastes and political affiliations,[49] few researchers
have shown how aesthetic tastes and political affiliations are inextricably
bound together. Activists' political and aesthetic tastes are fused through their
preferences for political art, crafts, and objects referencing Nobel Laureate
Pablo Neruda's homes; while moderate Catholics display their religious faith
and reverence for their ancestors' notable roles in government and wars.

Additionally, I found important differences in household aesthetic display
in Ñuñoa and La Florida homes, highlighting the concept of precarious privilege. Ñuñoa families had more elaborately decorated homes than their La
Florida counterparts. I argue, based on evidence provided in earlier chapters
as well as comparisons with marketing surveys, that these families are regularly exposed to wealthy families and thus consciously differentiate their own
styles from those of the elite in contrast to La Florida families.

A third perspective on household aesthetics examines the symbolic
boundaries families erect with others based on preferences for distinct aesthetic styles. Here, I found the concept of moral boundaries aptly described
my observations.[50] In contrast to my initial discovery of a shared middle-class
style and my second observation of variations across groups, here I found a
conflict-laden discursive field within which individuals from different groups

located themselves. Individuals expressed preferences for vernacular or modern decorative styles, and these differences were largely gendered. While men expressed confidence in their minimalist tastes, women felt judged for their craft preferences, though they developed counternarratives in response to these judgments. In spite of this sharp opposition between individuals, many shared an anti-consumption discourse that criticized social climbers' ostentatious display.

This chapter's findings dovetail with the next and final substantive chapter focused on cultural consumption and leisure activities. There, we will see further evidence of strong anti-consumption discourses that straddle different segments of the middle classes, ideological differences across middle-class groups, and distinct patterns of leisure and civic activities across the two communities.

6

Leisure Time Practices across Groups and Communities

WHEN I FIRST MET Clara at an LMS fundraiser, she and Rodrigo, another LMS alumnus, told me they were doing "political work" at the event. In our subsequent interview, she described her cultural activities: "I go to the theater and the movies monthly. Since I studied theater and was part of that world, I used to go much more often and could attend practically for free . . . This year, I took the kids to a modern dance performance at the University of Chile so they get in the habit and develop a taste for different [artistic] disciplines rather than just watching cartoons all the time." Clara also participated in a Ñuñoa citizens' campaign to restrict high-rise apartment construction there. She comments, "I get emails about the Ñuñoa Citizens' Network [*Red Ciudadana*] and participated in some marches where I ran into Víctor [another LMS parent] . . . The large builders only care about profits, and even Mayor Sabat is mixed up in this because he owns stock in some of the building firms." Clara's intense participation in the arts and local social movements illustrates a distinctive feature of Ñuñoa activists explored in this chapter.

Alejandra, a pragmatist, lives in her childhood home in La Florida with her mother and sister. She takes her son to the movies once a month and enjoys salsa dancing, but otherwise avoids other cultural activities. She explains, "Conversation is our main form of entertainment. When we're together, we chat. We don't like making plans to go out. We each do our preferred activity—my sister sews, and my mom does other crafts." She continues, "I'm a little different from some in my social circle because their life projects center on buying a car or a house. That's why my social circle is small. I seek authentic connections with others." Alejandra's preference for developing strong personal relationships with kin and close friends illustrates the tendency of activists, moderate Catholics, youngsters, and pragmatists in La Florida to adopt a more *domestic* pattern of leisure activity, in contrast to Ñuñoa residents' participation in public cultural consumption and social movements.

This final substantive chapter explores middle-class families' leisure activities, which tell us a great deal about their identities, patterns of inequality, and practices that may contribute to social change. Like chapter 5, this chapter describes shared middle-class leisure patterns, different practices across middle-class groups, and distinct cultural patterns in these two communities. The shared patterns of middle-class leisure activities integrate several themes developed in earlier chapters. The phenomenon of precarious privilege developed in chapters 1 and 2 results from job instability, career changes, and the high cost of housing. This phenomenon is apparent in middle-class adults' comments that they lack the time or money to enjoy many forms of cultural consumption (especially live performances). Moreover, parents' widespread use of concerted cultivation (described in chapter 3) resurfaces through their preferences for didactic leisure time activities over the purchase of material objects. This preference for "educational consumption" coincides with each group's identity investments built around their core political, religious, and meritocratic orientations: parents harshly criticize "consumerism" and counterpose their "virtuous" educational investments with other parents' focus on material things, as evident in Alejandra's comments.

In addition to these shared patterns, we observe distinct leisure practices across middle-class groups that reflect their different identity investments. Activists at Manuel de Salas and Raimapu expressed preferences for diverse musical styles (socially conscious folk, rock, classical, and world) and art film. They developed much of their social life through their children's schools. Activists at Raíces regularly participated in cultural activities but articulated less explicit tastes and developed fewer friendships at their children's school. Moderate Catholics at Calasanz and Rosario Concha expressed their religious and family values by viewing family-friendly films and restricting children's video game use, while supporting their musical education. Calasanz parents structured their social lives around their children's school, but Rosario parents had minimal participation in school life, as noted in chapter 4. Youngsters at LMS, Raíces, and Rosario Concha participated in public cultural consumption and didactic activities with their children but were not engaged with highbrow culture nor did they actively participate in school life. Finally, pragmatists at Raíces and Rosario focused their leisure practices on family time rather than cultural consumption or school activities.

We also observe place-specific differences in these two communities highlighted in chapters 2, 3, 4, and 5. Parents at Ñuñoa schools benefited from their proximity to cultural activities in the community and downtown, allowing them to attend more live performances and art galleries than their La Florida counterparts. Ñuñoa parents also participated in local social movements that relied on high levels of citizen organization in specific neighborhoods and responded to a building boom facilitated by a conservative mayor. Their activism formed part of the "inflection point" in Chilean politics described in the introduction and chapter 4. In contrast, La Florida has a less developed cultural infrastructure and more limited public green space. The community is also located further from downtown cultural institutions than Ñuñoa. The main cultural centers are two shopping malls that also host libraries, bookstores, and an art gallery. Its mixed-class character also influences cultural practices there. Hence, all groups in La Florida displayed a more "domestic" mode of leisure time activities focused at home rather than in public space. Additionally, La Florida residents engaged with contemporary popular musical styles that Ñuñoa families did not mention. Finally, apart from one interviewee involved in neighborhood activism, the La Florida families did not participate in community activism, which may reflect low levels of trust among neighbors.[1]

These findings make important contributions to current discussions of cultural consumption. Many scholars debate whether Bourdieu's model of cultural consumption that contrasts highbrow and lowbrow tastes has been superseded by a newer pattern.[2] Unlike Bourdieu, others contrast affluent cultural *omnivores* (who consume high- and lowbrow culture) with working-class *univores* (who only consume popular styles).[3] I found omnivorous tastes among activists, but not among the other groups, suggesting there are several contrasting forms of upper-middle-class cultural consumption.[4]

Additionally, activists' and moderate Catholics' cultural practices did not only reflect their incomes and education; rather, they resulted from their experiences within political and religious communities, a point largely overlooked in the literature on cultural consumption.[5] This chapter also shows how cultural activities at schools influence individuals' cultural participation. Finally, while others observe different patterns of cultural consumption across communities,[6] I also find important differences in political participation across communities that coincide with distinct patterns of cultural consumption.[7]

I begin with a brief review of cultural production and consumption in Chile to provide context for the tastes and practices described in the following sections. I continue with discussions of shared leisure patterns, differences across middle-class groups, and variations across the two communities. The conclusion revisits this chapter's findings and contributions to discussions of cultural practices.

Cultural Production and Consumption in Chile

Chile has an important heritage of artistic creation and is enmeshed in processes of cultural globalization that have increased the availability of artistic and cultural products. This brief overview of cultural production and consumption in Chile provides context for understanding middle-class Chileans' tastes and practices as well as some groups' hostility toward newer cultural practices that clash with traditional cultural icons and values.

Chile is the home of several internationally recognized artists, and its pre-1973 artistic tradition informs the tastes of activists I interviewed. Pablo Neruda (discussed in chapter 5) and Gabriela Mistral were both Nobel laureate poets.[8] José Donoso and Isabel Allende were part of the Latin American "literary boom" and its creation of the magical realist style.[9] Chile's *nueva canción* (New Song) left-wing folk music style created by Violeta Parra in the 1950s, and developed by Víctor Jara and others in the 1960s, gained international recognition. During socialist Salvador Allende's presidency (1970–1973), Inti-Illimani, Illapu, and Quilapayún integrated Andean indigenous music with folk and pop, and later gained international fame while in exile.[10] Chile also developed a rock music tradition that included innovative bands like *Los Jaivas* and *Los Blops* that were part of the global 1960s counterculture.[11] Roberto Matta was an internationally renowned surrealist painter who supported the Allende administration and painted murals in poor shantytowns. However, he spent most of his career in France.[12] Finally, Juan Downey, an acclaimed multimedia artist, spent much of his artistic career in New York.[13] In summary, prior to the coup, Chile's artistic production ranged across media, gained international acclaim, and artists were often tied to the political left.

Chile's military junta assassinated and expelled prominent artists that identified with the left, and promoted a patriotic aesthetic. One notable example is the government's support for conservative *cueca* (rural folk music) groups like *Los Huasos Quincheros* as regime surrogates. Starting in the late 1970s, artists who remained in Chile began to organize metaphorical public "happenings" that offered subtle criticism of the staid art world and the regime. Additionally, nueva cancion and later *canto nuevo* groups began to perform at strikes, protests, and semi-clandestine concerts (*peñas*); regime opponents circulated cassette recordings of these artists (including those who had died or were in exile) as well as Cuban *nueva trova* (folk) artists; and alternative radio stations played these musical styles. The Catholic Church and college students supported this oppositional artistic subculture. The activists I interviewed formed their musical tastes as college students in the 1980s and maintain strong attachments to these musical styles.[14]

Beginning in the 1990s, Chile and Latin America received an influx of US film and music, and saw the introduction of cable television and streaming services, although national and regional music and TV/film genres remain popular. The growing availability of US-based entertainment products helps contextualize moderate Catholics', youngsters', and pragmatists' consumption of Hollywood films and US-based cable channels. Chile is one of the few national locations of the Lollapalooza rock music festival, and MTV established a Latin American channel in the 1990s hosted by Mexican and Argentine nationals. The presence of MTV and rock festivals helps explain the popularity of *reggaeton* (the Puerto Rican rap/dance music style) and commercial artists like the Jonas Brothers among La Florida families. Finally, since 1990, Chilean directors have produced internationally acclaimed films serving to revive an industry the dictatorship had all but extinguished. Chile has become increasingly enmeshed in the global entertainment industry, and international cultural products influence local tastes.[15]

A decade into Chile's post-authoritarian rule, the Lagos administration (2000–2006) established a cultural policy that subsidized public performances to democratize arts access (the Santiago a Mil series of summertime outdoor performances, many of which are free), created new artistic spaces (like the Centro Cultural La Moneda, located in the basement of the presidential palace), and established funding agencies to support artists' work. These free and low-cost artistic spaces and performances are popular among middle-class families. Lagos's policy established the National Council on the Arts and

Culture (CNCA), which sponsors periodic surveys of cultural participation to guide cultural policy and scientific research.[16] Much current sociological research on cultural practices draws on surveys conducted in 2005, 2009, and 2012 (the most recent survey was completed in 2017).[17]

Scholars have used these surveys to analyze reading,[18] musical taste,[19] the overlap between political orientation and aesthetic taste,[20] and cultural consumption.[21] Researchers find that class is a strong predictor of both taste and engagement/disengagement in cultural consumption, but tastes and practices also reflect age, gender, and access to/expertise in digital technology use. Access to cultural goods and events (books, movie theaters, live performances) is more restricted than in more affluent countries, but it is growing, particularly in the areas of music, reading, and film attendance. While tastes vary across population groups, only a small group of highly educated, affluent individuals consume highbrow film, music, and art in combination with some popular forms, as evident through activists' cultural practices described later in this chapter. Artistic producers are much more culturally active and engaged with highbrow art forms.[22]

Shared Patterns of Leisure Activities across Middle-Class Groups

While much of this book focuses on different middle-class groups' distinct identity investments, like the previous chapter, I did find some shared middle-class attitudes and practices that speak to this book's larger themes. Members of all four groups complained that they either lacked time or money to go to the movies or live performances. The fact that these cultural events were inaccessible to upper- and lower-middle-class families underscores their precarious privilege: they are interested in these events but lack the time or resources to attend them. Additionally, many individuals highlight the didactic features of their leisure practices—they spent money on *important* goods (like books) and activities (like vacations or live performances) rather than on frivolous items like designer clothes, large television sets, or fancy cars. Their assignment of virtue to these didactic activities (which in fact enrich their children's cultural capital and may offer them advantages in college or on the job market) is related to their anti-consumption discourse introduced in earlier chapters. In contrast to more subtle expressions in other fields, middle-class individuals offered a full-throated condemnation of consumerism: the rise of new forms of consumption was unnerving because it threatened the legitimacy of the didactic and experiential consumption practices they had learned were appropriate for middle-class people.

The time and cost barriers restricting middle-class cultural consumption build on and extend others' findings. Analyses of survey data in Chile find that upper-middle-class adults state that they lack time to consume highbrow culture (e.g., visual arts, classical music, opera), while working-class and poor adults state they lack the money or the desire to consume consecrated cultural forms.[23] In contrast to these survey findings, I found that many upper-middle-class adults saw cost as a barrier to their participation in desirable cultural activities. While this finding is specific to my sample and cannot be generalized to the Chilean population, the upper-middle-class individuals I interviewed earned incomes in the 60th–90th percentiles of the distribution—these families had substantial discretionary funds. Thus, the fact that going to the movies or the theater was unattainable to them illustrates that live movies and performances are not accessible except to the most affluent Chileans and underscores the precarious privilege of those I studied: they want to attend live performances but cost barriers prevent them from doing so.

Ledda illustrates the time constraints upper-middle-class families face: "We would love to participate in more cultural activities, but with all of our daughters' extracurricular activities, there isn't enough time. Our four daughters are doing sports, English classes, art classes, piano lessons, two participate in a Catholic youth group, and the oldest is in a college preparatory class. It's a lot." Jimena, a Manuel de Salas parent, describes financial barriers limiting her cultural participation: "My daughter can pay the student rate to go to plays, which helps because the tickets are expensive, and if all four of us go, it's a lot of money." Pragmatists faced more severe cost constraints and consequently often opted to watch movies at home rather than go out. Thus, middle-class parents faced time and monetary constraints that limited their ability to attend movies or live performances.

Middle-class families' interest in providing their children with "didactic" or "enriching" activities also builds on scholarship reviewed in earlier chapters. The concept of concerted cultivation[24] can be extended beyond tutoring and enrichment activities to any family activity directed toward enhancing children's cultural capital.

Many parents spent much of their free time doing activities that were entertaining and educational. Parents described the importance of having books at home and reading to children or frequent visits to the library. Thus, Mario, a Raimapu parent, comments, "Each of our kids has their own bookshelf. We spend a lot of money on books [*laughs*]." It was also common for parents to use free outings to museums or vacations as educational opportunities. Dany describes a memorable vacation when her parents invited her and her children to visit Italy: "I made them read lots of books about the churches we would visit in Rome. They complained, but then when we actually visited the churches, their jaws dropped." Víctor described a preference for adventure tourism: "We traveled to the jungle in Bolivia. It was really meaningful because we went through the jungle like Tarzan—crossing rivers with snakes coming out of the rocks—it was very intense. My younger son was nine, and when we arrived to the national park, we learned he was the youngest person that had ever been there." Thus, any leisure activity can become a "teachable moment" through which parents fulfill their responsibilities to enrich their children's education and prepare them for the adult world.

Parents contrasted their preference for didactic leisure activities with those of "consumerist" parents. Others note the ascetic orientation of highly educated adults and their rejection of rich and working-class people's "crass" consumerism.[25] However, this anti-consumption discourse was evident across all middle-class groups. While this discourse dates back to the nineteenth century,[26] its current use reflects public repudiations of "consumerism" by prominent leaders and intellectuals as well as middle-class adults' discomfort with new expressions of ostentatious consumption. In 1990, Patricio Aylwin, the first democratically elected president after the dictatorship, refused to attend the inauguration of a shopping center, commenting that he "would never set foot in a mall" because he felt that malls clashed with Chile's cultural values.[27] Sociologist Tomás Moulian wrote scathing critiques of consumers' rising indebtedness and frequent visits to shopping malls as representing an abandonment of Chile's cultural traditions of austerity and as a force that discouraged Chileans from exercising their citizenship rights.[28] His polemical analyses gained widespread public attention, while other scholars empirically documented the growing supply of formal credit to middle- and low-income Chileans, shopping center expansion, and Chileans' accumulation of consumer debt.[29]

Some criticized Moulian's perspective for ignoring how working women's paid employment and purchases could give them greater bargaining power in their marriages, increase their personal autonomy, and fuel their social movement activism.[30] My research on working-class and poor families revealed that these groups adopted the same anti-consumption discourse Moulian articulated and showed that many poor families lost access to formal credit due to health emergencies and unemployment.[31]

Moulian's and others' generalizations about ostentatious consumption overlooked the conflicts between different groups of consumers that we have explored throughout this book. Middle-class adults counterposed their "virtuous" educational and experiential consumption to the idolatry of material goods they observed among others. Israel comments, "People see their cars as the expression of their hard work and how much they earn. You sometimes notice around here that people buy cars that are worth almost as much as their houses. It's really strange." Others criticized parents' "excessive" clothing and electronics purchases. Elba remarks, "There's a group of parents that spend their money on cellphones or a $150 pair of sneakers. I may earn the same salary, but I use my money for other things—education and providing my kids with experiences. These people don't buy books." Luis contends: "We show our kids a variety of international films because we want them to see that the world is more diverse and bigger than you could imagine. That's more important than having a brand new car." Lenka even referenced Moulian's work when criticizing showroom houses: "I stumbled across that little book *Consumption Consumes Me* [*El consumo me consume*], and it made me feel strange. That guy really caught my attention. I find it kind of pathetic, but very realistic in many ways."

These comments suggest that middle-class adults believe their preference for educational and experiential consumption is morally superior to their peers' focus on material things.[32] This observation underscores middle-class adults' determination that certain forms of consumption—those they had learned to prefer as children and young adults—are superior to newer forms of ostentation. These criticisms of materialism also serve as symbolic boundaries separating the middle class from the rich and less educated. Thus, these middle-class parents' anti-consumption attitudes reveal fissures within Chilean society centered around consumption. In contrast to Moulian's and others' generalizations regarding changing trends in consumption, we find salient disputes between different groups over appropriate forms of consumption that reflect their core values and identity investments. This anti-consumerist mindset is analogous to criticisms of "showroom houses" in chapters 2 and 5.

Variation in Cultural Practices across Groups

These shared leisure patterns and attitudes about consumption coincide with important differences across middle-class groups. Activists, moderate Catholics, youngsters, and pragmatists each display distinct leisure practices that hold different meanings for each group. Activists engaged in cultural activities that signaled their political identities, reflected the value they place on artistic expression, encouraged cultural practices among their children that allowed them to accumulate cultural capital, and highlighted the concept of authenticity. Moderate Catholics focused more on family-based film viewing, religious activities, and didactic children's enrichment activities. They encouraged children to engage in "wholesome" activities that deter them from drugs, alcohol, or violence. Youngsters mirrored some of moderate Catholics' cultural practices, but without expressing an explicitly ideological orientation toward consumption. Pragmatists enjoyed domestic leisure activities and movies as well as family gatherings, but participated less frequently in public cultural consumption.

The diversity of cultural consumption patterns across middle-class groups contrasts with the idea that "omnivorous cultural consumption" is a shared taste pattern for upper-middle-class adults.[33] In fact, only one of the four groups displays omnivorous tastes.[34] Other work outlining diverse patterns of cultural consumption does not offer interpretations of *why* middle-class tastes and practices vary. This section offers two answers to this question. First, different middle-class groups' identity investments based on their political, religious, cohort-based, and class identities lead them to adopt different cultural practices. Second, for many middle-class families, leisure time activities are anchored in their children's schools where group activities influence parents' consumption practices.

Activists

Many activists held degrees in teaching, graphic arts, or law. Some had parents that were doctors or came from affluent families, while others experienced upward mobility. Activists' intense levels of cultural participation and social life reflected their family and educational backgrounds as well as their desires to "live their lives fully" after their traumatic experiences during the dictatorship. These couples emphasized their attachments to the visual and performing arts and desire to expose their children to them. Simultaneously, they expressed a particular taste for left-wing folk music and art film, reflecting core identities. Raimapu and Manuel de Salas parents also found their main friendship groups through school, and hence their cultural practices coincided with school activities; Raíces parents were less strongly tied to other parents.

Several activists commented that they wanted to enjoy life after suffering during the dictatorship. Tamara remarks, "We lived through the 1980s when you didn't know if you were going to arrive home alive at night. We had a high level of commitment and risked our lives. Maybe that's why we enjoy everyday life and live intensely. We know the difference between trivialities and what's really important." Israel concurs: "After all those years of activism, I wanted to have a good time because I used to be so stoic and serious [*era un huevón grave*] [*laughs*]. Back then, I couldn't see many people because I was a clandestine activist, and I was organizing seven days a week. So, after that, I need to just relax. I've always tried to make new friends because otherwise, you'll grow old and won't even remember what you wanted to do in life."

These powerful narratives demonstrate that we cannot make sense of activists' cultural practices by only considering their educational and family backgrounds. Rather, their intense involvement in cultural consumption and socializing results from their efforts to heal after their traumatic experiences under the dictatorship. Their choices are also powerfully stamped by their political allegiances.

Activists were passionate music aficionados. While several activists attended live concerts and listened to classical music, jazz, and popular genres, they were most enthusiastic about nueva canción and nueva trova. Several individuals solidified their musical tastes in the 1980s during their college years. Lenka and Rodrigo comment:

> *Lenka:* We like nueva trova [socially conscious Cuban vocal music popularized by Silvio Rodríguez and Pablo Milanés]
> *Rodrigo:* That's right. I was very much shaped by Chilean song during the dictatorship.
> *Joel:* Any specific artists?
> *Rodrigo:* Inti-Illimani.
> *Lenka:* Quilapayún.
> *Rodrigo:* Víctor Jara.
> *Lenka:* Víctor Jara, Silvio Rodríguez.

Rodrigo: All the resistance music.

Rodrigo: I like boleros, too.

Lenka: We both listen to a lot of boleros and tango.

Rodrigo: Lenka introduced me to jazz and now I like it.

Lenka: I really like soul; I'm crazy about the blues.

Morgana similarly remarks: "I just went to a Serrat concert [Spanish trouba-dour]. I haven't missed any of his concerts—I'm a fanatic. It's like the music you grew up with. I like the 80s music, because it brings back fond memories. I enjoy nueva trova, like Silvio Rodríguez, Pablo Milanés, Inti-Illimani, Qui-lapayún, and Los Jaivas."

Activists' preference for political folk music supports other accounts noting that tastes are often solidified during young adulthood through college-based friendships.[35] It also aligns with findings that Chileans' cultural tastes are divided along partisan lines.[36] Nonetheless, two additional factors help us interpret this pattern. First, several activists' parents were communists who were blacklisted or killed after the 1973 military coup. Second, many of these individuals were prodemocracy activists in college, when nueva canción, canto nuevo, and nueva trova were frequently performed at protests, semi-clandestine performances (*peñas*), and circulated via pirated cassette recordings among activists.[37] Thus, activists' continued taste for nueva canción preserves their connection to their college years and signals the persistence of their political loyalties.

Some activists believed exposing children to diverse musical forms served a didactic function. Tamara, an LMS parent comments, "Music reflects people and cultures, so we play African music and tango, and the most famous artist from each country." Luis continues, "We play the *1812 Overture* for this young lady [*gestures toward their daughter*]—she loves it. When her sister studies math or physics, she puts on Beethoven's Ninth Symphony and it makes her happy." Luis later described how his daughter got him a ticket to a concert featuring the hard rock group Kiss: "You might look at me and think, 'Why does this progressive guy like rock?' but I've always loved rock music." He went on to describe that his daughters also enjoy Queen, Led Zeppelin, and Elvis Presley and had memorized their lyrics. "I tell them about the history of rock and jazz." Other activists described attending concerts by Spanish singers Joan Manuel Serrat and Miguel Bosé, nueva canción artists, and new wave band the Police. Activists share their tastes for a wide range of highbrow and popular music forms with their children as a means to enjoy a pleasurable activity but also to educate them about distinct musical styles, artists, and national cultures so they can become "well rounded" adults. They also have a "cerebral" appreciation for popular music as they locate artists within broader genres and modes of expression.[38]

While activists expressed strong tastes and passions for music, they did not all attend public performances. For many, cost was a limiting factor (as noted above), so many attended free concerts available through neighborhood cultural centers or large government-sponsored events like Santiago a Mil (a summer theater, music, and performance series including free events), which are part of recent administrations' efforts to democratize art access.[39]

Some activists received reduced price or free opera tickets from their employers, as Alicia, a university researcher comments: "Since we get discounted tickets through my job, we have been going to the opera monthly at the Municipal Theater [principal concert hall for classical music, opera, and ballet located in downtown Santiago]. We get the cheapest tickets. We've all enjoyed it. I had seen ballet at that theater before but had never been to the opera."[40] Aniluap, who had very limited means but was rich in social capital, still managed to hear live music: "When some of my classical musician friends are in the mood, they bring their violins and flutes to parties and perform classical music."

These same parents also consumed classic and art film with their children to acquaint them with "worthy" artworks in this medium. Art film is a highly exclusive taste in Chile. In 2005, only 13 percent of college educated Chileans expressed a preference for art film.[41] These parents watch art and classic films with their children to broaden their horizons. Evelyn, an art teacher, comments: "We have DVDs at home. Our daughters have seen art films by directors like Chaplin, Kusturica, and Kurosawa. They've seen a variety of movies, not just popular ones."[42] Others commented that they watched well-reviewed films, César or Academy Award winners, and European films. Two individuals were part of DVD clubs in which participants watched and discussed international art films. Aniluap comments, "We generally watch alternative films. A friend will come over and say, 'I've got a great film.' We watch international films, Kusturica's work, Argentine films, *Requiem for a Dream*—which I loved—and European films."

A few serious enthusiasts regularly attended art galleries and museums. Most enthusiasts were artists or had relatives or friends in the artist world.[43] In contrast, Morgana was not a visual artist but was a very serious enthusiast. She regularly attended museums and galleries: "I used to take my kids to galleries often. Now [that they are teenagers], they ignore me, so I go on my own. I'm going to the Frida Kahlo exhibition tomorrow at La Moneda Cultural Center." Members of the other three middle-class groups periodically visited the La Moneda Cultural Center and attended free tours of historic buildings, but did not visit art galleries or express an interest in consecrated visual art. Morgana's and others' visits to art museums and galleries form a complement to the progressive cosmopolitan art tastes evident in their home decorations.

Reading with children was an important leisure activity for all middle-class groups. However, activists were the only group that described omnivorous reading tastes. Gloria comments on her family's shared literary preferences: "I have to admit that we all love Harry Potter. My daughter likes Cortázar [Argentine surrealist author]. She's currently reading *Hopscotch* [an experimental novel]. She had to read a Cortázar story at school but we couldn't find it, so I bought her his collected works. After reading the assigned story, she just kept reading all of them. She loves them; we do, too." Gloria's family members enjoy both middlebrow and highbrow literature. Her inclusion of Cortázar is interesting as he is considered the father of the Latin American literary boom and because *Hopscotch* is an experimental novel with an unusual organization into two books with multiple "roadmaps" suggested by the author.[44] The family's interest in Cortázar reflects Gloria's training as an educator. Members of other middle-class groups did not articulate this interest in highbrow, experimental fiction.[45]

One distinctive feature of Manuel de Salas and Raimapu parents' social and cultural activities is that they spend much of their free time at school. Families develop strong friendships through their children's classes, volunteer, and serve in elected office in parent organizations. School cultural activities mirror and reinforce their aesthetic tastes.

Several activists were regular participants in school activities and parent organizations. Susana, a Raimapu parent, put this issue bluntly: "We live at the school. Sometimes we spend the whole weekend there. Our kids insist that we attend all the meetings. You have to do volunteer work, attend the parent meetings, and so on." In addition to their organizational responsibilities, parents build their friendship networks through school. Mario comments, "We share a lot more with Raimapu parents than with our neighbors. They are our main friendship group, and we see them all the time." Jimena remarks: "My daughters sometimes say that I participate too much at school. I'm the vice president of the alumni association. I also serve in the parent group in both my daughters' classes. I've never lost touch with the school since I studied there. The alumni always get together, and I don't just see those in my graduating class. I'm friends with graduates from other years, and I regularly attend gatherings."

This high level of volunteer participation and dense friendship networks coexist with a cultural milieu that reinforces activists' progressive cosmopolitan cultural tastes. When I attended a fundraiser at LMS, Aniluap, who served on the PTA board, commented, "My daughter will perform in a folk dance group later. I arranged for the National Folk Dancing Troupe to perform here. Later today, they will perform as part of the 'Homage to Allende' concert. Some Mapuche [indigenous] musicians will also perform." During this same school fundraiser, nueva canción and nueva trova played on loudspeakers. Additionally, on separate occasions, I went to well-attended performances of nueva canción group Inti-Illimani at both LMS and Raimapu. Thus, nueva canción was the "soundtrack" of campus activities and of activists' homes; school activities also highlighted indigenous themes.[46]

In contrast to LMS and Raimapu, where school was the core of parents' social lives, activist parents at Raíces had weaker social ties to other parents. Parents appreciated the school's leadership as well as the quality of debate at parent meetings, but they spent more free time with family and friends outside school.[47] This pattern likely reflects Raíces's multiclass character. Consider Israel's comment: "I have good relationships with parents at the school and we meet twice annually for a barbecue, but I don't have friendships at the school. One other member of the PTA came to our house once." Earlier in the interview, he explained, "I have friends from my college days. Because I was active in politics, I've maintained some strong ties with classmates." Tomás, another Raíces parent, concurs: "We don't have friends through the school. I have four college friends, and we get together with their families."

The "strong ties" LMS and Raimapu parents develop through school highlight similarities with chapter 2's discussion of activists' and moderate Catholics' desires to live in a "community of peers." Parents in these two schools selected into school communities of "people like us," and so it is understandable that they build friendships in these settings. Further, several LMS parents I interviewed were alumni, and thus had long-term involvement in the community, while some Raimapu parents were part of the school's early history.

Finally, these parents' political networks and identities often intersected with those of other parents. In contrast, while the activists I interviewed at Raíces had similar backgrounds to parents in these other two schools, they sent children to a school that was more socioeconomically diverse and did not have a strong identity. They also lived in a mixed income community. Consequently, their college friends were much more likely to share their interests than parents at the school. We see a similar contrast in the two Catholic schools.

Moderate Catholics

Moderate Catholics had similar levels of education and often higher incomes than activists, but participated in different leisure activities. They preferred "family-friendly" art and entertainment rather than highbrow art. Like activists, moderate Catholics frequently viewed films with their children. However, rather than using film viewing to introduce children to movies as an art form, parents deferred to their children's tastes, while restricting content to "age-appropriate" themes. Marcelo comments, "We've gone to see *Wall-E*, *Madagascar*, and *Star Wars*. I'm a *Lord of the Rings* fanatic. I love the integration of fiction with magic. We've read and discussed the Harry Potter books, so it was enjoyable to see the movies together." Moderate Catholics' preference for Hollywood children's films contrasts with activists' taste for classic and art films.

However, these parents see video games as a potentially negative influence on children. Gonzalo and Dany remark,

> *Dany:* We discourage the kids from playing Japanese video games.
> *Gonzalo:* The violent ones.
> *Dany:* They have Nintendo game consoles but can only use them on the weekends. I don't like those games. Our kids are well balanced.
> *Gonzalo:* Childhood is brief. Let them live each stage of their life, and they will have all the time in the world for other things as adults.

Ernesto has similar concerns: "They have a Nintendo console and they can play Super Mario Brothers, but we don't allow them to play any violent games where they can shoot and kill someone. If some kid in Germany kills nineteen of his classmates, he is taking what he learned in the video game and carrying it out in real life." Other moderate Catholics restricted their children's video game use. Gonzalo and Ernesto believe that media can lead their healthy, moral children astray. Thus, in contrast to activists, who sought to *expose* their children to diverse cultural activities, activists made sure to *restrict* their children's access to potentially corrupting influences. Moderate Catholics see video games as a potentially "healthy" outlet for their children, while restricting their use to prevent addiction or exposure to harmful influences.

Moderate Catholics did not articulate specific musical preferences. Rather, they noted their children's musical interests and study. Like with film, parents defer to their children's tastes. Elba, a Rosario parent, comments, "My son loves music. I bought him a drum set, and he learned to play on his own. He plays rock music very well." Marcelo makes a similar comment: "Our daughter has taken drumming classes. If you look inside her bedroom, you'll find an organ, a keyboard, a violin, an accordion, and a guitar." Thus, members of this group supported their children's music education, but did not articulate their own musical tastes or expose their children to specific musical styles.

Moderate Catholics had modest participation in public cultural events. Several take children to the Day of National Heritage and museums. Claudia comments: "Museum visits are almost required because otherwise, my kids get bored. I can't afford to take them to concerts because the prices are exorbitant." Others have taken children to free theater performances. Romina remarks: "We used to take the kids to the theater in Ñuñoa a lot. The problem was that since it's free, the other kids would stand up so we couldn't see or hear the productions." Dany comments, "We don't go to concerts very often because they are too crowded. My niece dances in the Bafochi folk dance festival, so we went to see her perform." These individuals expose their children to art, music, and theater, but do not display extensive knowledge of these genres, nor do they seek to introduce their children to specific works or styles.

A few families had personal connections to the art world. For example, Patricia, a Calasanz parent, comments, "Andrés Palvez is setting up his painting studio at a Trappist monastery. We visited because the nanny that took care of my husband when he was a child has a son that works there. So, the kids got to see paintings. It was beautiful. He gifted us this painting. So, we don't go to exhibits but we can access art that way." As noted in chapter 5, for moderate Catholics, art is more a representation of family connections than a vehicle for abstract contemplation.

While some activists engaged in regular exercise with their children, this was much more common among moderate Catholics, who listed bicycling, walking, swimming, and ping pong as frequent family activities. Ernesto comments, "Every weekend, they get up early, eat breakfast, put on their exercise clothes, and go outside to run, ride bikes, jump rope, and stretch. I don't like sports, but that doesn't stop me from instilling a taste for physical activity in my kids." Álvaro comments, "The only thing I try to push my daughters to participate in is sports. I'm trying to teach them to play tennis. We play ping-pong, too—anything to help them get moving." Just as activist families hope their children develop a taste for art film, moderate Catholics want their children to enjoy sports as a healthy activity.

Like activists, moderate Catholics encourage their children to read. Elba comments, "I invest a ton of money in books. My fourteen-year-old daughter asks me for books like crazy. She likes the classics. She's reading *Sense and Sensibility* and loves the famous vampire books [presumably the *Twilight* series]. She just asked me for *Wuthering Heights*. She read *Romeo and Juliet* as part of a collection, and she would like a collection of those classic novels." It is noteworthy that Elba describes book purchases as an "investment," highlighting her didactic goals. Ernesto concurs: "My wife had the mission of buying books, books, and more books when they were two or three years old before they even knew how to read . . . Maybe it's a little excessive, but thanks to our efforts, we've made some accomplishments. For example, the kids listen to the morning news. It's unusual that a kid their age [elementary school] will read the newspaper and say, 'Mom, the Education Minister resigned,' or 'Gas prices are going up.'" Moderate Catholics encourage their children's reading, but unlike activists, do not express an interest in experimental fiction. Rather, they see reading primarily as a means to promote their children's academic success.

Like the alternative schools described in the last section, Calasanz and Rosario Concha displayed a clear split with regard to parents' involvement in schools. Many Calasanz parents spent much of their free time at the school. Claudia comments, "I love the pastoral activities at school. I wish they were required, but they are voluntary. I was a catechist last year and this year." Marcelo remarks: "Our friends are parents at the school. My wife and I belong to the Catholic Marriage Encounter group, which focuses on marital and family growth and is open to families at the school. We have a lot of friends at school but none through work." Deyda and Dany's daughter both participate in a volunteer program, as noted in the last chapter. Deyda comments, "I participate in the Street Pastoral program every Wednesday. We prepare food and distribute it to the poor on the street. The school gives us canned goods and lends us the kitchen. Personally, I feel that the school has given me the opportunity to participate in an activity that I really enjoy."[48]

The strong community at Calasanz based on religious rituals, volunteer activities, and friendship is not present among moderate Catholics at Rosario Concha. Adults attend parent meetings but note that they have few friendships through the school. Elba comments, "I talk to two mothers I see at the parent meetings whose children are my daughter's friends. My kids find friends who are similar to them. They say the other kids are different. Of course, they are—they drink and smoke! My kids keep their distance from them." Ana makes a similar remark: "We have a couple of friends through the school whose children are friends with my eldest son." Thus, Rosario parents, whose children attend a mixed-class school, have weaker social ties to the school, much like their Raíces counterparts. Revisiting the discussion above, Calasanz parents were more likely to see other parents as "people like us" than in Rosario's diverse and fractious community. Consequently, Calasanz parents' cultural participation centered around school activities whereas Rosario parents had limited connection to their peers.

Youngsters

Youngsters had a similar cultural repertoire to moderate Catholics, but without the focus on religious or school-based activities. They engaged in concerted cultivation to support their children's academic development and made periodic visits to museums and movie theaters. They did not, for the most part, express specific cultural tastes and did not volunteer on a regular basis. In addition to their age-specific cultural attitudes, youngsters may have been less active in public cultural consumption because they had elementary school-aged children that might not have understood or appreciated more "adult" activities like concerts or art films.

Janneth comments, "We have a video collection, but we only have films that my son likes, mainly animated films, like *How to Train Your Dragon* and *Seven Deadly Sins*. I can't have any horror movies or other inappropriate adult films in the house." Others described regular movie viewing at home or at theaters but did not express strong preferences for genres or directors. María enjoyed available free activities: "The House of Culture sometimes has free theater performances and movies. There's a theater nearby that's not cheap, but it's good. It's very convenient."[49] Thus, youngsters exposed their children to age-appropriate film but did not articulate specific tastes for individual titles or genres.

Youngsters, like moderate Catholics, offered their children private lessons or after-school activities and, like activists, articulated a mix of popular tastes. Mickey remarks, "Manuel de Salas has a big focus on culture. They really promote music and theater. My daughter really likes the school's photography and film after-school programs." Lisette focuses more on her husband's music playing: "When we have people over, my husband and his friends like to play music. We might have a sing along to a Quilapayún [nueva canción group] or a pop song that everyone knows." Gladys described attending alternative rock and pop music concerts once per year (described in more detail in the next section). However, in contrast with activist parents, rather than stating tastes for specific artists and genres, she mainly focused on her annual attendance at live events.

In contrast, Nelson, a Rosario parent, likes baroque music and rejects popular genres: "We like Jordi Savall, who performed the early French baroque music for the film score to *All the Mornings of the World*. It's not popular classical music, but we play it for our kids and they like it. They don't hear any reggaeton. We don't listen to popular music—we're *outliers* [uses the English word]." Here, Nelson describes his preference for baroque music as a way to state his rejection of popular music. However, unlike activists, he does not express knowledge of or interest in a wide range of musical styles. Rather, his preference for baroque music serves mainly to differentiate him from the crowd. Moreover, this perspective was unique among youngsters, who did not express strong musical tastes.

Youngsters also sometimes took their children to the theater, especially if venues were conveniently located and affordable. Lisette comments, "I used to take my son to see a children's theater troupe in La Reina [affluent community in eastern Santiago]. They were a group of theater aficionados that performed for kids. It was very affordable in contrast to most plays in town. When we lived in Talca, I used to take him more often because it was less expensive. I also haven't stayed on top of what shows are playing in Santiago." Thus, parents exposed their children to theater, but did not express strong preferences or interests.

Youngsters periodically take their children to museums, especially those tailored to children. Lisette comments, "I've taken my son to the Interactive Museum. We also went to a museum in the Entrepreneurial City [a business park and residential complex in northern Santiago] to a museum with a dinosaur exhibit." Mickey, due to her training as a historian and pursuit of an advanced degree in museum studies, emphasizes historical museums: "When we went on vacation to Iquique [in northern Chile], we saw the ruins of the Humberstone nitrate mines [that produced Chile's main export from 1880 to 1929] and museums. They are gorgeous—they have so much history, historic buildings, and museums. That's the area we've explored the most."

Youngsters did not spend much of their social lives in schools. María, an LMS parent, remarks, "My friends are from my college years. Since I was injured and am off work, I started having coffee with some of the mothers. When I was working, I rushed to drop my daughter at school and had no idea the mothers met regularly. It's been nice to get to know them." Others centered their social life around family and coworkers. Gladys remarks, "Sometimes I'll have coworkers, friends from college, or other parents over to the house for a barbecue." While youngsters have friendly social connections with other parents, they do not display the same intense involvement in school activities as activists and moderate Catholics at LMS, Raimapu, and Calasanz. Nelson remarks, "I have a problem with the other parents because all they talk about at the meetings is collecting money for fundraisers." Youngsters had more distant ties with their children's schools, and their leisure pursuits were centered around the home and outings with friends from other social settings.

Pragmatists

Pragmatists described a more limited range of cultural activities than the other three groups. They were less engaged in cultural consumption. However, this group expressed satisfaction with their leisure activities, particularly in the opportunities they afforded for connection with immediate family and extended kin.[50]

While not all pragmatists identified clear musical tastes, those who did so liked popular music styles noted in survey research on working- and lower-middle-class Chileans.[51] Alejandra comments, "I like ballads. I really like to dance to salsa music. It's a guilty pleasure because Chileans are not very into dancing. I finally found a partner, so I go dancing with him regularly. I must admit I like some reggaeton songs, too." Alejandra's interest in music is connected to an activity—dancing—rather than to a more contemplative form of listening evident among the activists and one youngster couple (Nelson and Tania). Paulina remarks, "I like music for meditation and relaxation— orchestral music. I like Luis Miguel [Mexican romantic pop singer], too. My son listens to rock and reggaeton on the computer." The omnipresence of reggaeton in La Florida as the dominant youth dance music style is evident in this and other interviews. Paulina's use of classical music for relaxation suggests that she either listens to "light classical" material or uses original classical compositions as background music rather than giving it focused attention.[52]

Some pragmatists enjoyed (or tolerated) children's films to accommodate their children's tastes. Alejandra remarks, "My son and I try to schedule a monthly visit to the movies. We go to the films he likes, so I have to sit there with a happy face. Sometimes I fall asleep because the movies aren't very good, but it's a chance for us to be together away from the house." Others displayed gendered tastes noted in other research.[53] Thus, Paulina comments, "He likes vampire and war movies; I prefer romantic and historical films." Iván comments, "I enjoy watching children's movies with my kids. I love *Ice Age*. We often watch *The Simpsons* together and die laughing at the stupid things they do! I enjoy classics like *Star Wars*, and epic films like *Braveheart*. I like *Dances with Wolves* about Native American history . . . I also like *Tony Manero*, which came out recently. It was fantastic—I really enjoyed the cinematic techniques and plot."

In addition to the gendered pattern noted above, Alejandra and Iván form an interesting counterpoint to other pragmatists. Both were trained as teachers, but earn modest incomes and live in their childhood homes. They send their children to the same alternative school where they interact with upper-middle-class families. Hence, their educational background helps explain Alejandra's displeasure with attending children's films and Iván's interest in Chilean films. In particular, *Tony Manero* traces the life of a man obsessed with impersonating John Travolta's *Saturday Night Fever* character and that commits several murders to acquire clothing and props for a performance. The film took place during the dictatorship and was widely viewed as depicting the erosion of citizens' moral character under military rule. Thus, Alejandra's and Iván's tastes and distastes occupy an intermediate point between pragmatists and activists.

Unlike other groups, some pragmatists could not afford to go to the movies, much like approximately 60 percent of Chileans.[54] Rossana comments, "We rarely go to the movies. I made a special effort on summer vacation, but during the year, I just can't afford it." Nelly remarks, "My son asked me to go to the movies yesterday. I had to tell him no because I hadn't sold much in the street market and need to save money to pay bills. It's a pity because it was the premiere showing of *Iron Man* and he wanted to go, but we have to keep our priorities straight."

Pragmatists were also less likely to attend museums or plays, though some occasionally attended concerts. Olga comments, "Museums never really caught my attention. I go along with my daughter to the reggae concerts she enjoys." Marcela remarks, "When we go to see my family in the Elqui Valley [northern Chile] during summer vacations, I take the kids to Andean music concerts." These parents attend concerts in response to their children's tastes or while on vacation, but do not express a strong interest in hearing live music.

Pragmatists expressed the most intense feelings about family gatherings. Alejandra comments, "We often have barbecues with my mother and siblings. You know, everything revolves around meat and beer for my brother, just like the typical Chilean male." Iván similarly comments, "I remember having barbecues every week when I was a kid. We went to the country to get a lamb, chicken, or pig to roast. Last week we had a barbecue for my grandmother's ninetieth birthday. My daughter plays guitar. Other guitarists joined her, and we all sang and displayed our talents." Paulina comments, "I often invite my sisters and their families to the apartment for barbecues. Fourteen of us gather for these events. We've vacationed together as well." Thus, for pragmatists that had strong extended kin networks, family gatherings were an important source of joy and social connection. This emphasis on socializing with extended family contrasts with the upper-middle-class groups that gathered with both family and friends from different social settings. Pragmatists found joy in family gatherings and were also more discerning in establishing close friendships outside the family, as Alejandra noted in this chapter's introduction.

Not all pragmatists had the opportunity to participate in large family gatherings. Single mothers with more limited social networks enjoyed cozy gatherings with children at home. Marcela remarks, "Sometimes in the winter when we don't have to go out, we get up late and stay in bed with our pajamas on all day. I plan lunch ahead of time so I don't need to shop. It's fun to wear pajamas all day." Nelly makes a similar comment: "Sometimes my son will climb into bed, and we'll watch *The Simpsons* together. Because money is so tight, I can't invite people to the apartment." Thus, while we noted above that cost is a barrier preventing some families from going to the movies, Nelly can barely make ends meet. These severe financial limitations restrict these women's social circles and concomitant sources of social and moral support.

Pragmatists had limited participation in school-based social events or volunteer activities. As noted in chapter 4, women particularly felt the weight of perceived microaggressions in parent meetings where they were asked to contribute their limited funds for school events. Marcela and Nelly felt humiliated by other parents' insistence that they contribute money to school activities when they faced severe financial restrictions. Paulina offered a more relaxed perspective: "If I don't care for someone, I just avoid them. I don't need to get all hot and bothered about it." Thus, pragmatists' experience of social exclusion at school led them to withdraw from social interactions there.

Two pragmatists had participated in volunteer activities in the past or did so outside their children's school. Alejandra describes volunteer work she did as a teen: "I used to do pastoral work with at-risk and homeless youth, I participated in confirmation classes and did mission work in rural towns in the metro area." Iván also describes a vocation for social service: "In addition to my direct sales work, I teach at-risk youth for the Chile Sports organization, building on my training in education." Their volunteer participation likely reflects their profession as educators as well as their empathy with the poor. Alejandra and Iván live in their family homes in a working-class community and hence do not dis-identify with the poor, in contrast to other pragmatists that experienced downward mobility.

To conclude this section, we see each group's distinct identity investments in cultural consumption and volunteering. Activists are voracious consumers of highbrow and popular music genres, art film, and the visual and performing arts. Activists in Raimapu and Manuel de Salas also focus their leisure time on school activities that reinforce their tastes for progressive folk music and political identities, while their counterparts at Raíces are more weakly tied to the school. Moderate Catholics focus their leisure time on family-friendly cultural activities and take pains to shield their children from corrupting influences like violent video games. They do not express strong tastes in artistic genres, but devote time and energy to their children's exposure to music and literature. A similar split was observed between Calasanz parents' heavy involvement with school activities and Rosario parents' more distant ties to school. Youngsters participate in public cultural events while preferring a mix of folk and popular music genres. This group was also weakly connected to schools. Finally, pragmatists focused their social activities on spending time with extended kin groups and preferred popular film and music forms. Some in this group were unable to attend films or invite others to their homes due to resource constraints.

These distinct patterns show that members of only one of the four middle-class groups were voracious omnivores. This taste pattern reflected their educational and occupational backgrounds as well as their political experiences. Additionally, important differences in leisure time activities resulted from the distinct school communities in which adults participated. More socially homogeneous schools lent themselves to high levels of parental participation and strong social ties among parents while mixed-class schools tended to yield more fragmented school communities. These findings depart from much of the literature on cultural consumption that focuses primarily on distinct taste patterns across different class, gender, and age groups. The discussion in this section suggests that in addition to demographic differences across groups, participation in religious and political subcultures strongly influences cultural practices. Finally, the distinct school communities influence the character of parents' social ties and cultural practices.

Place-Based Cultural Practices

Thus far, we have explored shared patterns of leisure activities within the middle class as well as differences across groups based on their distinct identity investments. However, in line with our findings in chapters 2, 3, 4, and 5, the different characteristics of Ñuñoa and La Florida were evident in distinct types of leisure pursuits in the two communities. Thus, members of the same middle-class group engaged in distinct activities during their free time in each community. Ñuñoa residents participated in public cultural consumption and were also active in urban social movements. This pattern reflected Ñuñoa's rich cultural infrastructure, proximity to downtown cultural institutions, affluent social makeup, and important conflicts related to housing and urban planning. In contrast, La Florida residents had a more "domestic" pattern of leisure activities, engaged more directly with popular music, and were less active in volunteering outside their children's schools. These distinct forms of cultural activities reflect La Florida's more limited cultural amenities, suburban location, and mixed-class population.

A few works examine variations in cultural consumption across communities. Some note the distinct cultural orientations and practices of young couples living in mixed-income urban settings and those residing in suburbs. Urban professionals were much more active in night life and artistic activities than their suburban counterparts.[55] Others suggest that some "amateur" omnivores have high levels of cultural participation because they live in urban areas that subsidize museum fees. In contrast, busy suburban families engage in "ordinary consumption."[56] Similarly, researchers find that "voracious omnivores" tend to live near the main cultural district in London and that omnivores are more prevalent in wealthier urban areas in South England.[57] Further, students of urban revitalization, historic shopping streets, and retail gentrification note that the presence of independent boutiques, art galleries, restaurants, and musical venues in urban areas attracts middle-class pedestrians, consumers, and residents while fostering community vitality.[58] Taken together, these studies suggest that high cultural participation may reflect not only individuals' education and family experiences, but also the availability of artistic scenes near their homes.

Some recent studies of "citizens' movements" in Santiago emphasize upper-middle-class residents' protagonism in protests seeking to improve neighborhood quality of life and to prevent construction of highways or other infrastructure that could undermine their communities. Numerous citizens' movements emerged in Santiago beginning in the late 1990s to block highway construction, high-rise apartment development, and gentrification due to their potential negative effects on historic housing, neighborhood cohesion, and quality of life.[59] These movements were led by upper-middle-class citizens but emerged in socioeconomically diverse communities.[60] In this section, we consider both place-based patterns of cultural consumption and citizen participation.

Cultural Consumption

There was a notable contrast in cultural consumption patterns in the two communities. Activists, moderate Catholics, and youngsters living in Ñuñoa more actively participated in public cultural activities than those in La Florida, even though some in the latter community also attended concerts, museums, and performances. This likely reflects the rich physical and cultural infrastructure in Ñuñoa, including numerous parks and plazas, a cultural center, two university campuses (the Catholic University and the University of Chile), the National Stadium (featuring concerts and soccer games), and several theaters. Additionally, Ñuñoa is closer to downtown museums, the Lastarria arts district, and galleries located in wealthy eastern Santiago communities like Las Condes and Vitacura. Several Ñuñoa families noted the easy availability of activities in cultural centers or free outdoor events during the summer. For example, María comments, "There's lots of culture here. The Cultural Center has many activities. We've got restaurants. There's so much to do here. I really

like the fact that it's a livable, walkable community with neighborhood life."
Morgana concurs, "A year or two ago a theater near here offered free movies,
musicals, and flamenco dance performances. I took the kids every Wednesday." Thus, the proximity (and low cost) of cultural activities is one factor
contributing to Ñuñoa activists' voracious cultural consumption as well as
moderate Catholics' and youngsters' attendance at public events.

In contrast, the main cultural activities in La Florida were available at the
two shopping malls. Both have movie theaters and bookstores, and the largest
of the two even has a small gallery managed by Santiago's Fine Art Museum.
La Florida established a cultural center in 2003, but none of the interviewees
mentioned it; Ñuñoa's cultural center was inaugurated in 1988 and its House
of Culture (now part of the cultural center) was founded in 1952 in a historic
mansion. The cultural center crops up in several interviews.[61] La Florida's
rapid and unplanned urban development under the dictatorship mean it has
few plazas and parks where residents can congregate.[62]

As noted in chapter 5, Ñuñoa activists also criticized malls as standardized retail environments that promote ostentatious consumption. Clara, interviewed in this chapter's introduction, comments, "Shopping malls and
grocery stores encourage impulse purchases. It's the typical Sunday outing for
many Chileans, but it's not the same as shopping at the corner greengrocer,
which is slower paced. The lights and music at the mall stupefy you [*entre que
te pones huevón*], are tiring, and also make you hyper and anxious." Clara
contrasts Ñuñoa's familiar urban amenities with malls' negative psychological
effects on consumers.

In contrast, Raimapu and Raíces parents describe suburban-style leisure
activities focused on the domestic sphere, and their outings (like visits to the
bookstore) tended to occur in shopping malls. (Malls were the central focal
point for moderate Catholics' and pragmatists' public leisure activities there
as well.) For example, Tomás comments, "Sometimes the family likes 'lazy
Sundays' [*fomingos*][63] where we all lay around at home." Like Alejandra, whose
comments appear in this chapter's introduction, Evelyn, a Raimapu parent,
also enjoys sewing and knitting: "My daughters and I sit down and knit or
sew, which people don't do much anymore. My mother and grandmother
used to sew and knit. It's important for all children to do something with
their hands." Ricardo, whose daughter is an avid reader, remarks, "We go to
the bookstores a lot. We like to linger there. We go to the bookstores at the
two malls here." Malls were also hangout spots for teenagers. Elba comments,

"Sometimes my daughter will go to the mall with her friends to get ice cream." Thus, indoor activities and trips to the mall were more common in La Florida than in Ñuñoa.

Additionally, La Florida activists more frequently mentioned sing-alongs at house parties (reminiscent of the dictatorship era) than attending concerts. Israel comments, "On the weekends, we like to have friends over for a barbecue, drinks, and guitar playing." In the previous section, Lisette described similar gatherings. Interestingly, the most culturally active family residing in La Florida (Luis and Tamara) had moved there from Ñuñoa, sent their children to Raimapu, and later moved them to Manuel de Salas in Ñuñoa. Tamara was also employed in Ñuñoa at the time. Given their active involvement in the school and close friendships with LMS parents, it is unsurprising that their cultural consumption is similar to their Ñuñoa counterparts. Place importantly shapes variations in cultural activities among interviewees with similar educations and incomes.

Musical Taste

Place also affects interviewees' cultural references. This was particularly notable with regard to musical tastes in the two communities. As noted above, most of the Ñuñoa activists expressed an interest in Chilean nueva canción alongside classical music and rock groups, and the moderate Catholics in that community were primarily involved in music via their children's lessons. In contrast, several contemporary popular music forms and artists surfaced in discussions with La Florida residents across all groups. As noted above, youngsters and pragmatists positioned themselves in relation to reggaeton, the Puerto Rican electronic dance music style mixing sexualized rap lyrics with Jamaican dance hall rhythms. Some pragmatists simply noted that their children liked it, others (like Alejandra) expressed embarrassment that they enjoyed it (perhaps because of its sexist, lower-class image), and other youngsters (like Nelson) rejected it as anathema. Notably, reggaeton did not surface at all in the Ñuñoa interviews.

The Jonas Brothers is another band La Florida residents mentioned several times but Ñuñoa residents never acknowledged. At the time research was conducted, the band was primarily known through their Disney television program targeting young adolescents. They continue performing today, but the television show was discontinued. Gladys, a youngster, remarks, "If I can get tickets to the Jonas Brothers show, I'll be there . . . I took the girls to hear

Julieta Venegas [Mexican pop singer] last year or the year before. Before that, I took them to the Los Jaivas [Chilean rock band] concert. They loved it. My daughter who is deaf was blown away by their drummer." Gladys, a Raimapu parent, has diverse musical tastes, but was unique in mentioning this popular music group among parents interviewed at that school.

Two other participants in the snowball sample also attended Jonas Brothers concerts. Pamela, a pragmatist, invited her daughters to participate in the interview, and they told me they planned to attend their concert. Roberto, an activist, lamented, "The first time my daughter asked me to go to a concert, she wanted to hear the Jonas Brothers, so I took her and paid for that stuff. I don't really promote that kind of thing. If it came up again, I would think twice about whether or not to bring her."[64]

Commercial pop music is pervasive in La Florida. Pragmatists are happy to listen to it, some youngsters enjoy it alongside Chilean rock, while other activists and youngsters chafe at the genre. The point of interest is that La Florida residents mentioned the Jonas Brothers, who I would imagine most teenage Chileans were exposed to at the time,[65] but Ñuñoa residents did not. The popularity of reggaeton likely reflects La Florida's larger poor population given its popularity among lower-income Chileans, while the Jonas Brothers' popularity can be interpreted as reflecting the weaker presence of highbrow musical forms given the community's limited cultural infrastructure.

Civic Participation

Finally, there were important differences in residents' public participation in the two communities, which reflected the emergence of a significant housing conflict in Ñuñoa and no similar dispute in La Florida. In 2004, the municipality of Ñuñoa changed its master plan to encourage high rise apartment development given the community's population loss. There was a massive building boom following the change, causing traffic congestion and other impacts on quality of life. Residents created the Citizens' Network of Ñuñoa in response and in 2007 secured a freeze on new building in residential areas, though construction continued on the community's southern border.[66]

José, an architect, was a Manuel de Salas parent who played a leadership role in the mobilization. Along with a team of activists, he visited neighborhoods across the municipality to solicit opinions regarding the building boom and to seek support for efforts to freeze high rise construction: "We visited one community that was surrounded by high rise apartments, and the people were very active. The network held a massive meeting at Manuel de Salas with 500–600 people attending. We also organized two marches, the first of which had 1,000 participants." José was ultimately disappointed with loopholes in the agreement to halt new high rise construction and the movement's slow decline, but was hopeful it could be reactivated in the future.

As indicated in Clara's comments in this chapter's introduction, several LMS parents participated in the mobilization. Morgana remarks, "I supported the movement, signed petitions, and went to the marches. The communities that are full of apartments have become more impersonal." Jimena highlights the movement's broad appeal: "They had some meetings across the street, and the good thing is that they were able to freeze new construction. People across the political spectrum were opposed to the building boom, especially long-term residents." Marcelo was the only Calasanz parent I interviewed who participated. He recalls, "I went to a neighborhood association meeting about this. I like to stay informed about these issues, and I do anything I can to support these activities. I'm absolutely opposed to high rise construction because it leads to major traffic and parking problems that the street infrastructure isn't equipped to handle."

Activists' and moderate Catholics' participation in this movement can be understood as an extension of their cultural consumption and intense participation in school activities. It is notable that an LMS parent was an important organizer of the Citizen's Network, LMS parents participated in protests, and a large meeting was held in the school. Activists' and one moderate Catholic's participation reflect their identity investments as well as these schools' connection to civic issues within the community. Ñuñoa was not just a culturally lively setting, but also a site of strong citizen participation, in this case with the goal of restricting high rise construction to maintain the community's quality of life. This participation is closely aligned with activists' and moderate Catholics' efforts to "push back" against unregulated markets and competition.

Interestingly, the lively citizen participation in Ñuñoa was not evident among those I interviewed in La Florida, in spite of the fact that many of the parents were seasoned activists and party militants. Indeed, Mario was the only La Florida resident that was involved in volunteer or civic activities outside of school. He describes the difficulty of garnering his neighbors' participation in community activities: "I'm a leader in the neighborhood association and just got back from a meeting. The main thing people talk about is safety. They live in fear, build fences around their homes, and stay indoors. It makes it so hard to develop relationships with people. That has led us to make friends at the school we were unable to establish elsewhere." Other La Florida residents commented on the prevalence of crime. Evelyn, a Raimapu parent, remarked, "We've been robbed several times. At first, we didn't have a fence. We later added a fence and an alarm. In the past, we've lived in homes without theft protection." Luis, an LMS parent, similarly remarks, "Our pickup truck was stolen. We bought a new one, and people took the roof and tires. We need to take care of it because it's a durable vehicle."[67]

The contrast between these two settings suggests that Ñuñoa residents enjoy collective efficacy[68]—the ability to engage in group action at a community level. This collective efficacy depends on a sense of security, trust, and regular interactions in public. Ñuñoa residents' frequent participation in public cultural consumption and social movements likely enhances trust among neighbors while demonstrating that citizens are capable of achieving results through collaboration. In contrast, the fear of crime in La Florida, evident in the above discussion as well as pragmatists' discussions of schools in chapters 3 and 4, likely undermines La Floridians' civic orientation and willingness to work with neighbors.

To conclude this section, in addition to different patterns of cultural practices across middle-class groups, we have also observed distinct patterns of leisure time activities in the two communities among those interviewed. Ñuñoa residents engage in public cultural consumption and community activism more frequently than their La Florida counterparts. These differences reflect distinct cultural infrastructures, political contexts, and levels of collective efficacy. They suggest that what it means to be middle class is place specific— middle-class experiences, practices, and identities vary across communities based on their distinct populations, cultural infrastructures, and patterns of social relations.

Conclusion

This chapter has examined how different middle-class groups' identity investments take shape through their cultural practices. In many ways, the leisure activities I observed among middle-class Chileans drew on similar cultural attitudes and practices observed in previous chapters on work, housing, schools, and home decoration. They provide a final window into the dynamics of identity investments and precarious privilege.

I first explored common attitudes and practices of cultural participation across middle-class families. Here, I observed evidence of these families' precarious privilege through time and cost barriers that limited their cultural activity. In contrast to other studies that only see cost as a barrier for working-class people's cultural participation,[69] I observed that upper-middle-class families found attendance at live events cost prohibitive. Additionally, middle-class adults emphasized the educational qualities of their leisure activities and contrasted them with the "crass consumerism" they observed among others. This opposition reflects broader public debates regarding consumerism in Chile;[70] but in contrast to scholarly generalizations regarding ostentatious consumption, I found that middle-class Chileans *oppose* ostentation as antithetical to their values of asceticism and consumption as an uplifting practice. This opposition fits with critiques of showroom houses and materialism discussed in earlier chapters and highlights middle-class anxieties about new forms of consumption that challenge the legitimacy of their values and practices.

Second, I observed distinct identity investments across middle-class groups that closely mirror patterns of aesthetic taste explored in chapter 5. In contrast to studies finding a unified pattern of omnivorous taste among upper-middle-class people,[71] I found this pattern only among activists. Further, activists' omnivorous tastes in part reflected their *political biographies*: they did not solely result from their educational and occupational backgrounds. Moderate Catholics and youngsters actively engaged in cultural consumption, but did not express tastes for highbrow culture, and pragmatists preferred popular cultural forms and family-based consumption. I also found an important difference between parents across schools: parents in socially homogeneous schools spent most of their free time doing school-sponsored activities while those at mixed-class schools had more distant ties to these organizations. Thus, school life can potentially influence the quantity and quality of cultural activities parents engage in.

Third, I found salient place-based differences between parents residing in Ñuñoa and La Florida. Those in the former community engaged in more public cultural consumption and civic participation, reflecting a rich infrastructure of cultural institutions and a sense of collective efficacy. La Florida residents had more suburban and domestic patterns of leisure activities, were more receptive to popular music forms, and were less active in community affairs. These patterns reflected La Florida's weaker cultural infrastructure, mixed-class composition, and limited collective efficacy. While others have noted variations in cultural practices across communities, few have considered how these differences coincide with distinct levels of civic participation.[72]

This chapter completes our review of middle-class identity investments. Throughout this book, we have highlighted fissures within the middle class emerging from some segments' socialization within political and religious subcultures, variations across age cohorts, and differences in education and income. This discussion of cultural practices brings to the fore how these differences take shape in family life, cultural practices, and civic participation. It reveals the fruitfulness of examining the assets (economic, cultural, and social capital), ideological orientations, and residential settings of middle-class groups to understand their values, practices, and life projects. In turn, these findings tell us a great deal about the inflection point in Chilean politics during the mid-2000s to which we return in the conclusion.

Conclusion
Identity Investments, Precarious Privilege, and Chile's Political Transformation

ALEJANDRO IS A VETERAN educator who conducts trainings for the national teachers' union. He comments, "I've seen the pattern of educational development in different parts of the country. In that context, Raimapu offers a small laboratory of an 'alternative' project that can push back against the neoliberal challenge, without being completely contaminated by it . . . Raimapu isn't an island, but it has protective elements [against the influence of neoliberalism]. One important element is our shared activities." Here, Alejandro draws on his experience as a teacher and observer of different schools to highlight his identity investments in the alternative education provided at Raimapu as well as the school's anti-neoliberal ideology.

Claudio offers a similar critique of Chile's market-based education system: "A long time ago the government forgot about public education. In the Pinochet period, they gave a little money to local governments, and the result was a mess. Under democratic governments, there haven't been any changes . . . At first, you could blame the problems of education and healthcare on Pinochet, but after twenty years—no way! At a certain point [the government] needs to realize that the [free market] model doesn't work." While Claudio does not see Calasanz as an "alternative to neoliberalism," he shares Alejandro's critique of the military's free market educational model. In his critique of education policy, Claudio highlights his identity investments in poverty alleviation efforts, evident in his volunteer activities with the blind and commitment to Calasanz school's social mission as described in chapters 4 and 6.

Alejandro and Claudio speak to the past, present, and future of education in Chile and how they intersect with political identities and public policies. Their intense feelings regarding education reference themes from previous chapters and set the stage for this final chapter. Individuals in this book described their educational experiences as key influences on their identities and occupational choices; placed great emphasis on their children's schooling; and their educational investments often intersected with their participation in occupational, housing, home decoration, and cultural markets. Of all the fields studied, education is the central site of investment, interpersonal relations, and conflict that connects with these other markets.

School reform was a central component of the Pinochet regime's free market policy revolution that also sparked two student movements and the "social explosion" between 2006 and 2019. It is fitting, if ironic, that one of the junta's "policy triumphs" may lead to the unravelling of the "economic model" through the 2021 election of Gabriel Boric, a progressive congressman and former student activist, and a new Constitution that voters will approve or reject in September 2022. Indeed, one of this book's central findings is that parents born in the 1960s who were college activists during the 1980s supported their children's activism in the 2006–2008 Penguin Revolution. That mobilization catalyzed a fifteen-year protest cycle culminating in Boric's victory and the drafting of a new Constitution.

Building on this initial theme of education and social change, this chapter has several goals. First, I review the main findings in previous chapters and explore how they support the book's central argument. Second, I explore the implications of these findings for theoretical debates on middle classes. Third, I compare these findings with research on middle classes in other middle-income countries to identify commonalities and differences between these cases. I close with an exploration of the implications of this book's findings for contemporary Chilean politics and culture.

Core Findings on Chilean Middle Classes

This book has developed the concepts of identity investments and precarious privilege to understand how members of different segments of the middle classes participate in employment, housing, education, aesthetic, and cultural markets. In contrast to many analyses in Chile and elsewhere that focus on middle-class families' opportunity hoarding and upward mobility projects, I have argued that some segments of the middle classes respond to their circumstance of precarious privilege through identity investments that draw on strongly held convictions and differentiate them from other segments of the middle classes as well as the poor.

As outlined in the introduction, each middle-class group I identified faced a different set of threats to their identities in Chile's market society. Growing incomes from 1990 to 2010 sparked greater competition between different segments of the middle class, as some families moved out of poverty, others experienced upward mobility, and incumbents in the upper middle experienced threats to the legitimacy of their social position. Simultaneously, teachers and engineers experienced job instability because their educational training did not provide stable rewards in a labor market with few job protections.

Each segment of the middle classes studied here experienced precarious privilege differently. We recall that the term *precarious privilege* refers to individuals that do not experience absolute poverty, but retain a fragile hold on their jobs and social status. Middle-class individuals faced job and career instability, were often pushed out of desirable communities, and witnessed demographic changes in their children's schools.

While precarious privilege describes individuals' tenuous hold on their middle-class positions, the individuals studied in this book responded to their precarious privilege by drawing on cultural resources cultivated in their childhoods and young adult lives. They made identity investments in distinct fields to make sense of their current circumstances and to criticize the social settings they inhabited because these settings diverged from their childhood experiences. Activists drew on their political identities and educational training to place their children in alternative schools and developed a *political critique* of the wealthy and upwardly mobile. Moderate Catholics drew on their religious identities and educational backgrounds to send children to Catholic schools and developed a *moral critique* of the upwardly mobile while noting their exclusion from the upper class. Youngsters relied on their educational backgrounds and occupational success to select alternative and religious schools while developing an *anti-elitist critique* of incumbents in the upper-middle class and the wealthy. Finally, pragmatists emphasized their hard work and decency to criticize *exclusionary* attitudes of the upper-middle class and the *moral depravity* of the poor.

The concepts of precarious privilege and identity investments help us understand why upper-middle-class families prioritized values over performance in their children's schools, youngsters and pragmatists placed greater emphasis on school performance, and all groups clashed with individuals occupying other segments of the middle classes. While drawing on Bourdieu's concepts of capital volume and composition to understand the distinct dispositions of different middle-class groups, identity investments and precarious privilege explore a less developed aspect of Bourdieu's writing by showing how religious, political, and age cohort–based identities are fused with the orientations he linked to distinct class fractions.[1]

As argued in previous chapters, identity investments reflect the enduring religious and class cleavages solidified within Chile's political parties and internalized by members of the middle classes studied here. These ideological orientations interacted with the inflection point in Chilean politics during Michelle Bachelet's first administration (2006–2010) when a wave of social protest gathered steam and eventually threatened to tear down the neoliberal order created during military rule. While activists and moderate Catholics leaned toward the left- and center-left parties, pragmatists leaned to the right. Youngsters, who were born after the Allende administration and did not attend college during the 1980s wave of prodemocracy activism, illustrate the waning party identifications of younger Chileans that other scholars identified beginning in the 1990s.[2]

The concepts of precarious privilege and identity investments form an important counterpoint to current work on Chile's middle classes. Rather than focusing primarily on lower-middle-class families' pursuit of upward mobility or upper-middle-class families' efforts to protect their privileges, these concepts show how partisan, organizational, and ideological legacies of an earlier era strongly influence some middle-class adults' investments in distinct markets that mark them as different from other middle-class groups. While other scholars have aptly studied how middle-class families struggle to accumulate wealth and secure advantages for their children, this book has shown how an important segment of middle-class families use identity investments as a means of symbolic struggle against more economically successful families and to manage fraught relationships with the poor. This book has thus sought to revisit the political and symbolic struggles between middle-class groups that most sociologists studying Chile have overlooked.[3]

Throughout the book, I have also argued that *place* importantly influences the experiences, practices, and attitudes of middle-class families. Individuals' identity investments and the symbolic boundaries they constructed differed in Ñuñoa and La Florida based on those communities' distinct populations, land markets, school markets, and cultural infrastructures. Thus, individuals I interviewed with similar backgrounds had different experiences of being middle class in these two communities. This finding suggests the importance of understanding middle classes in the context of their local settings rather than seeking overarching patterns that are not place-specific.[4]

There are important similarities in middle-class families' identity investments across the employment, housing, education, home decoration, and cultural consumption fields. The first two chapters explore middle-class families' access to economic capital through their jobs and homes. The middle-class families' economic positions and struggles serve as a platform for understanding market decisions in educational and aesthetic markets. In chapter 1, we learned that, after a decade of growing incomes and wealth in the 1990s, slowing economic and income growth coincided with middle-class families' experiences of precarious privilege on the labor market. While the highest paid professionals in medicine, law, and finance enjoyed financial stability, others had a weak hold on the job market. Teachers shifted careers, engineers faced unemployment, and clerical workers churned through low-paid jobs. Women faced challenges in lower-paying sex-segregated jobs, with establishing work-life balance, and in making ends meet as single parents. Left-wing activists had slow career trajectories due to their high-risk activism during the dictatorship.

Activists and moderate Catholics responded to their precarious privilege by emotionally withdrawing from a competitive workplace. In contrast, youngsters experienced an upward labor market trajectory, and pragmatists mainly focused on staying afloat in an unforgiving labor market. These findings highlight the fragility of some middle-class jobs, underscore the long-term employment consequences for participants in "high-risk" activism, illustrate gender inequality on the labor market, and point to the workplace as an important site of age-based symbolic conflicts.

Chapter 2 examined families' decisions in the housing market. We divided the discussion into questions of housing access, housing taste, and symbolic boundaries. Couples' entry into the housing market revealed their dependence on extended kin for financial and in-kind support, following a pattern observed in southern Europe and post-Soviet Russia.[5] Activists and moderate Catholics that used housing as an investment highlighted their financial acumen. Upper-middle-class couples that relied on parental support during tough times perceived housing as a gift. Couples entering the mortgage market for the first time wondered if they could ever pay down their mortgages. Pragmatists that lived in their family home saw housing as a shared resource, whereas renters highlighted their sense of vulnerability. With the exception of those that used housing as an investment, complex housing pathways revealed middle-class families' precarious privilege due to their dependence on family, landlords, or long-term mortgages.

Families faced financial constraints regarding where they could live: members of the Ñuñoa diaspora were pushed out of that desirable community. In the context of those constraints, families selected communities for their amenities, the sense of place they provided, and/or the quality of their schools. Activists, moderate Catholics, and pragmatists constructed symbolic boundaries with others via the housing market, revealing their group identities much as they did in the labor market. Activists rejected peers' selection of ostentatious or standardized homes in wealthy communities, moderate Catholics criticized high density apartments and gated communities for their corrosive effects on residential ties, and pragmatists avoided contact with the poor. Youngsters, by contrast, expressed satisfaction with their homes and communities, but did not contrast themselves with other groups in this field.

The next two chapters focused on schooling as a central element in middle-class identity investments. Chapter 3 reviewed important findings regarding middle-class school choice. While most work studying Chile and other societies argues that middle-class families use educational markets to their own advantage and to the detriment of working-class and poor students, this chapter revealed a more contradictory picture. All members of this sample selected charter or private schools, but their decision-making patterns and interactions with peers depart from other accounts.

School choice "micro-climates"[6] varied between Ñuñoa, where interviewees selected private schools but contrasted themselves with elites; and La Florida, where they selected charter schools and constructed boundaries with the new rich and the poor. In Ñuñoa, alumni could continue a family tradition in Manuel de Salas or Calasanz, while others looked to these schools' reputations for guidance on school selection; La Florida parents turned to trusted contacts for help with choosing a school.

Activists sending children to alternative schools looked for holistic teaching styles, artistic training, and a space where students and parents could freely debate. Parents at LMS and Raimapu saw their decision as a political choice, while Raíces parents focused on the school's pedagogical approach and inclusive culture. Moderate Catholics sending children to traditional Catholic schools (Calasanz and Rosario Concha) wanted a school that teaches the "whole child" by combining academic excellence with a focus on moral guidance. Youngsters found the pedagogical programs at alternative and Catholic schools appealing, but their choices were not informed by partisan or religious identities. Pragmatists, most of whom sent their children to traditional Catholic schools, saw school as a means to upward mobility, and thus prioritized order, discipline, academic rigor, and protection from poor students.

Activists and moderate Catholics deliberately rejected public and private elite schools due to their competitive environments and excessive costs. To counteract perceived deficiencies in the schools they selected, they "hedged their bets" by engaging in concerted cultivation. Providing children with tutoring, help with homework, and enrichment activities allowed these individuals to adhere to their values when they selected schools while still supporting their children's educational opportunities. Youngsters also engaged in concerted cultivation but did not think of this practice as a tradeoff between their values and their children's educational success. Pragmatists supported their children outside school to the extent it was feasible, but saw schools as the main sources of educational guidance and support.

In chapter 4, we explored how schools functioned as communities, were sites of symbolic conflicts, and served as platforms for the exercise of citizenship. Activists and moderate Catholics at LMS, Raimapu, and Calasanz built strong friendship ties at school, while Raíces and Rosario parents had more distant ties to their school communities due to their mixed-class character. Parents also constructed symbolic boundaries with others inside schools. Activists found younger peers lacked intellectual curiosity and sought to instrumentalize their children's education for personal gain. Moderate Catholics also criticized younger peers for their poor manners and competitive attitudes. Youngsters, in contrast, found alternative schools disorganized and rife with bullying. Finally, pragmatists rejected microaggressions from more affluent parents and often felt marginalized at parent meetings. These findings highlight conflicts *within* the middle classes in contrast to other studies arguing that parents sort themselves into class-homogeneous schools.

In contrast to scholars' views that middle-class families use schools primarily as tools for class reproduction, some activists and moderate Catholics engaged in activism and social action with egalitarian goals alongside their

children. Activists at LMS and Raimapu fought to save their schools and encouraged their children to participate in the Penguin Revolution and subsequent protests. These schools also emphasized indigenous rights, a theme that
resurfaced during the 2019 social explosion. Moderate Catholics at Calasanz
participated in social action with the poor and supported special needs populations both inside and outside school. This finding contrasts with other critiques of liberal parents' hypocrisy: parents in three of the schools studied
acted based on their value commitments rather than merely giving lip service
to them. In contrast, student activism sparked criticism from some moderate
Catholics, youngsters, and pragmatists, who argued that protests created cha-
otic school environments and protesters did not appreciate their privileges.

The final two chapters shifted to an examination of aesthetic tastes and
leisure time practices. Chapter 5 explored middle-class aesthetic tastes in home
decorations through three lenses. First, middle-class families had a shared aesthetic focused on rustic furniture, functional decorations, and inherited or
gifted objects. This shared aesthetic aligned with *relational* perspectives on home
furnishings that understand them as part of a *gift economy*. Second, middle-
class families displayed contrasting tastes that broadly reflected differences in
capital composition, capital volume, and age cohort membership. Moderate
Catholics displayed a traditional, religious taste; activists had a progressive,
cosmopolitan aesthetic; youngsters displayed genre-spanning preferences;
and pragmatists had a DIY aesthetic. Third, middle-class families constructed
symbolic boundaries with others using ideas from a *shared discursive field*.
Individuals' distastes displayed clear *gender divisions*. Most individuals that
rejected minimalist design or showroom houses were female, while most of
those that preferred minimalism were male. However, individuals across this
divide shared an "anti-consumption" discourse that criticized ostentation and
social climbing. This chapter showed the fusion of aesthetic taste with political/
ideological loyalties that are central to identity investments.

Chapter 6 continued our discussion of aesthetic taste through its focus on
cultural consumption and leisure practices. Here, we examined three different
dimensions of cultural consumption. First, middle-class families had some
common tastes and practices: they had limited access to live performances
due to cost and time constraints, preferred educational forms of cultural consumption, and once again displayed an "anti-consumption" discourse that
contrasted their own preferences with morally suspect forms of ostentation
and materialism.

Second, these families had distinct patterns of cultural consumption that mirrored their aesthetic orientations in the home. Activists displayed omnivorous tastes, but their most deeply felt attachments were to nueva canción protest music and art film, reflecting their cultural capital and political identities. Moderate Catholics actively engaged in cultural consumption with a religious emphasis, though they often deferred to their children's tastes in film and music. This group saw cultural consumption as having both a didactic and a protective function, as they sought to shield children from moral threats through sports and restrictions on video game use. Youngsters took children to movies and museums, but did not articulate clear cultural tastes. Finally, pragmatists' free time focused primarily on meetings and celebrations with extended family as they expressed no concern about the ennobling features of cultural consumption. These practices also varied by school as parents in more socially homogeneous schools spent much of their free time there, while those in more economically diverse schools had more distant relations with other parents, as noted in chapter 4.

Third, these activities varied across the two communities studied, as Ñuñoa hosted a richer cultural infrastructure and is located close to museums and galleries, while La Florida has more limited cultural amenities. Thus, Ñuñoa families engaged in more public cultural consumption, while La Florida families displayed a more domestic, suburban pattern of leisure activities. These differences were also present in residents' civic activities, whereby Ñuñoa residents participated in social movements, while La Florida residents' lower levels of collective efficacy led them to avoid encounters with neighbors. This chapter further displayed distinct cultural practices across middle-class groups reflecting each group's identity investments and variations across two communities with different social characteristics and cultural amenities.

Taken together, these chapters offer a new picture of Chile's middle classes that departs from much research that sees middle-class adults as primarily focused on opportunity hoarding and economic advancement at the expense of the working class and poor. In contrast, I found that activists and moderate Catholics expressed strong criticisms of market-based inequalities in Chile and that these views were enmeshed in their economic, cultural, and emotional investments across distinct fields. These criticisms were not merely lip service, either: activists mobilized in their own schools, engaged in "political work," and encouraged their children's activism; while moderate Catholics participated in volunteer work to support the poor and special needs popu-

lations. Youngsters, too, expressed insightful analyses of education-based inequality by criticizing elitism among upper-class students and parents as well
as racist practices by school administrators, although their criticisms were not
as all-encompassing as those of activists and moderate Catholics. Pragmatists,
who barely maintained a foothold in the middle class, used schools as tools
for upward mobility and expressed hostility toward the poor, but these attitudes and practices reflected their limited resources and daily encounters with
poor people. Pragmatists also felt the sting of microaggressions from other
upper-middle-class parents, while finding solace in valued relationships with
extended kin and close friends.

Theoretical Contributions to the Study of Middle Classes

As outlined in this book's introduction, scholars have primarily focused on
middle-class adults' efforts to secure their economic and social privileges,
and lower-middle-class individuals' aspirations of upward mobility. While
these analyses are illuminating, this book has endeavored to build more fine-
grained distinctions within the middle classes to reveal powerful symbolic
and political tensions between these subgroups. I did so by integrating three
conceptual approaches. I identified occupational and ideological differences
within the upper-middle class based on capital composition (activists versus
moderate Catholics). I then examined differences in capital volume that separate these first two groups from the lower-middle class (pragmatists).[7] Second,
I discovered salient differences across age cohorts within the upper-middle
class separating the first two groups from youngsters.[8] The contrasts and
conflicts between these four groups reveal a much more dynamic portrait
than previous accounts. Third, I examined differences across space to show
how these four groups take different shape in distinct urban communities.[9]
The integration of these three approaches has revealed a unique portrait of
the middle classes that moves beyond earlier studies through its sensitivity to
history, politics, and place.

   This study makes important contributions to analyses of cohort replace-
ment and differences across cohorts that are a key to understanding conflicts
within Chile's upper-middle classes. As I have argued, upper-middle-class
individuals born in the 1960s were exposed to communist and progressive
Catholic subcultures through their families and schools. In contrast, those
born in the 1970s spent their childhoods under the dictatorship when party

life was prohibited and did not attend college until the 1990s during a period of political calm following the democratic transition. Thus, activists and moderate Catholics retain humanistic, egalitarian values based on political and religious identities and reject market-based behaviors and metrics of success among youngsters. Additionally, activists encouraged their children's participation in the Penguin Revolution, and some moderate Catholics promoted their children's involvement in volunteer work with the homeless. Youngsters criticized discrimination, bullying, and student activism, but did not express strong political or religious identities. Pragmatists, who were mostly part of the older cohort, espoused meritocratic values in the hopes that their children would gain greater success than they had, though the few younger members of this group who also had college educations expressed attitudes that mirrored the youngsters. Pragmatists' attitudes coincide with analyses arguing that the lower-middle-class vote contributed to conservative Sebastián Piñera's presidential election in 2010 and 2018.[10]

These findings bear some similarities to Fishman and Lizardo's argument that patterns of political change influence younger generations' cultural tastes and participation.[11] They find high levels of cultural omnivorism among youths following the Portuguese Revolution and the opposite pattern after Spain's elite-driven democratic transition. I observed parallels to their study with the relative depoliticization of youngsters who came of age in the 1990s after the dictatorship privatized schools and universities and censored oppositional cultural expression. In contrast, however, I find that *opponents* of the dictatorship that were exposed to leftist and intellectual subcultures before 1973 displayed high levels of politicization and cultural omnivorism. Further, their children followed in their parents' footsteps through their activism, much like the highly educated youthful fans of Ché Guevara in contemporary Spain.[12]

This identification of conflicts between older and younger cohorts is reminiscent of Abramson and Inglehart's argument that societies undergoing high rates of economic growth (like Chile since the 1980s) display sharp value differences between cohorts based on distinct experiences in their pre-adult years.[13] However, it would be important to qualify these authors' argument that there is a *general* trend toward greater post-materialist values across societies, at least for the Chilean case. Youngsters highlight concerns about racism that are not explicitly mentioned by the older cohorts, though some activists articulate support for indigenous people's rights. However, we also observe the persistence of "materialist" values among activists through their support for the Communist Party, and the push by student activists since 2006[14] for broadly redistributive policies (Manuel de Salas and Raimapu students were among these activists). These loyalties echo long-held materialist values in center and left parties in Chile dating back to the early twentieth century. This pattern challenges the idea that there has been a broad shift from materialist to post-materialist values in Chile.

My analysis also diverges from several critiques of "progressive" parents.[15] While these authors suggest that progressive middle-class adults give lip service to goals of social change while cementing their own privilege, I found a different pattern. Activists and moderate Catholics were products of institutionalized partisan and religious subcultures. Because they were part of these collectivities, their avowed political and moral sentiments coincided with their activism and volunteerism. Further, adults' political participation and volunteerism in schools encouraged their children to participate inside and outside their schools. In this regard, private and charter schools, like the well-known public schools that ignited student protests, were not only "engines of social reproduction," but also "incubators of social transformation." These findings suggest that when middle-class adults are part of broader movements, parties, or religious organizations dedicated to social change, their "alternative consumption" may not be limited to an individual lifestyle choice but rather will be embedded in cultures of resistance. These cultures also include contradictions—private school parents are not willing to sacrifice their privilege by enrolling their children in public schools, but they participate in protests that temporarily shutter their children's schools as part of broader social movements. I revisit this point below.

Finally, this study has contributed to understandings of middle-class participation in different fields by showing how economic practices vary across residential communities. Specifically, I found that local school "microclimates"[16] offered parents with similar backgrounds different "choice sets" across residential communities, and individuals' participation in public cultural consumption also varied across neighborhoods. These variations reflect the distinct school submarkets and cultural infrastructures in these communities as well as their relative proximity to museum and art gallery districts.[17] This finding suggests that spatial configurations constrain how individuals with similar educational or occupational backgrounds engage in market behavior. While this point is fairly obvious with regard to housing markets—choices are price sensitive—it is less widely recognized for school and cultural markets. This finding suggests the need to move beyond sociodemographic factors (education, occupation, gender, age) to explore how space and place shape variations in middle-class identities and practices.[18]

Chilean Middle Classes in Comparative Perspective

This study reveals important similarities and differences with analyses of middle classes in other national settings. Here, I develop these comparisons with a focus on the shift from "old" to "new" middle classes, middle-class politics, and the construction of intra- and interclass symbolic boundaries.

The political and ideological heritage of Chilean activists and moderate Catholics in this study shares important features with other postcolonial, middle-income societies where middle classes began to shape social policies in the early- to mid-twentieth century. Like their counterparts in México,[19] Perú,[20] Egypt,[21] India,[22] and elsewhere, Chilean middle classes developed nationalist, anti-oligarchic ideologies in the early twentieth century to justify their new role in public office.[23] The growing middle classes were trained primarily in public schools, and an important segment of this group were public and private employees.[24] The image of middle-class people as highly educated individuals that served as a modernizing force in society was widely shared.

As the texts cited above attest, this "old" middle class has lost influence in these countries[25] in recent decades in the context of economic liberalization policies that have eroded welfare states and dynamized private sector growth, a structural shift from industrial to service employment, and a globalized consumer market. This study, like others, points to the tensions between the "old" and "new" middle classes, but more than other accounts, I highlight the continued importance of the "old" middle class as a political and cultural force pushing back against free market policies and their consequences for education, labor, and consumption markets as well as interpersonal coexistence in society.[26]

This study has highlighted the importance of middle-class politics for understanding broader changes and continuities in Chilean society. The persistence of activism by Communist Party members in the present finds its counterpart in México's 1968 student activist generation's involvement in protests over the 1985 earthquake that led to that country's democratization.[27] However, where Walker finds that the middle classes shifted politically over time in relation to changing political and economic events, I find the persistence of political, religious, and age cohort divisions within the Chilean middle classes inherited from the past.

Chile's middle-class activism also diverges from Argentina's "anti-party" mobilization during that country's 2001–2003 financial crisis as the activists in this study were closely aligned with political parties.[28] This difference likely reflects the Argentine middle class's political development in opposition to working-class organizations and the dominant Peronist (*Justicialista*) Party. In contrast to these two cases, the institutionalization of a pluralistic party system dating back to the nineteenth century in which some parties represented multiple social classes likely explains the continued tensions within the Chilean middle classes.[29]

Finally, this study reveals similarities to and differences from other analyses of middle-class individuals' construction of symbolic boundaries.[30] Like the middle classes in São Paulo, Brazil, I find that lower-middle-class pragmatists express hostility toward the poor, which may result from their precarious foothold on their middle-class positions.[31] Additionally, like Lima, Perú's middle classes, I identified strong conflicts across cohorts between activists and moderate Catholics, on the one hand, and youngsters, on the other.[32] However, unlike Perú, these conflicts were not explicitly racialized. Further, I found that activists and moderate Catholics also constructed boundaries with elites, in line with many studies' finding that middle-class people differentiate themselves from "those above and those below."[33]

This study's cross-cohort analysis of upper- and lower-middle-class Chileans moves beyond these other studies, however, by highlighting the voices of not only the upper-middle classes that engage in practices of social closure, but also lower-middle classes that feel excluded. Further, this study highlights the ambiguity of progressive upper-middle-class identities as these families push for greater social equity through activism and volunteer activity while "hedging their bets" by engaging in concerted cultivation to support their children's educational success. This finding counters the generally pessimistic view of members of the middle classes as self-centered and encourages us to reconsider the tradition of middle-class idealism, activism, and political participation.

The Middle Classes and Contemporary Political Change in Chile

As I consider this book's implications for understanding Chile's middle classes and widespread social change, its most profound and powerful insights refer to events that occurred after I completed fieldwork in 2010. While the Penguin Revolution still reverberated at LMS and Raimapu when I conducted interviews and observed school events, the much larger and more influential college student movement appeared in 2011.

Although some research sees the Penguin Revolution as the beginning of the contemporary student movement,[34] the mobilization actually had its roots in the 1990s.[35] College, and later high school students, slowly developed organizations that led to the massive 2011 college student protests provoking important changes in K–12 and college policy designed to create greater educational equity. Much of the discussion focuses on the Penguin Revolution's origins in elite public schools (the so-called "emblematic" schools like the National Institute and Liceo #1) and in traditional research universities like the University of Chile and the Catholic University that had a long history of student organization and protest.

However, alternative private schools were another source of leadership of the 2011 movement. As noted in chapters 3 and 4, Camila Vallejo, a Raimapu graduate, was one of the most visible student leaders. She was later elected to Congress and currently serves in Gabriel Boric's presidential cabinet. Additionally, as discussed in chapter 4, Raimapu and LMS students participated in the 2006, 2011, and subsequent student mobilizations and produced several national high school and college leaders. Prominent college student leaders— Vallejo, Karol Cariola, Giorgio Jackson, and Gabriel Boric—were elected to Congress in 2014, and Boric was elected president in 2021. Vallejo and Cariola are both members of the Communist Party, and Cariola attended a public high school. Jackson and Boric participate in new left wing parties that emerged after the student movement and played a pivotal role in the 2019 social explosion, election of members to the Constitutional Convention, and Boric's 2021 presidential victory. Both Boric and Jackson attended private schools.[36]

Additionally, other scholars argue that the parents of student activists or adults that lived through the dictatorship had traumatic memories of authoritarian rule that made them afraid to participate in politics, reluctant to discuss their past political participation with their activist children, or initially hesitant to support their children's activism.[37] However, this study finds that parents who were members or sympathizers of the Communist Party continued their political participation after the democratic transition and actively encouraged their children's activism. Thus, while some argue that recent student movements reflect a generational break between adults and children with regard to their children's participation in the student movement, I found the *intergenerational transmission* of partisan identities in activist families. I did observe youngsters' and pragmatists' criticisms of student activists, as discussed in chapter 4.

The story gets even more interesting as we move forward toward the present. In October 2019, National Institute students called for subway fare evasion to protest rising ticket prices. The movement caught fire and brought together students, feminists, pension reform activists, environmentalists, and other groups. Within a week, activists had organized the largest protest in Chilean history, with over one million participants in Santiago, in spite of a state of emergency declared by President Piñera and flagrant human rights abuses by police and soldiers. At protests, it was common to hear participants singing the late nueva canción artist Víctor Jara's "The Right to Live in Peace" (*El derecho de vivir en paz*).

The 2019 movement brought to a head Chileans' rising discontent with the market model enshrined in Pinochet's 1980 Constitution. Activists trained their sights on the charter's protection of private property and the concept of the "subsidiary state" that alleviated the central government of the responsibility of providing public goods like education, healthcare, pensions, and public utilities. Once again, as noted above, a Manuel de Salas student played a central leadership role in the protests. Seventeen year-old Víctor Chanfreau was a visible leader of the protests, appearing on television programs and leading protests in early 2020 against college entrance exams, for which the government placed criminal charges against him under a Pinochet era anti-terrorist law.[38]

It was only fitting that high school students from the National Institute and Manuel de Salas, among other schools, should call democratic governments to account for what many knew to be the failures of Chile's experiment with privatized K–12 and college education. College students suffered from debt after attending schools of uneven quality, and Chile's K–12 education market that was supposedly designed to improve educational outcomes via competition between schools yields standardized test results far below the average of OECD countries. These disappointing results should come as no surprise as

Chile has among the highest levels of inequality in school investment based on student socioeconomic status among OECD and Latin American countries.[39] The movement gathered steam because it moved beyond education to address the paltry pensions retirees receive under Chile's oligopolistic pension funds that charge high service fees,[40] feminist demands that emerged from Chile's #MeToo movement,[41] and demands for environmental regulation and indigenous rights.[42]

Most scholarship on the movement focuses on neoliberal policies as the catalyst for mobilization. While this explanation undoubtedly has a grain of truth, I have argued that we can only understand these protests by considering political and religious identities that predate the dictatorship and continue to animate growing segments of the middle and working classes to oppose free market policies. Moreover, while scholars and activists traditionally looked to organized labor and shantytown dwellers as the principal popular social movements in Chile, student movements have existed for a century and have a long history of alliances with labor and left-wing parties.[43] Additionally, teachers played an important role in middle-class activism, identity, and party development beginning in the 1920s,[44] and their national union's militancy and success have grown in recent decades after a steep decline under the dictatorship.[45] Teachers and students, alongside many other groups who participated in the social explosion, are pushing for public policies they hope can ameliorate the terrible inequalities and injustices that Chile has endured since the military coup of September 11, 1973.

The protests continued until the following March when COVID-19 infections reached Chile, and the protesters achieved something unprecedented—the government's agreement to hold a plebiscite on a new Constitution. The October 2020 referendum received the support of 78 percent of voters, and in 2021, Chileans elected a majority of independents and leftists to the Constitutional Convention charged with drafting the new charter. The elections were structured to guarantee gender parity of representation and reserved seventeen seats for indigenous representatives.[46]

That year also witnessed a heated presidential contest in which the political polarization that first emerged in 2006 took center stage. Gabriel Boric, a former student leader and congressman who headed a small coalition of new left-wing parties that emerged during the 2011 student movement, faced off against far-right congressman José Antonio Kast, who also led a new conservative party and styled his right-wing, populist campaign after Donald Trump and Brazil's Jair Bolsonaro. In the November elections, Kast prevailed with 27.9 percent of the vote to Boric's 25.8 percent. Candidates representing the center-right and center-left party coalitions that had dominated Chilean politics since 1990 fell far behind.[47] In the runoff the following month (neither candidate exceeded the required 50 percent threshold of the vote in the first round), Boric triumphed with 55.8 percent of the vote to Kast's 44.1 percent, which makes him the youngest president in Chilean history.[48] The triumph of a former student leader who fronted a coalition of small, new leftist parties symbolized the collapse of the "politics of consensus" secured by traditional parties in the previous three decades, and demonstrated how students had become the leading edge of movements that had effectively challenged Chile's long period of neoliberal, technocratic rule. Boric's victory was secured with votes from women, youth, the poor, and residents of mining zones that have suffered from environmental devastation. He received 56 percent of the vote in Ñuñoa and 65 percent of the vote in La Florida, demonstrating strong support from voters in the two communities examined in this book and highlighting the durability of middle-class citizens' identity investments.[49]

Boric's victory would be inconceivable without the groundswell of multi-sector social movement mobilization beginning with the Penguin Revolution. Activists at schools like LMS and Raimapu were important leaders in those protests, providing a powerful counterexample to accounts suggesting that middle-class Chileans are primarily interested in securing their own advantages. At these fully private and charter schools, upper-middle-class students mobilized to demand greater educational equity in support of public and charter school students. They were part of the movement that elected Gabriel Boric president and made fellow student leaders Camila Vallejo and Giorgio Jackson his two main cabinet spokespeople. Boric also named a majority female cabinet, acknowledging the crucial 2018 feminist mobilization that preceded the social explosion as well as his ample electoral support from women.[50] Boric crowdsourced his presidential platform via 600 citizen meetings and paid homage to the social movements that made his victory possible in his 53-point plan of proposed changes focused on education, gender equality, human rights, labor rights, health, LGBTQ+ equality, and other issues.[51]

Boric's victory coincided with the first steps in the development of Chile's new Constitution. At the time of this book's completion (June 2022), the final draft of the proposed charter has been published. The new Constitution would make Chile's government regional, plurinational, intercultural, and provide autonomy for indigenous territories; reform the judiciary and give authority to indigenous judicial systems in native territories; eliminate the Senate and create a regional legislative chamber; and enshrine social rights rather than individual property rights. The provisional charter's emphasis on indigenous rights reflects the centrality of these issues in the 2019 social explosion but also likely builds on the support for native peoples at schools like LMS and Raimapu dating back to the first Bachelet administration. In a September 2022 referendum, voters will decide to approve or reject the proposed charter.[52]

This book has argued that Chile's weakly regulated labor market, market-based economy, and privatized educational and social services have created precarious privilege among middle-class families. These families have drawn on cultural resources from earlier stages of their lives to engage in identity investments in distinct markets. These identity investments were part and parcel of middle-class adults' and youths' activism during Chile's political inflection point during the early 2000s. While conservative middle-class voters helped elect billionaire Sebastián Piñera president in 2010 and 2018, progressive middle-class activists contributed to the wave of protest culminating in Chile's constitutional referendum and convention as well as former student leader Gabriel Boric's resounding presidential victory in 2021. Far from being a primarily conservative and materialistic group, different segments of the middle class have pushed back against free market policies, and their activism has contributed to Chile's stunning repudiation of neoliberal policies as evident in Boric's presidential plan and a possible new Constitution.

Appendix   Research Design and Methods

I BEGAN THIS PROJECT with the goal of contrasting the "old" middle class tied to public employment with the "emerging" middle class of private sector employees and freelancers identified by many scholars and journalists in Chile, Latin America, and other countries of the Global South.[1] I suspected that members of the old and new middle classes would hold different values, occupy distinct occupational positions, and have different lifestyles, as research suggests. As I collected data, it became clear that the salient divisions were *within* the upper-middle class (between private and public employees), across age cohorts, and between the upper- and lower-middle classes (based on income and education).

To capture the contrast between different segments of the middle class, I examined families in distinct schools across two communities. From 2008 to 2010, I conducted sixty-eight semistructured interviews with seventy-seven parents (several interviews included both spouses) aged thirty-one to fifty-nine years old. Additionally, I conducted one interview with a Ñuñoa housing activist and one interview with a housing market analyst. Most interviewees were in their early to mid-forties at the time of the interview. The study focused on parents with children attending schools in Ñuñoa, an eastern Santiago municipality historically settled by professionals, intellectuals, and immigrant (Jewish and Middle Eastern) businessmen that has an extensive educational and cultural infrastructure;[2] and La Florida, a growing southern Santiago suburb with limited cultural amenities and a growing middle class.[3] Both municipalities host mixed-class populations, though Ñuñoa residents have higher average incomes.

I began the study with snowball samples in Ñuñoa and La Florida before gaining access to schools in each area. I suspected that contrasting traditional Catholic and secular alternative schools in each community would allow me to interview public and private employees and explore the religious-secular cleavage that has been important to Chilean culture and politics since the nineteenth century. Additionally, since Ñuñoa is more affluent than La Florida, I anticipated that I might find more upper-middle-class families in the former and more lower-middle-class families in the latter.

Some school-based studies compare children from the same age group.[4] Since I sought to use distinct schools as entry points to examine different dimensions of middle-class identities and lifestyles, I did not restrict the study to families with children of a specific age. In the end, I interviewed parents with elementary and high school students in four of the five schools I studied (Raíces only continued to the eighth grade). Gaining access to each school presented unique challenges. After some preliminary interviews, I developed connections with parents at Liceo Experimental Manuel de Salas (Manuel de Salas Experimental School, LMS) in Ñuñoa through a colleague whose children attended there. He introduced me to Víctor, who connected me to other parents of elementary and high school students, Aniluap (a member of the parents' association), and a school administrator. Aniluap was an activist, but because she had a daughter in elementary school, she introduced me to several youngsters that broadened the range of parents I interviewed at the school. I also attended a parents' association board meeting, visited a school fundraiser, attended a concert at the school, and visited a family at their vacation home.

A few months after beginning research at LMS, I gained access to Calasanz school through my wife (a former history teacher). I met with the school's principal, who gave me a list of parents with children in elementary and high school. In addition to parents, I interviewed a school administrator and attended a weekly "street pastoral" event during which parents provided homeless people with food they had prepared in the school's kitchen.

Because I had stronger personal connections with Ñuñoa schools, it took a few more months to gain access to schools in La Florida, though I interviewed individual parents via a snowball sample beforehand. I established connections with parents at Raimapu through a friend whose daughter was a parent there. One of my interviewees was also a Raimapu teacher. She introduced me to the principal and took me on a tour of the school. In addition to interviews, I also attended a concert at the school.

While conducting fieldwork at Raimapu, a colleague recommended I interview parents at Raíces Altazor, where he had a personal connection. I met with one of the school's two founders (they are sisters). She sketched the school's identity and mission and issued me a list of parents with children of different ages.

Finally, a graduate student who was an alumna of Rosario Concha introduced me to the school's principal. Rosario included the largest proportion of lower-middle-class interviewees of all the schools where I conducted research. The principal invited me to attend parent teacher conferences so I could recruit study participants. In addition to recruiting volunteers from two classes, the visit gave me a feel for the school through observation and informal conversations with parents and teachers.[5]

All told, I conducted sixteen interviews with eighteen parents (including an administrator) at LMS, thirteen interviews with sixteen parents (and one administrator) at Calasanz, six interviews with eight parents at Raimapu, six interviews with eight parents at Raíces, and eight interviews with ten parents at Rosario Concha. In other words, I interviewed a roughly equivalent number of individuals in Catholic and alternative schools (if we combine Raimapu and Raíces) in the two communities. Additionally, the snowball samples yielded twelve interviews in Ñuñoa (including the two housing interviews noted above) and seven interviews in La Florida and nearby communities. These interviews provided additional context for the focused comparison of the five schools. Some of the parents attending Ñuñoa and La Florida schools lived outside the municipality where their school is located.

Like many qualitative researchers, I did not construct a random sample of parents or a comparison of parents with children of the same age. Rather, I sampled for range by examining parents with children of different ages in two types of schools across two communities.[6] The data allowed me to identify important contrasts between activist and Catholic upper-middle-class parents, upper- and lower-middle-class parents, parents from different age cohorts, men and women, as well as residents in the two communities.

School fees are significantly lower in the La Florida schools, reflecting their status as charter schools with public subsidies and the higher percentage of parents with modest incomes in that municipality. However, with the exception of Calasanz, where all the study participants were upper-middle-class, I interviewed upper- and lower-middle-class parents in all of the remaining schools. Hence, the tuition differential between communities did not result in vast differences in families' financial circumstances from each area. Table A.1 summarizes some basic features of the five schools.

I conducted interviews with study participants at schools, restaurants, workplaces, or homes based on their preferences and availability. My goal was to maximize the number of interviews conducted in participants' homes because I sought to observe and analyze home furnishings and decorations. In the end, I photographed thirty-one living rooms or a little less than 40 percent of the sample.

The study's goal was to examine how parents' family, educational, and occupational backgrounds shape their selection of schools, housing, home decorations, and participation in cultural consumption. I sought to examine these fields to revisit Bourdieu's hypothesis that there is a "homology between positions and position-taking," that is, that individuals in the same occupational position would likely adopt a similar attitude toward investments and consumption in different areas like housing or schools.[7]

Many studies have focused on a single field, but few have conducted comparisons across several fields. One mixed methods study focuses on various fields of cultural consumption and work life in Australia using a mixed-methods (survey and interview) design,[8] and a qualitative study examines diverse fields in Manchester, UK,[9] though it does not explore home decorations. Another mixed-methods study explores various fields of cultural consumption in the

School Name	Year Established	Monthly tuition in U.S. dollars (2009)	Number of students	Fourth-grade standardized test scores: language, math, social studies (top ranked school averaged 348 per section)	College entrance exam scores (top ranked school averaged 720)
Manuel de Salas	1932	$320	1500	286, 287, 295	616.9
Calasanz	1951	$320	1600	315, 303, 304	650.4
Raimapu	1982	$120	600	299, 300, 308	566.3
Raíces Altazor	1985	$120	210	277, 263, 268	K–8 only
Rosario Concha	1913	$70	900	270, 260, 265	561

Table A.1 Characteristics of Schools Studied. Sources: *El Mercurio* 2008; Colegio Particular COEDUC 2009; Chile, Ministerio de Educación 2015a, 2015b.

UK but does not study housing, school choice, or home decoration.[10] A recent work examines school choice, housing selection, and cultural consumption in Santiago, Chile, though it relies on survey data, does not explore home interiors, and examines more affluent communities than those studied here.[11] This book draws on the insights from these earlier studies, while also making unique contributions through its qualitative analysis of these distinct fields and focus on political and religious identities.

I used semistructured interviews, photos of home interiors, and partici-pant observation of school events to gain insights regarding these fields. Inter-views focused on the educational and occupational backgrounds of the person interviewed, as well as their spouse, siblings, and parents; family income; their rationales for housing and neighborhood choices; a description of living room decorations and their meanings for the interviewee; school selection, school satisfaction, and relationships with staff and parents; family leisure pursuits, including children's enrichment activities; how the interviewee compared him or herself to peers; and their hypothetical wish for a better home, school, or neighborhood should resources become available.

Photographs are my second data source. Photos provide a visual record of material culture possessed by different families that supplements and enriches interview transcripts. Because I interviewed all participants regarding their home furnishings, I could compare their narratives regarding their home dec-orations to my own interpretations of the visual data. The photos provide a unique window into participants' aesthetic tastes, how they represent their home to outsiders, and how they perceive their relationships with persons who gifted them objects. My interpretation of home decorations and artworks ben-efited from previous studies.[12]

Finally, I conducted participant observation at school fundraisers, con-certs, as well as a volunteer activity with homeless individuals; and visited a family at their vacation home. After completing one year in the field, I in-vited participants to attend a focus group where I presented preliminary re-search findings, and we discussed their reactions and perspectives. Finally, two participants attended a university seminar I co-organized featuring two well-known authors who summarized their books on class and status in Chile. I had follow-up conversations and email exchanges with a small number of participants after completing fieldwork. Each of these opportunities comple-mented the formal interview by permitting observation of participants in a natural, unscripted setting.[13]

The focus group was also fruitful (though awkward) as participants challenged the category of middle class used in the study (upper-middle-class
participants did not think lower-middle-class people were "truly" middle
class). This criticism echoed comments during formal interviews when upper-
middle-class participants questioned the idea that they were part of the same
middle class as people who earned much less than they did. Similarly, the two
participants that attended the seminar found the speakers' use of the term *clas-
sism* offensive because they believed the presentation implicitly and unfairly
criticized them for harboring discriminatory attitudes toward the working
class and poor. While these were challenging encounters, they provided useful
data points highlighting how upper-middle-class participants draw symbolic
boundaries with the wealthy and the lower-middle class.

I used a modified grounded theory approach to code and interpret interviews, photos, and field notes.[14] I first examined each field separately (e.g.,
school choice, housing choice, etc.) with an open coding technique until I
identified initial themes. Then, I developed broader analytical categories
based on these themes. After analyzing each field separately, I revisited the
data numerous times, which allowed me to construct the typology of activists,
moderate Catholics, youngsters, and pragmatists as well as develop the core
concepts of identity investments and precarious privilege. While I used
some grounded theory coding and interpretive techniques, I depart from
this approach in that I began the study with theoretical questions on culture
and inequality that shaped the development of interview questions and data
interpretation.[15] Hence, my approach approximates "abduction"—an iterative
dialogue between data and theories that alternates between induction and
deduction to generate new ideas.[16] I triangulated across individual interviews
as well as between interviews, publicly available data, and scholarly sources to
minimize possible distortions in the retrospective accounts I collected.

Ethnographers often reflect on their "positionality" in the field.[17] This
term refers to their social background and how this may have influenced
both how those they study perceive them and how they can establish trust
with interviewees across social and cultural boundaries. I am a white, Jewish,
American, middle-class man. Thus, I am culturally quite different from the
individuals in this book. However, I came to this study after a long history of
conducting qualitative, multimethod research in Chile. I began dissertation
research on labor activism in 1993 that employed oral histories, participant
observation, and archival research;[18] and subsequently did several studies

throughout the 2000s on consumer practices and settings that utilized semi-structured interviews and participant observation.[19] Thus, this is the third large research project I have conducted in Chile. I am thus quite familiar with Chile's language and culture and came to this project as a seasoned researcher. Additionally, my wife is Chilean, her family lives in Santiago, and my two daughters attended school while we lived in Chile from 2008 until 2010.

All of these experiences thus served as bridges that helped me connect with those I interviewed. I could rely on my previous research experience and institutional affiliation (first at the Catholic University and then at Diego Portales University) to legitimize my role as a researcher. Additionally, my children's experiences in school there also served as a common theme when discussing school-related issues. My personal ties with friends or relatives of the "gatekeepers" at each school (principal informants or school officials) also helped "get me in the door" with potential interviewees. Because my wife was a former teacher and graduate of both the Liceo #1 and Metropolitan University of Educational Sciences, this was a point of commonality that built rapport with people I interviewed who were graduates of those institutions.

These were all advantages that facilitated the research process. However, because my previous research experience was with working-class and poor people and/or activists, I had to learn how to build rapport with my middle-class interviewees who had a different cultural style than those I had studied in the past. In some instances, this was jarring at first. My past working-class interviewees were far more effusive and informal than my at times detached and formal middle-class interviewees. That said, as I became more acquainted with the culture of each school, the initially "stiff" nature of our conversations subsided and became more relaxed, comfortable, and friendly. Some interviewees thanked me after the interview for providing the opportunity to reflect on their experiences, and a few that attended the focus group or read earlier publications from this project found the analyses rang true and provided food for thought.

Some of those I interviewed were very welcoming and a few even became friends. This was the case with Víctor and Alicia, who attended our going away party when we returned to the U.S. Víctor was a very enthusiastic promoter of the study at LMS and spent a lot of time recruiting interviewees. I was able to return the favor when he asked me to serve as a personal connection for a teaching opportunity that interested him. Tamara and Luis offered me wine and olives during our interview that lasted more than two hours. They later invited me to their summer cottage. During another marathon interview with Susana and Alejandro, we enjoyed a glass of rum together. It was an intense discussion, but by the end, we were laughing and joking. Nelson and Tania offered me olives during our interview. I was also impressed and moved by some individuals' choice to reveal frightening and painful experiences under the dictatorship, like Ledda's comment in the introduction that the dictatorship "disappeared" (likely assassinated) some of her mother's colleagues, or Mario's remarks in chapter 1 that his family needed to live in safe houses when his father was released from prison for his political activities.

Because the material in this book is highly personal and intimate (as it explores incomes, child-rearing, political and religious identities, and home decoration) and also covers issues about which these individuals may feel judged (the size and location of their homes, their consumption practices), some of those I interviewed seemed "on their guard," thus generating a less relaxed interview encounter. When I perceived such concerns or fears, I tried to redirect our discussions or reframe questions that seemed uncomfortable to the interviewee. Ultimately, because I observed consistent patterns and discourses across subgroups of the sample as well as broader shared discourses, I think that most interviewees overcame their initial wariness and were as open as they could be in an interview encounter with a stranger. This is all to say that qualitative research hinges on the quality of relationships the researcher forms with her, his, or their interviewees, and I marshaled all of the resources at my disposal to elicit honest answers from the individuals I interviewed. In turn, I tried to be as open and honest as possible when they asked me questions about my family, research, and life in the U.S.

Notes

Introduction

1. To paraphrase Tilly (1998, 10), opportunity hoarding is the ability of members of a group to access a valuable resource that can be monopolized and renewed to support its activities. For a critique and update of Tilly's ideas, see Tomaskovic-Devey and Avent-Holt 2019.

2. Interview, April 14, 2009. I conducted and digitally recorded all interviews in Spanish and translated extracts to English. Miguel Pérez Ahumada and Leila Juzam Pucheu transcribed all recorded interviews.

3. Interview, March 24, 2009.

4. Interview, April 27, 2010.

5. Interview, November 9, 2008.

6. McAdam 1986.

7. Bourdieu 1984, 1993, 1996.

8. Bennett et al. 2009; Atkinson 2017; Savage et al. 2015; Savage et al. 2005.

9. Bennett et al. 1999.

10. Flemmen et al. 2019.

11. Méndez and Gayo 2019.

12. Bourdieu (1984) dedicated a chapter to "Culture and Politics." There, he primarily focused on middle- and upper-class domination of political parties and the construction of public opinion, although he also examined how political affiliations vary across occupational groups. Bourdieu (1996, 158–187) explored variations in political affiliations among students across different fields in France's elite graduate schools, or *grandes écoles*, though his main focus was on the shifting contours of France's elite universities. Bourdieu (1988) examined how professors in different universities responded to France's 1968 student and labor mobilization. Recent applications and extensions of Bourdieu's political analyses include Atkinson (2017) and Jarness et al. (2019).

13. Zelizer 1989; 2005.

14. Wherry 2012.

15. Cunningham 2002.

16. Snow and Anderson 1987.

17. In a recent UN report, Barozet et al. (2021) highlight middle-class support for more egalitarian political change in the 2019–2021 period. However, this book argues that some segments of the middle classes pushed for this change more than a decade earlier, and their attitudes reflected political and religious experiences dating back to their college years in the 1980s. See Mau (2015) for an analysis of middle classes as increasingly self-interested actors that support market-based policies.

18. Lamont 1992.

19. Rey et al. 2020.

20. Roy 2021.

21. Mosoetsa et al. 2016.

22. Solimano 2012; Barozet et al. 2021.

23. Lamont 1992.

24. Constable and Valenzuela 1991.

25. Schneider 1995; Winn 1986.

26. Martínez and Díaz 1996.

27. Zeitlin and Ratcliffe 1988.

28. Stern (2021) and Hutchison and Zárate Campos (2017) chronicle an earlier wave of research in the 1950s

29. Banerjee and Duflo 2008; Kharas 2010; Ferreira et al. 2013; Dayton-Johnson 2019; Kochhar 2020.

30. Bellin 2010.

31. Biekart 2015.

32. Banco Mundial and Gobierno de Chile 2020.

33. Castillo et al. 2013.

34. Banco Mundial and Gobierno de Chile 2020; López-Calva and Ortiz-Suarez 2014; Dayton-Johnson 2019. In contrast to these absolute measures, some economists prefer to use relative measures of the middle class that examine those with incomes 50 percent below and above the median income. See Dayton-Johnson 2019.

35. See Erickson and Goldthorpe 1992.

36. Torche 2005.

37. Espinoza and Núñez 2014.

38. Barozet et al. 2021; Banco Mundial and Gobierno de Chile 2021.

39. Savage et al. 1992. Savage et al. (2015) provide a more detailed class breakdown while also highlighting the importance of social capital (connections) as a valuable resource.

40. Méndez and Gayo 2019; Méndez 2008; Fuentes and Mac-Clure 2019; Castillo 2016.

41. Dayton-Johnson 2019.

42. See Johnson 1958; Lipset 1959.

43. Villegas 2010; Ekiert 2010.

44. Bellin 2010.

45. Ray 2010; Mau (2015) makes a similar argument for Western Europe.

46. Davis 2010; Savage et al. 1992.

47. López-Pedreros 2019.

48. Savage et al. 2005; Bridge 2003; Butler and Robson 2003; Jackson and Benson 2014; Márquez and Pérez 2008; Bacqué et al. 2015.

49. Andreotti et al. 2015.

50. Butler and Robson 2003; Jackson and Benson 2014; Sabatini and Salcedo 2007; Ruiz-Tagle 2016.

51. Abramson and Inglehart 1995.

52. Fishman and Lizardo 2013.

53. Bourdieu 1984.

54. Holt 1998; Weinberger et al. 2017.

55. Lareau 2003; Pugh 2009.

56. Jarness 2017.

57. Abramson and Inglehart 1995; Fishman and Lizardo 2013.

58. Other studies identify anti-elitist and egalitarian attitudes within the middle classes as well as the increasing fragility within the middle classes after I completed my 2008–2010 fieldwork. See Mac-Clure et al. 2015; Barozet et al. 2021.

59. Barr-Melej 2001; Silva 2000.

60. Serrano 2018; Barr-Melej 2001; Rosemblatt 2000; Stern 2021.

61. Barr-Melej 2001; Stern 2021; compare Garcia-Bryce 2012 on Perú.

62. Angell 1972; DeShazo 1983.

63. Silva 2000.

64. Hutchison and Zárate Campos 2017.

65. Silva 2007; Serrano 2018.

66. Loveman 1986; Fleet 1985; Hutchison and Zárate Campos 2017.

67. Winn 1986; Teichman 2015.

68. Huneeus 2001; Gárate Chateau 2012; Martínez and Tironi 1985.

69. Donoso 2013; Roberts 2017; Parraguez 2016.

70. Loveman 1998; Constable and Valenzuela 1991; Schneider 1995; Oxhorn 1995; Hipsher 1998; Garreton 1989; Roberts 1998; Rosemblatt 2013.

71. Siavelis 2010, 2014; Solimano 2012; Lechner 2002. These laws included, most importantly, the 1980 Constitution that restricted the government's role in providing social welfare and guaranteed the sanctity of private property; eleven nonelected senators appointed by the armed forces, Supreme Court, and the president; a binomial electoral law that created congressional districts with two seats that favored the two dominant political coalitions and excluded the Communist, Green, and Humanist parties from congressional representation; and other laws that restricted full democratic participation and representation. Congress eliminated the designated senators in 2005 and the binomial electoral law in 2013 (Solimano 2012; Siavelis 2014). After massive protests in 2019, Congress agreed to a referendum on a new Constitution, in

2020, voters approved it, and in 2021, Chileans elected a Constitutional Assembly to write a new charter that includes a majority of independents and leftists. See Ríos 2021.

72. Solimano 2012; Roberts 2017; Torche and López-Calva 2013.

73. Roberts 2011; Solimano 2012.

74. Moulian 1997, 1998; Lechner 2002.

75. Solimano 2012.

76. Solimano 2012; Barozet et al. 2021.

77. Solimano 2012; Barozet et al. 2021.

78. The movement was dubbed the "Penguin Revolution" because the students' school uniforms of navy blue sport jackets (or dresses), white shirts, and ties made them look like penguins.

79. Donoso 2013.

80. Donoso 2013; Roberts 2017; Parraguez 2016; Von Bülow and Bidegain Ponte 2015; Funk 2010, 57.

81. Franco and Leon 2010; Elacqua and Aninat 2013; Castillo 2014; Solimano 2012; Barozet et al. 2021.

82. Palacios-Valladares 2016; Roberts 2017; Parraguez 2016.

83. Mayol 2020; Heiss 2020; Cuadra 2020; Ríos 2021.

84. BBC 2021b.

85. Núcleo de Sociología Contingente 2020.

86. Barozet et al. 2021.

87. Barozet et al. 2021; Barozet and Espinoza 2016.

88. Barr-Melej 2001; Johnson 1958.

89. Glaser and Strauss 1967; Tavory and Timmermans 2014.

90. Qualitative studies include Calarco 2018; Lacy 2007; Lareau 2003; Pugh 2009; and Holt 1998. Although this study uses a nonrandom sample designed to uncover situated meanings and practices within a specific group of people rather than to create generalizations about the middle class as a whole, I was interested in locating the individuals in this study within Chile's class hierarchy to develop hypotheses about how their backgrounds influenced their behavior and to facilitate comparisons with other scholarship on the middle classes.

91. See Rasse et al. 2009 and Barozet et al. 2021 for rationales regarding this classification. While this may seem like a large salary range, economists and sociologists consider this group as part of the upper-middle class. Because the incomes and wealth of the top 1, 5, and 10 percent of earners are substantially higher than the bulk of the population, the differences in incomes in the bottom 90 percent are relatively small by comparison. To illustrate, in 2010, four billionaires held wealth equivalent to 20 percent of Chile's gross domestic product (Solimano 2012, 81, 123). See Torche 2005 and Espinoza and Núñez 2014 for similar analyses.

92. AIM 2008, 2018.

93. Rasse et al. 2009; Barozet et al. 2021.

94. Small 2009.

95. Burawoy 1998.

96. Tavory and Timmermans 2014.

97. Thumala 2012; Bellei et al. 2020.

98. Loveman 1986; Loveman 1998; Tinsman 2014.

99. Méndez and Gayo 2019.

100. See Barozet and Espinoza (2016) and Barozet et al. (2021) for exceptions. Méndez and Gayo (2019) offer an interesting analysis of political attitudes among their wealthy study participants, but do not explore processes of political mobilization within and beyond their sample. Marín et al. (2019) briefly note political differences among middle-class residents in distinct communities, but do not explore this topic in depth.

101. Araujo and Martucelli 2012; Lechner 2002; Moulian 1997, 1998; Castillo et al. 2013. The slowdown in economic growth, 2019 social explosion, Constitutional Convention, and economic effects of the Covid-19 pandemic have recently led scholars to focus more closely on middle-class precarity and politicization. See Barozet et al. 2021; Banco Mundial and Gobierno de Chile 2020; World Bank 2021.

102. Moulian 1997, 1998; Lechner 2002; PNUD 2002.

103. McAdam 1986, 1989; Loveman 1998.

104. Reay et al. 2011; Sherman 2017.

105. Lena and Peterson 2011.

106. Warde et al. 2007.

Chapter 1

1. Interview, April 29, 2009.

2. PNUD 2017; Solimano 2012.

3. Torche and López-Calva 2013; Banco Mundial and Gobierno de Chile 2020.

4. Barozet et al. 2021.

5. Sehnbruch 2006, 2010, 2014.

6. See McAdam (1986, 1989) and Loveman (1998) on "high-risk activism" and its personal consequences later in life.

7. Bourdieu (1977) deploys this term to describe the disorientation individuals experience when their habitus developed in childhood does not match the social settings they encounter in adulthood.

8. Erickson 1996.

9. Barr-Melej 2001; Silva 2000; Stern 2021.

10. Solimano 2012.

11. Torche 2005.

12. Espinoza and Núñez 2014.

13. Franco and León 2010.

14. PNUD 2017.

15. Barozet et al. 2021; Banco Mundial and Gobierno de Chile 2020; World Bank 2021.

16. Torche and López-Cálva 2013; Banco Mundial and Gobierno de Chile 2020; Barozet et al. 2021.

17. These included El Liceo # 1 de Niñas, El Liceo #7 de Niñas, Carmela Carvajal, National Institute, and Salvador Sanfuentes Experimental School.

18. Friedman and Laurison 2019.

19. Interview, May 4, 2009.

20. Interview, November 18, 2008.

21. Interview, April 8, 2009.

22. Interview, March 23, 2009.

23. Interview, March 24, 2009.

24. Interview, April 22, 2009.

25. Interview, June 16, 2009.

26. Interview, May 14, 2009.

27. Compare Bourdieu 1996.

28. Interview, May 20, 2009.

29. PNUD 2010.

30. Adler Lomnitz and Melnick 1994.

31. PNUD 2017.

32. Interview, December 1, 2008.

33. Interview, May 4, 2010.

34. Interview May 27, 2009.

35. Interview, October 7, 2008.

36. Barr-Melej 2001; Silva 2000; Stern 2021.

37. PNUD 2017; Sehnbruch 2006.

38. Interview, November 20, 2008.

39. Interview, March 12, 2009.

40. Interview, May 3, 2010.

41. Franco and León 2010; Barozet and Espinoza 2008.

42. On fragility, see: Ferreira et al. 2013; Banco Mundial and Gobierno de Chile 2020; López-Calva and Ortiz Juárez 2014. For studies emphasizing upward mobility, see Castillo 2016; Mac-Clure 2012; Méndez and Gayo 2019.

43. PNUD 2010; Torche and López-Calva 2014; Barozet et al. 2021.

44. Hegewisch and Hartmann 2014.

45. Banco Mundial and Gobierno de Chile 2020; Barozet et al. 2021.

46. Interview, March 13, 2009.

47. Interview, March 6, 2009.

48. PNUD 2010; see Hutchison and Zárate Campos (2017) on professional women's distrust of nannies dating back to the 1960s.

49. Interview, June 16, 2009.

50. Hegewisch and Hartmann 2014; Williams 1995; PNUD 2010; PNUD 2017.

51. Interview, April 27, 2010.

52. Interview, May 15, 2009.

53. Interview, September 12, 2008.

54. Interview, June 5, 2009.

55. Gouldner 1979.

56. Brooks and Manza 1997.

57. Brint et al. 1997.

58. Parkin 1968; Weeden and Grusky 2012.

59. McAdam 1986.

60. Loveman 1998. See Vela Castañeda (2021) for use of this concept to understand high-risk activism during Guatemala's 1980s civil war.

61. McAdam 1989. Van Dyke et al. (2000) extend these findings by observing different biographical consequences of activism for men and women.

62. See Castillo 2016.

63. Interview, April 14, 2009.

64. Hutchison and Zárate Campos (2017, 281) note that as far back as the 1930s, observers recognized the fragile position of those receiving public jobs through political patronage.

65. Lamont 1992.

66. Bourdieu 1977.

67. Bourdieu 1996.

68. Weeden and Grusky 2012; Friedman and Laurison 2019. As noted above, earlier work argued that highly educated activists opt-in to educational and human services occupations: Parkin 1968.

69. Erickson 1996. While this author frames her analysis as a critique of Bourdieu's focus on cultural capital as an important resource in the labor market, I believe he would argue that high culture is a "field specific resource" that can be deployed effectively in some work settings (higher education, the public sector) and not others (private business). This view finds support in the contrast Friedman and Laurison (2019) draw between fields that emphasize high culture for screening and promoting employees, and those that require technical competence.

70. Interview, May 26, 2009.

71. Interview, November 10, 2008.

72. Un Techo Para Chile (2021) is a nonprofit founded in 1997 when student volunteers helped build a church in a small community. The organization uses donations and volunteer labor to build homes for the poor, much like Habitat for Humanity in the U.S. Since its founding, the organization expanded to other Latin American countries.

73. Brunner 2009.

74. Von Bülow and Bidegain Ponte 2015.

75. Brunner 2009.

76. The other two institutions referenced in his editorial are Universidad Adolfo Ibañez and the Universidad de los Andes. See Brunner 2009.

77. Interview, April 14, 2009.

78. Interview, June 8, 2009.

79. Solimano 2012.

80. Banco Mundial and Gobierno de Chile 2020; PNUD 2017; Barozet et al. 2021.

81. Compare Barozet et al. 2021.

82. Warde et al. 2007.

Chapter 2

1. Poggio 2008; Andreotti et al. 2015.

2. Savage et al. 2005.

3. Davis 1990; Caldeira 2000; Márquez and Pérez 2008; Svampa 2001; Álvarez-Rivadulla 2007.

4. Brown-Saracino 2017; Benson and Jackson 2018; Butler and Robson 2003; Lin 2019; Ocejo 2014.

5. Márquez and Pérez 2008.

6. Sabatini and Salcedo 2007.

7. López-Morales 2015, 2016.

8. Andreotti et al. 2015.

9. Bourdieu 1984; Holt 1998.

10. Alvayay and Schwartz 1997; Micco et al. 2012; Schneider 1995; Stern 2021; Martínez and Díaz 1996.

11. López-Morales 2015, 2016; Sabatini and Cáceres 2004; Salcedo 2004; Portes 1989; Marín et al. 2019; Ruiz-Tagle 2016; Rasse 2015; Sabatini et al. 2012; Méndez and Gayo 2019; Stern 2021.

12. López-Morales et al. 2014; López-Morales and Meza-Corvalán 2015; Stern 2021; Aguirre and León 2007.

13. Ruiz Tagle 2016; Pérez 2017, 2019.

14. Stillerman 2017.

15. See Boterman (2012), Hochstenbach and Boterman (2015), Clapham (2005), and Ford et al. (2002) for elaboration and application of the concept of housing pathways.

16. Compare Moor and Friedman 2021.

17. Poggio 2008; Andreotti et al. 2015.

18. Zavisca 2012.

19. Chile's private retirement fund managers charge notoriously high fees and offer meager monthly pay outs. Citizens and social movements have criticized the system established under the dictatorship, and only modest reforms have been enacted to date. Those protesting the pension plans participated in Chile's 2019 "social explosion." See Solimano 2012; Borzutsky 2010; Márquez 2020.

20. Interview, November 24, 2008.

21. Interview, May 29, 2009.

22. For overviews and examples, see: Brown-Saracino 2017; Lees et al. 2015; Caldera 2000.

23. Butler and Robson 2003.

24. Savage et al. 2005.

25. Benson 2014.

26. Bacqué et al. 2015; Andreotti et al. 2015.

27. Gieryn 2000; Anguelovski 2014.

28. See Firey (1945) for a classic analysis of this phenomenon.

29. Pierce et al. 2011.

30. Interview, November 17, 2008.

31. Interview, April 26, 2010.

32. Interview, December 22, 2008.

33. Interview, May 15, 2009.

34. Andreotti et al. 2015.

35. Savage 2014.

36. Compare Jackson and Benson 2014.

37. Contreras et al. 2010.

38. Méndez and Gayo 2019.

39. Interview, March 24, 2009.

40. Interview, March 13, 2009.

41. Interview, October 30, 2008.

42. Bourdieu 1984, 56.

43. Lamont 1992.

44. Interview, October 1, 2008.

45. Baudrillard 1996.

46. Holt 1998.

47. McCracken 2005.

48. Compare Pereyra 2015 on Lima, Perú.

49. Interview, March 11, 2009.

50. Interview, March 27, 2009.

51. Interview, May 18, 2009.

52. See Andreotti et al. 2015.

53. Poggio 2008; Andreotti et al. 2016.

54. Zavisca 2012.

55. On the flight from bland suburbs, see Butler and Robson (2003). On the desire to remain in urban communities near family, see Andreotti et al. (2015). In contrast, Lees et al. (2015) make the case for a broader definition of gentrification that would include the move to gated communities in poor suburbs. It is unclear, however, whether this development actually leads to displacement of poor residents, which is a keystone to understandings of urban gentrification. See Sabatini and Salcedo (2007).

Chapter 3

1. An earlier version of this chapter written in Spanish appeared in Stillerman (2016).

2. Bourdieu and Passeron 1979, 1990; Bourdieu 1984, 1996.

3. Ball et al. 1995; Ball and Vincent 1998; Ball 2003; Pugh 2009.

4. Lareau 2003.

5. Reay et al. 2011; Raveaud and Van Zanten 2007.

6. Contreras et al. 2010.

7. Elacqua et al. 2006.

8. PNUD 2017, 301.

9. Raczynski et al. 2010; Rojas 2018; Leyton and Rojas 2017.

10. Chile joined the OECD in 2010 based on its economic performance, but its ed-

ucational outcomes lag behind other member countries: Solimano 2012; PNUD 2017; Barozet et al. 2021.

11. Lareau 2014.

12. Lareau 2003.

13. Carrasco et al. 2017.

14. Álves et al. 2015.

15. While charter performance is better than that of public schools at the high school level, this may reflect parents' class background more than the quality of education provided: Mizala and Torche 2017. Further, recent improvements in test scores (from 2002–2013) reflect rising educational attainment among parents rather than market competition generating improved school performance: Hofflinger and von Hippel 2020.

16. Rojas 2018; Carrasco et al. 2017; Santos and Elacqua 2016.

17. There is conflicting evidence about whether or not low income students' test scores improved in schools that opted into SEP: Mizala and Torche 2017; Elacqua and Santos 2013; Rojas 2018; Aguirre 2022. On the 2015 School Inclusion Law, see: Muñoz 2017; Rojas 2018; Carrasco et al. 2021.

18. Contreras et al. 2010; Carrasco et al. 2017; Zancajo 2019.

19. Gayo et al. 2019; Bellei et al. 2020.

20. Thieme and Treviño 2013; Bellei et al. 2020; Contreras et al. 2010; Elacqua et al. 2006; Hsieh and Urquiola 2006.

21. Raczynski et al. 2010.

22. Flores and Carrasco 2013.

23. Valenzuela and Somma 2018; Stern 2021.

24. Lareau 2014. As noted in the previous chapter, some parents select a school first and must settle some distance from that school due to the lack of affordable housing near those schools, but her concept of microclimates still captures specific features of local school markets.

25. Biblioteca del Congreso Nacional de Chile 2015a; Chile, Ministerio de Educación 2015a.

26. It would be intriguing to compare parents' choices across the three types of schools in this community. One family in the sample that had migrated to Santiago from the provinces first sent their daughter to a public school but then moved her to a private school after they were disappointed with the results. The two school administrators I interviewed in Ñuñoa saw public schools as competitors, so they do play an important role in Ñuñoa's market and are thus worthy of study by future researchers.

27. Stern 2021: 170; Hutchison and Zárate Campos 2017; Rosemblatt 2000; Labarca 2009. (Labarca's article originally appeared in 1950.)

28. Liceo Experimental Manuel de Salas 2020; Serrano 2018. Stern (2021) describes the school's first three decades, highlighting how its innovations shaped Chilean public education.

29. This activism built on a tradition dating back to the 1950s: Stern 2021.

30. Interview, November 12, 2008.

31. Fleet and Smith 1997.

32. Valenzuela and Somma 2018; Stern 2021.

33. Méndez and Gayo 2019; Gayo et al. 2019; Bellei et al. 2020.

34. Solimano 2012, 104.

35. Escuelas Pias—Colegio Calasanz 2022.

36. Interview with Carlos, a school administrator, April 6, 2009.

37. A Chilean priest dedicated to the poor that was beatified in recent years.

38. For more details on Calasanz's persecution, later acceptance by church authorities, and friendship with Galileo, see Church of St. Helena (2021).

39. Sofia's sister's children attended the Grange school, one of the top elite private
schools. She commented that this school was unaffordable for her.

40. Patricia considered sending her son to St. George, a prominent elite school
where her husband's family members sent their children. However, she commented
that it was both too expensive and too inconveniently located for her. Ernesto, like
Marcelo, also considered Kent School, but determined it was too expensive.

41. Interview, March 25, 2009.

42. Biblioteca del Congreso Nacional de Chile 2015b; Chile, Ministerio de Educación 2015b.

43. Colegio Raimapu 2022; Romero 2011; Bartlett 2022.

44. El Colegio Latinoamericano de la Integración is located near La Florida. It
became well known when military officials assassinated a communist teacher there
along with two of his associates: Memoria Chilena 2020. Francisco de Miranda is a
well-known progressive school where some parents at LMS sent their children for a
time.

45. Interview, May 3, 2009.

46. Colegio Raíces Altazor 2022.

47. Field notes, April 30, 2009.

48. Interview, May 26, 2009.

49. Colegio Rosario Concha 2022.

50. Field notes, May 5, 2009.

51. I conducted a small number of interviews at Colegio Alcántara, and the son of
one of the Raíces parents attended their high school. Alcántara is a secular charter
school focused on academic excellence. I did not conduct a sufficient number of interviews at this school to gain a clear sense of its mission and social dynamics, but I
refer to these interviews periodically because they added to my smaller pool of lower-
middle-class parents, and the individuals I interviewed offered important perspectives and insights on education and symbolic boundaries in La Florida. My initial
snowball sample of parents in Ñuñoa and La Florida likewise yielded helpful context
regarding traditional and alternative schools in these two communities, and I make
periodic reference to these interviews where appropriate.

52. Interview, June 15, 2009.

53. Interview, April 26, 2010.

54. On concerted cultivation, see: Lareau 2003. To paraphrase Hayes (1991), inten-

sive mothering is a laborious, time-consuming, and emotionally demanding style of childrearing that requires extensive expertise. Compare Kimelberg (2014b) regarding parents "hedging their bets."

55. Méndez and Gayo 2019; Bellei et al. 2020; Gubbins Foxley 2014.

56. Bourdieu 1984; Atkinson 2017.

57. Weinberger et al. 2017; Rivera 2015; Friedman and Laurison 2019.

58. Miguel seems to refer to the fact that only students at state-supported universities, which have the most selective admissions policies, are eligible for low interest loans—so called "solidarity credits." Students at private universities rely on parents' resources and/or government-backed loans with higher interest rates. See Von Bülow and Bidegain Ponte 2015.

59. PNUD 2017; Barozet et al. 2021.

60. The two exceptions were both lower-middle-class teachers, who offered similar, but less elaborate reasons for sending their children to Raíces as did more affluent activists.

Chapter 4

1. Interview, March 11, 2009.

2. Interview, May 13, 2009.

3. Pugh 2009.

4. Sherman 2017.

5. Raveaud and Van Zanten 2007.

6. Reay et al. 2011.

7. Kimelberg 2014a.

8. Rojas 2018; Raczynski 2010; Canales et al. 2016.

9. Ocejo 2014.

10. Elias and Scotson 1994.

11. Lamont 1992.

12. Elias and Scotson 1994.

13. Bellei et al. 2019; Gayo et al. 2019.

14. Interview, March 13, 2009.

15. Interview, April 7, 2009.

16. Interview, April 6, 2009.

17. Interview, May 13, 2009.

18. Riquelme 2018.

19. Mauricio, the LMS school administrator I interviewed, commented, "We used to have 1,200 students and now we have 1,500, but other schools nearby have lost some students. We're all competing to attract the same students because fertility rates are lower and the government has invested in high-performing public schools." Interview, April 7, 2009.

20. Lamont 1992.

21. Olga, an Alcántara parent, similarly remarks, "My daughter used to go to another school. It was good at first, but once she got into third grade, it started going

downhill. They began admitting poorly behaved children [*niños más conflictivos*]. I also thought the principal didn't take his job very seriously, so I moved her to Alcántara." Rossana, also an Alcántara parent, describes her own self-isolation: "I used to be very active in the kids' schools, but I've distanced myself from other parents because I don't feel like my life is very interesting. It's tedious because it seems like one bad thing happens after another. My work is nonstop, the environment isn't always the best, we have problems at home, and so sometimes I just pull back." As noted in chapter 1, Rossana is a breast cancer survivor and single mother.

22. Pugh 2009; Reay et al. 2011.

23. Lareau 2003; Calarco 2018.

24. Contreras et al. 2010.

25. Rojas 2018.

26. Borzutsky and Weeks 2010; Aravena and Núñez 2009; Kubal 2010; Silva and Rodrigo 2010; Donoso 2013; Ríos 2021.

27. Sehnbruch 2010.

28. Funk 2010, 57.

29. Von Bülow and Bidegain Ponte 2015, 187.

30. See Stern (2021, 198–209) for evidence of student and parent activism at LMS dating back to the 1950s.

31. Focus group with study participants, June 20, 2009.

32. Ciper 2016.

33. Liceo Experimental Manuel de Salas 2018.

34. Chanfreau's grandfather, a University of Chile philosophy professor and militant of the Movement of the Revolutionary Left party (MIR, a guerrilla party inspired by the Cuban Revolution) was disappeared during the dictatorship. Chanfreau was a regular figure on television during Chile's months-long social explosion as he expertly debated news program hosts and helped organize a student boycott of college entrance exams (Muñoz and Fava 2020).

35. Romero 2011; Bartlett 2022.

36. Interview with Mauricio, April 7, 2009; Colegio Raimapu 2022.

37. Reay et al. 2011; Pugh 2009; Sherman 2017.

38. Field notes, April 14, 2009.

39. See Brunner 2009.

40. Von Bülow and Bidegain Ponte 2015, 188.

41. Elacqua and Aninat 2013; Barozet et al. 2021.

42. As explained in the last chapter, activists and moderate Catholics were confident that they could "hedge their bets" through concerted cultivation to supplement any academic deficits at their children's schools. This dual-track approach to education allowed them to adhere to their moral and political values while continuing to support their children's education.

43. Weber 1978. Compare Bellei et al. 2020; Gayo et al. 2019.

44. Compare Coser 1954; Simmel 1955.

45. Bourdieu 1984, 1993, 2005.

46. See: Bourdieu and Passeron 1990.

47. Valenzuela and Somma 2018; Stern 2021.

Chapter 5

1. Fundación Pablo Neruda 2022.

2. Loveman 1986.

3. Bourdieu 1984. For updates to Bourdieu's argument that identify differences in aesthetic tastes based on class, gender, age, and ethnicity, see Bennett et al. 1999, Bennett et al. 2009, and Madigan and Munro 1996.

4. Halle 1993.

5. Woodward 2001, 2003.

6. Csikszentmihalyi and Rochberg-Halton 1981; McCracken 2005; Money 2007.

7. Holt 1998.

8. Atkinson 2017; Jarness et al. 2019.

9. See Woodward 2001, 2003.

10. Holt 1998.

11. Money 2007.

12. Madigan and Munro 1996; Silva and Wright 2009; Savage 2014; Bennett et al. 2009.

13. Money 2007.

14. Holt 1998.

15. Money 2007.

16. Bourdieu 1984.

17. Halle 1993.

18. Bourdieu 1984. While I found distinct patterns of identity investments across different occupational, age cohort, and income groups, I do not claim that we can generalize based on these inductively derived patterns that occupational position *causes* specific types of identity investments, given the statistically small and nonrandom character of this sample. Rather, my goal is to identify and interpret patterns in the qualitative sample as a way to improve existing theories (Burawoy 1998) and to develop new theoretical ideas (Tavory and Timmermans 2014). This exercise in theory development using a qualitative sample divided between upper- and lower-middle-class individuals (others make similar distinctions between high- and low-cultural-capital individuals or middle-class and working-class persons) mirrors theoretically innovative studies: see Holt 1998; Üstüner and Holt 2010; Lareau 2003; Weinberger et al. 2017; and Cairns and Johnston 2015, among others.

19. Jarness et al. 2019; Atkinson 2017.

20. Warde et al. 2007.

21. See McCracken 1988; Berta 2019.

22. Conny, an activist psychiatrist married to a physician, was part of the initial snowball sample. Her husband received a painting from his relative, the widow of Juan Downey, an internationally famous Chilean multi-multimedia artist who spent much of his career in New York City: Artnet 2020. This seems to fit the pattern described

above, but Conny and her husband are very involved in the arts. She took several art courses and exhibited her work, had various art books on her living room table and reproductions hanging on her walls, had numerous artist friends, and routinely visited galleries with her husband. Conny and her husband were voracious consumers of music, fiction, poetry, and highbrow sports like tennis. Their orientation fits more closely with activists discussed below who display cultural capital through their artistic knowledge. Her scholastic interest in art likely reflects the fact that her parents are college professors rather than businesspersons.

23. The Schönstatt movement honoring the Virgin Mary originated in Germany in 1914. Nuns belonging to the movement established chapters in South America beginning in 1933 in response to Hitler's rise to power: Schönstatt Sisters of Mary 2022.

24. Mujeres Bacanas 2021.

25. Paci, who was part of the initial snowball sample, owns six paintings produced by artist friends: "I've gone to all of their exhibitions. If I had more money, I would buy more artwork. I love sculpture, but I don't have a house that is big enough to display one. To have art, you need to own a house. Art is elitist."

26. Servicio Nacional del Patrimonio Cultural (2015) provides an overview of Carreño's work and its importance within the Chilean artistic field.

27. Mapuche is an umbrella category for the largest group of indigenous nations in Chile. Members of this group have historically resided in rural southern Chile, but the majority of Mapuches now live in cities. Mapuche activists have waged a decades' long struggle to recuperate ancestral lands in southern Chile, and in 2021, they finally gained political representation in the Constitutional Convention. See Silva and Rodrigo 2010; Richards 2010; Torres-Salinas 2016; Sepúlveda and Zúñiga 2015; Warren 2017; and Ríos 2021.

28. Lara-Lara 2019.

29. Rodríguez-Merino 2018.

30. Two individuals in the La Florida snowball sample displayed Guayasamín reproductions in their home and office, respectively, in addition to several Manuel de Salas parents.

31. Compare Wherry 2008.

32. While Tamara and Luis live in La Florida, they are part of the Ñuñoa diaspora described in chapter 2, and they have a strong social network at Manuel de Salas. Ricardo and Gloria live in Puente Alto, near La Florida, but Gloria grew up in the affluent community of Las Condes.

33. This hypothesis is based on the visual features of the homes I observed as well as the symbolic boundaries individuals constructed with others as described throughout this book. Additionally, the contrasts in home interiors between the communities that I observed approximate the distinctions developed by Chilean market researchers between those in the 80th and 90th percentile of earnings and living in Ñuñoa and nearby communities (C1 segment), with those earning between the 60th and 80th percentiles of income and living in or near La Florida (C2 segment). However, in my sample, upper-middle-class incomes did not vary substantially across communities.

My hypothesis is that upper-middle-class La Florida families in the sample assimilated the more modest style of home decoration that was common in the community. Other researchers may wish to explore this hypothesis further by developing larger scale research designs. See AIM 2008, 19–22.

34. Bellavance 2016.

35. Bourdieu and Darbel 1990. Lisette's mother is an art teacher, but she lives in a provincial city and hence was less connected to dominant artistic institutions and networks in Santiago.

36. I observed Egyptian prints in two moderate Catholics' homes, but the homeowners did not express a strong emotional attachment to these items.

37. Woodward 2001, 2003.

38. Compare McCracken 2005.

39. Compare Ariztía 2014.

40. Holt 1998.

41. Compare Madigan and Munro 1996; McCracken 2005.

42. Compare Madigan and Munro 1996; Laumann and House 1970.

43. Compare Parker 2012; Lamont 1992; Stern 2021.

44. Woodward 2001, 2003.

45. Money 2007; McCracken 2005; Csikszentmihalyi and Rochberg-Halton 1981.

46. Holt 1998.

47. Bourdieu 1984.

48. Halle 1993.

49. Atkinson 2017; Jarness et al. 2019.

50. Woodward 2001, 2003; Lamont 1992.

Chapter 6

1. Dreier et al. 2014. Others have observed middle-class activism to restrict new low income housing construction and poor people's housing activism in the community: Ruiz-Tagle 2016; Pérez 2017, 2019.

2. Bourdieu 1984.

3. Peterson and Kern 1996.

4. Warde et al. 2007; Savage and Gayo 2011; Ollivier 2008.

5. See Roy 2010 and Gayo 2011 for exceptions.

6. Warde et al. 2007; Cutts and Widdop 2017.

7. Compare Peters 2012.

8. Serrano 2018.

9. Notimex 2014; Revista Don 2020.

10. Jordán 2009.

11. Barr-Melej 2017.

12. The Art Story 2020.

13. Artnet 2020.

14. Errázuriz 2009; Errázuriz and Leiva Quijada 2012; Jordán 2009; Barbancho 2014; Vega 2013; Bresnahan 2002; González 2016.

15. García Canclini 2001; Straubhaar 2007; Santibáñez et al. 2012; Wang et al. 2000; Hopewell and Lang 2019.

16. De Cea 2018; Santibañez et al. 2012.

17. See Consejo Nacional de la Cultura y el Arte (CNCA) 2018.

18. Torche 2007.

19. Gayo and Teitelboim 2009; Leguina et al. 2017.

20. Gayo 2011.

21. Torche 2010; Santibáñez et al. 2012; Gayo et al. 2009, 2013, 2016; Gayo 2017; Méndez and Gayo 2019; Murray and Ureta 2005.

22. P. Torche 2005; Bellavance 2016.

23. Gayo 2017; Campos Medina 2012.

24. Lareau 2003.

25. Holt 1998; Bourdieu 1984.

26. Parker 2012; Stern 2021.

27. Cáceres et al. 2006.

28. Moulian 1997, 1998; compare Van Bavel and Sell-Trujillo 2003; Lechner 2002.

29. Stillerman and Salcedo 2012; Ossandón 2014; González 2018; Marambio Tapia 2018; Barozet et al. 2021.

30. Tinsman 2014.

31. Stillerman 2004, 2012.

32. Compare Pugh 2009; Sherman 2017.

33. Peterson and Kern 1996.

34. Compare Warde et al. 2007; Savage and Gayo 2011; Gayo et al. 2013.

35. Friedman 2012; Lahire 2016.

36. Gayo 2011; Marín et al. 2019.

37. Jordán 2009; González 2016; Bresnahan 2002.

38. Atkinson 2011.

39. Murray and Ureta 2005.

40. Interview, November 10, 2008.

41. Murray and Ureta 2005.

42. Interview, May 6, 2009.

43. In the previous chapter, Luis and Tamara described purchasing a painting at a charity auction. Several Ñuñoa activists in the snowball sample attended art galleries regularly. These individuals were either practicing visual artists or had close friendships with creative professionals.

44. Irby 1967.

45. Others highlight their children's interest in current events. Tomás, a Raíces parent, remarks: "Our three kids are well informed. They follow the news on the internet, television, and through print media. They're not just reading the crime pages; they are seeking out the latest scientific advances. Since I work with biotechnology and am learning about the latest discoveries and research results in the field, I discuss it with them. They're curious and well informed." Tomás's work in science and technology influences his children's interests in this field rather than in literature.

46. Field notes, November 8, 2008; April 17, 2009; May 22, 2009.

47. A few Raíces parents did have friends through school as noted in chapter 4. However, their main friendship network was outside of school.

48. Claudio and Javiera, both Calasanz parents, also do volunteer work outside school with the blind and at a hospital.

49. In a contrasting view, Nelson, a Rosario parent, is reluctant to take his children to the movies due to his rejection of commercial entertainment: "Most of the movies are made in Hollywood. It's like taking them to McDonald's. Culturally, it's a waste of time. It's similar to when you watch TV: you stop communicating—it's problematic." This comment is reminiscent of activists' views that art must enlighten and moderate Catholics' fears of the corrupting influence of video games. However, this was a minority view among youngsters.

50. Compare Bennett et al. 2009 and Savage 2014.

51. Leguina et al. 2017; Gayo and Teitelboim 2009; Gayo et al. 2016; Murray and Ureta 2005; Santibáñez et al. 2012.

52. Bennett et al. 2009; Savage and Gayo 2011.

53. Bennett et al. 2009; Murray and Ureta 2005.

54. Murray and Ureta 2005.

55. Savage et al. 2005; Butler and Robson 2003; Bacqué et al. 2015.

56. Warde et al. 2007.

57. Cutts and Widdop 2017.

58. Zukin 2012; Lloyd 2010; Ocejo 2014; Lin 2019: Schlack and Turnbull 2015.

59. Poduje 2008.

60. Compare Sagaris 2014; Méndez 2018; Angelcos 2021; Hölzl 2018.

61. Centro Cultural La Florida 2020; Corporación Cultural de Ñuñoa 2020a, 2020b.

62. Reyes Päcke et al. (2010) show that Santiago's three wealthiest communities (Las Condes, Vitacura, and La Reina) contain the largest, most accessible green areas, and these areas are smaller and less accessible in communities with lower incomes.

63. Here, Tomás combines the Chilean colloquial term *fome*, which means "boring," with *domingo* (Sunday).

64. Interview, April 30, 2009.

65. Cable TV was widely available at the time. In fact, my daughter watched their show on television while we lived in Providencia, located near Ñuñoa.

66. López-Morales et al. 2014; López-Morales and Meza-Corvalán 2015; Poduje 2008; Aguirre and León 2007.

67. In contrast, Ruiz-Tagle (2016) describes middle-class residents' efforts to block social housing construction near their homes. Pérez (2017, 2019) describes poor residents' demands for access to low-income housing that builds on earlier housing struggles in the community. These conflicts highlight more intense cross-class tensions in La Florida that undermine trust among neighbors, as I have argued.

68. Dreier et al. 2014. Méndez et al. 2021 argue that neighborhood cohesion is strongly associated with the advantages enjoyed by residents of privileged communities. The Ñuñoa mobilization may have benefited from such resources, though the community hosts a mixed-income population.

69. Gayo 2017.

70. See: Moulian 1997, 1998.

71. Peterson and Kern 1996.

72. See Méndez et al. 2021 for an exception.

Conclusion

1. Bourdieu 1984.

2. Lechner 2002; Moulian 1997, 1998.

3. Méndez 2018, Barozet and Espinoza 2016, and Barozet et al. 2021 are exceptions to this general trend.

4. For place-based understandings of middle classes, see: Méndez et al. 2021; Butler and Robson 2003; Bacqué et al. 2015; Savage et al. 2005; Andreotti et al. 2015.

5. Andreotti et al. 2015; Poggio 2008; Zavisca 2012.

6. Lareau 2014.

7. Bourdieu 1984.

8. Abramson and Inglehart 1995; Fishman and Lizardo 2013.

9. Méndez et al. 2021; Butler and Robson 2003; Bacqué et al. 2015; Savage et al. 2005; Andreotti et al. 2015.

10. Barozet and Espinoza 2016; Elacqua and Aninat 2013; Barozet et al. 2021.

11. Fishman and Lizardo 2013.

12. Larson and Lizardo 2007.

13. Abramson and Inglehart 1995.

14. Donoso 2013; Roberts 2017; Palacios-Valladares 2016.

15. Reay et al. 2011; Sherman 2017; Raveaud and Van Zanten 2007.

16. Lareau 2014.

17. Cutts and Widdop 2017; Warde et al. 2007; Savage et al. 2005.

18. Compare Méndez et al. 2021; Bacqué et al. 2015; Zukin 2012; Ocejo 2014; Lin 2019.

19. Walker 2013.

20. García-Bryce 2012.

21. Schielke 2012.

22. Srivastava 2012.

23. Barr-Melej 2001; Silva 2000; Drake 1978; Rosemblatt 2000; Stern 2021.

24. Stern (2021) argues that the mid-twentieth-century middle classes included public and private employees as well as small business owners.

25. This process has also occurred in wealthy nations: Savage et al. 1992.

26. Compare Davis 2010.

27. Walker 2013.

28. Ozarow 2019.

29. Collier and Collier 1991.

30. Lamont 1992; Lamont 2000.

31. Caldeira 2000.

32. Pereyra 2015.

33. Lamont 2000; Jackson and Benson 2014.

34. See Parraguez 2016.

35. Palacios-Valladares 2016.

36. Parraguez 2016: 86–87; Biblioteca del Congreso Nacional 2020a, 2020b, 2020c; Palacios-Valladares 2016; Von Bülow and Bidegain Ponte 2015.

37. Parraguez 2016; Araujo and Martucelli 2012.

38. Muñoz and Fava 2020.

39. Parraguez 2016; Palacios Valladares 2016; Bellei et al. 2020; PNUD 2017.

40. Borzutsky 2005; Rozas and Maillet 2019.

41. González and Figueroa 2019.

42. Torres-Salinas et al. 2016.

43. Serrano 2018; DeShazo 1983.

44. Silva 2000; Stern 2021.

45. Barozet and Silva 2016.

46. Mayol 2020; Márquez 2020; Villalobos-Ruminott 2020; Leiva 2020; BBC 2021a; Ríos 2021; Molina 2020.

47. Statista 2021a.

48. Statista 2021b.

49. Valenzuela Levi 2021; T13 2021.

50. Bartlett 2022.

51. Boric and Apruebo Dignidad 2021.

52. La Tercera 2022; Montes 2022.

Appendix

1. Franco and León 2010; Castillo 2016; Méndez 2008; Heiman et al. 2012; Üstüner and Holt 2010; Davis 2010.

2. Stern 2021.

3. Ruiz-Tagle 2016; Pérez 2017, 2019.

4. Calarco 2018; Pugh 2009.

5. I conducted three interviews at Alcántara Cordillera, a secular traditional school. I had less success recruiting parents there and thus focused on the other three La Florida schools. The interviews did serve as a valuable contrast to the other La Florida schools.

6. Small 2009.

7. Bourdieu 1984.

8. Bennett et al. 1999.

9. Savage et al. 2005.

10. Bennett et al. 2009.

11. Méndez and Gayo 2019.

12. Halle 1993; Woodward 2001, 2003; Money 2007; Csikszentmihalyi and Rochberg-Halton 1981.

13. Duneier 1999; Desmond 2016.

14. Glaser and Strauss 1967.

15. Burawoy 1998; Tavory and Timmermans 2014.

16. Tavory and Timmermans 2014.

17. Duneier 1999; Desmond 2016; Fridman 2016; Reyes 2019; Contreras 2013.

18. Stillerman 2003.

19. Stillerman 2004; Stillerman 2012; Stillerman and Salcedo 2012.

References

Abramson, Paul R., and Ronald Inglehart. 1995. *Value Change in Global Perspective.* Ann Arbor: University of Michigan Press.

Adler Lomnitz, Larissa, and Ana Melnick. 1994. "La Clase Media, las Redes Sociales y el Modelo Neo-liberal: El Caso de los Profesores Chilenos (1973–1988)." *Reforma y Democracia* (July): 1–12.

Aguirre, Josefa. 2022. "How Can Progressive Vouchers Help the Poor Benefit from School Choice? Evidence from the Chilean Voucher System." *Journal of Human Resources* 57(3): 956-997.

Aguirre N., Carlos, and Daniela León L. 2007. "Analisis descriptivo de la evolución urbana de la comuna de Ñuñoa 2001 a 2006." *Urbano* 10(16): 60–72.

Álvarez-Rivadulla, María José. 2007. "Golden Ghettos: Gated Communities and Class Residential Segregation in Montevideo, Uruguay." *Environment and Planning A* 39(1): 47–63.

Alvayay, Jaime R., and Arthur L. Schwartz. 1997. "Housing and Mortgage Market Policies in Chile." *Journal of Real Estate Literature* 5(1): 47–55.

Álves, Fatima, Gregory Elacqua, Mariane Koslinki, Matias Martinez, Humberto Santos, and Daniela Urbina. 2015. "Winners and Losers of School Choice: Evidence from Rio de Janeiro, Brazil and Santiago, Chile." *International Journal of Educational Development* 41: 25–34.

Andreotti, Alberta, Patrick Le Galès, and Francisco Javier Moreno-Fuentes. 2015. *Globalised Minds, Roots in the City: Urban Upper-Middle Classes in Europe.* Malden, MA: John Wiley & Sons.

Angelcos, Nicolás. 2021. "Luchas por el significado del derecho a la ciudad: el caso de la coordinadora 'Plebiscito por La Reina,' Santiago de Chile." *EURE* 47(140): 179–197.

Angell, Alan. 1972. *Politics and the Labor Movement in Chile*. Oxford: Oxford University Press.

Anguelovski, Isabelle. 2014. *Neighborhood as Refuge: Community Reconstruction, Place Remaking, and Environmental Justice in the City*. Cambridge, MA: MIT Press.

Araujo, Kathya, and Danilo Martucelli. 2012. *Desafíos communes: Retrato de la sociedad chilena y sus individuos*. 2 vols. Santiago, Chile: LOM.

Aravena, A., and Daniel Núñez, eds. 2009. *El renacer de la huelga obrera en Chile*. Santiago: Instituto de Ciencias Alejandro Lipschutz.

Ariztía, Tomás. 2014. "Housing Markets Performing Class: Middle-Class Cultures and Market Professionals in Chile." *Sociological Review* 62(2): 400–420.

Artnet. 2020. "Juan Downey (Chilean, 1940–1993)." http://www.artnet.com/artists/juan-downey/ (accessed June 1, 2020).

The Art Story. 2020. "Roberto Matta." https://www.theartstory.org/artist/matta-roberto/life-and-legacy/#biography_header (accessed June 1, 2020).

Asociación Chilena de Empresas Investigadores de Mercado (AIM). 2008. *Grupos Socioeconomicos 2008*. http://www.aimchile.cl/wp-content/uploads/2011/12/Grupos_Socioeconomicos_AIM-2008.pdf (accessed August 26, 2019).

Asociación de Investigadores de Mercado (AIM). 2018. *Nuevos Grupos Socioeconómicos 2018 AIM CHILE* (February). http://www.aimchile.cl/wp-content/uploads/Nuevos-Grupos-Socioeconomicos-AIM-febrero-2018-FINAL-2.pdf (accessed August 26, 2019).

Atkinson Will. 2011. "The Context and Genesis of Musical Tastes: Omnivorousness Debunked, Bourdieu Buttressed." *Poetics* 39(3): 169–186.

Atkinson, Will. 2017. *Class in the New Millennium: The Structure, Homologies and Experience of the British Social Space*. London: Routledge.

Bacqué, Marie-Hélène, Gary Bridge, Michaela Benson, Tim Butler, Eric Charmes, Yankel Fijalkow, Emma Jackson, Lydie Launay, and Stéphanie Vermeersch. 2015. *The Middle Classes and the City: A Study of Paris and London*. Houndmills: Palgrave Macmillan.

Ball, Stephen. 2003. *Class Strategies and the Education Market: The Middle Classes and Social Advantage*. London: Routledge Falmer.

Ball, Stephen J., Richard Bowe, and Sharon Gewirtz. 1995. "Circuits of Schooling: A Sociological Exploration of Parental Choice of School in Social Class Contexts." *Sociological Review* 43(1): 52–78.

Ball, Stephen J., and Carol Vincent. 1998. "'I Heard It on the Grapevine': 'Hot' Knowledge and School Choice." *British Journal of Sociology of Education* 19(3): 377–400.

Banco Mundial and Gobierno de Chile. 2020. *Producto 1. Conceptos de medición de los sectores medios, y análisis de movilidad descendiente en Chile*. Santiago: World Bank and Government of Chile. https://documents1.worldbank.org/curated/en/361791615533082000/pdf/Conceptos-de-Medicion-de-los-Sectores-Medios-y-Analisis-de-Movilidad-Descendiente-en-Chile.pdf (accessed September 5, 2021).

Banerjee, Abhijit V., and Esther Duflo. 2008. "What Is Middle Class about the Middle Classes around the World?" *Journal of Economic Perspectives* 22(2): 3–28.

Barbancho, Juan Ramón. 2014. "Arte, sociedad y política: otras formas de protesta." *Arte y Sociedad: Revista de Investigación* 6: 1–7.

Barozet, Emmanuelle, Dante Contreras, Vicente Espinoza, Modesto Gayo, and María Luisa Méndez. 2021. "Clases medias en tiempos de crisis: Vulnerabilidad persistente, desafíos para la cohesión y un nuevo pacto social en Chile." *Documentos de Proyectos* (LC/TS.2021/101). Santiago, Comisión Económica para América Latina y el Caribe (CEPAL).

Barozet, Emmanuelle, and Vicente Espinoza. 2008. "Quienes pertenecen a la clase media en Chile? Una aproximación metodológica." *Ecuador Debate* (Abril): 103–122.

Barozet, Emmanuelle, and Vicente Espinoza. 2016. "Current Issues on the Political Representation of Middle Classes in Chile." *Journal of Politics in Latin America* 8(3): 95–123.

Barr-Melej, Patrick. 2001. *Reforming Chile: Cultural Politics, Nationalism, and the Rise of the Middle Class.* Chapel Hill: University of North Carolina Press.

Barr-Melej, Patrick. 2017. *Psychedelic Chile: Youth, Counterculture, and Politics on the Road to Socialism and Dictatorship.* Chapel Hill, NC: University of North Carolina Press.

Bartlett, John. 2022. "Chile's President-Elect Names Progressive, Majority-Women Cabinet." *The Guardian,* January 21, 2022. https://www.theguardian.com/world/2022/jan/21/chile-gabriel-boric-cabinet-majority-women.

Baudrillard, Jean. 1996. *The System of Objects.* Translated by James Benedict. Verso: New York.

BBC. 2021a. "Elecciones en Chile: candidatos independientes y de la oposición dominan la asamblea que redactará la nueva Constitución." *BBC,* May 17, 2021. https://www.bbc.com/mundo/noticias-america-latina-57139669 .

BBC. 2021b. "Elecciones Chile 2021: Boric logra un contundente triunfo sobre Kast y es el presidente electo del país." *BBC,* December 20, 2021. https://www.bbc.com/mundo/noticias-america-latina-59722345.

Bellavance, Guy. 2016. "The Multiplicity of Highbrow Culture: Taste Boundaries among the New Upper Middle Class." In *Routledge International Handbook of the Sociology of Art and Culture,* edited by Laurie Hanquinet and Mike Savage, 324–336. London: Routledge.

Bellei, Cristián, Víctor Orellana, and Manuel Canales. 2020 "Elección de escuela en la clase alta chilena: comunidad, identidad y cierre social." *Archivos analíticos de políticas educativas* 27(5): 1–22.

Bellin, Eva. 2010. "The Dog That Didn't Bark: The Political Complacence of the Emerging Middle Class (with Illustrations from the Middle East)." *Political Power and Social Theory* 21: 125–141.

Benson, Michaela. 2014. "Trajectories of Middle-Class Belonging: The Dynamics of Place Attachment and Classed Identities." *Urban Studies* 51(14): 3097–3112.

Benson, Michaela, and Emma Jackson. 2018. "From Class to Gentrification and Back Again." In *The Handbook of Gentrification Studies,* edited by Loretta Lees and Martin Phillips, 63–80. London: Edward Elgar.

Bennett, Tony, Michael Emmison, and John Frow. 1999. *Accounting for Tastes: Australian Everyday Cultures*. Cambridge: Cambridge University Press.

Bennett, Tony, Mike Savage, Elisabeth Silva, Alan Warde, Modesto Gayo-Cal, and David Wright. 2009. *Culture, Class, Distinction*. London: Routledge.

Berta, Péter. 2019. *Materializing Difference: Consumer Culture, Politics, and Ethnicity among Romanian Roma*. Toronto: University of Toronto Press.

Biblioteca del Congreso Nacional de Chile. 2015a. "Población por grupos de edad 2002 y proyectada 2012 INE." http://reportescomunales.bcn.cl/2012/index.php/%C3%91u%C3%B1oa#Poblaci.C3.B3n_por_grupos_de_edad_2002_y_proyectada_2012_INE (accessed August 16, 2015).

Biblioteca del Congreso Nacional de Chile. 2015b. "Población por grupos de edad 2002 y proyectada 2012 INE." http://reportescomunales.bcn.cl/2012/index.php/La_Florida#Poblaci.C3.B3n_por_grupos_de_edad_2002_y_proyectada_2012_INE (accessed August 16, 2015).

Biblioteca del Congreso Nacional de Chile. 2020a. "Karol Aída Cariola Oliva: Reseñas biográficas parlamentarias." https://www.bcn.cl/historiapolitica/resenas_parlamentarias/wiki/Karol_A%C3%ADda_Cariola_Oliva (accessed August 12, 2020).

Biblioteca del Congreso Nacional de Chile. 2020b. "Kenneth Giorgio Jackson Drago: Reseñas biográficas parlamentarias." https://www.bcn.cl/historiapolitica/resenas_parlamentarias/wiki/Kenneth_Giorgio_Jackson_Drago (accessed August 12, 2020).

Biblioteca del Congreso Nacional de Chile. 2020c. "Gabriel Boric Font: Reseñas biográficas parlamentarias." https://www.bcn.cl/historiapolitica/resenas_parlamentarias/wiki/Gabriel_Boric_Font (accessed August 12, 2020).

Biekart, Kees. 2015. "The Choice of the New Latin American Middle Classes: Sharing or Self-Caring." *European Journal of Development Research* 27(2): 238–245.

Boric, Gabriel, and Apruebo Dignidad. 2021. *Programa de Gobierno Apruebo Dignidad*. https://s3.amazonaws.com/cdn.boricpresidente.cl/web/programa/Plan+de+gobierno+AD+2022-2026+(2).pdf (accessed January 26, 2020).

Borzutsky, Silvia. 2005. "From Chicago to Santiago: Neoliberalism and Social Security Privatization in Chile." *Governance: An International Journal of Policy, Administration, and Institutions* 18(4): 655–674.

Borzutsky, Silvia. 2010. "Socioeconomic Policies: Taming the Market in a Globalized Economy." In *The Bachelet Government: Conflict and Consensus in Post-Pinochet Chile*, edited by Silvia Borzutsky and Gregory Weeks, 87–116. Gainesville: University Press of Florida.

Borzutsky, Silva, and Gregory Weeks. 2010. "Introduction." In *The Bachelet Government: Conflict and Consensus in Post-Pinochet Chile*, edited by Silvia Borzutsky and Gregory Weeks, 1–26. Gainesville: University Press of Florida.

Boterman, Willem R. 2012. "Deconstructing Coincidence: How Middle-Class Households Use Various Forms of Capital to Find a Home." *Housing, Theory and Society* 29(3): 321–338.

Bourdieu, Pierre. 1977. *Outline of a Theory of Practice*. Translated by Richard Nice. Cambridge, UK: Cambridge University Press.

Bourdieu, Pierre. 1984. *Distinction: A Social Critique of the Judgment of Taste.* Translated by Richard Nice. Cambridge, MA: Harvard University Press.

Bourdieu, Pierre. 1988. *Homo Academicus.* Translated by Peter Collier. Cambridge, UK: Polity.

Bourdieu, Pierre. 1993. *The Field of Cultural Production: Essays on Art and Literature.* Translated by Randal Johnson. New York: Columbia University Press.

Bourdieu, Pierre. 1996. *The State Nobility.* Translated by Lauretta C. Clough. Cambridge, UK: Polity.

Bourdieu, Pierre. 2005. *The Social Structures of the Economy.* Translated by Chris Turner. Cambridge, UK: Polity.

Bourdieu, Pierre, and Alain Darbel. 1990. *The Love of Art: European Art Museums and Their Public.* Translated by Caroline Beattie and Nick Merriman. Stanford, CA: Stanford University Press.

Bourdieu, Pierre, and Jean-Claude Passeron. 1979. *The Inheritors: French Students and Their Relation to Culture.* Translated by Richard Nice. Chicago: University of Chicago Press.

Bourdieu, Pierre, and Jean-Claude Passeron. 1990. *Reproduction in Education, Society and Culture.* 2nd ed. Translated by Richard Nice. London: Sage.

Bresnahan, Rosalind. 2002. "Radio and the Democratic Movement in Chile 1973–1990: Independent and Grass Roots Voices during the Pinochet Dictatorship." *Journal of Radio Studies* 9(1):161–181.

Bridge, Gary. 2003 "Time-Space Trajectories in Provincial Gentrification." *Urban Studies* 40(12): 2545–2556.

Brint, Steven, William L. Cunningham, and Rebecca S. K. Li. 1997. "The Politics of Professionals in Five Advanced Industrial Societies." In *Citizen Politics in Post-Industrial Societies,* edited by Terry N. Clarke and Michael Rempel, 113–141. Boulder, CO: Westview Press.

Brooks, Clem, and Jeff Manza," 1997. "Partisan Alignments of 'Old' and 'New' Middle Classes in Post-industrial America." In *Citizen Politics in Post-Industrial Societies,* edited by Terry N. Clarke and Michael Rempel, 143–54. Boulder, CO: Westview Press.

Brown-Saracino, Japonica. 2017. "Explicating Divided Approaches to Gentrification and Growing Income Inequality." *Annual Review of Sociology* 43: 515–539.

Brunner, José Joaquin. 2009. "Universidades 'Cota Mil.'" January 18, 2009. http://www.brunner.cl/?p=1172 (accessed June 6, 2022).

Burawoy, Michael. 1998. "The Extended Case Method." *Sociological Theory* 16(1): 4–33.

Butler, Tim, and Garry Robson. 2003. *London Calling: The Middle Classes and the Re-making of Inner London.* Oxford, UK: Berg.

Cáceres, Gonzalo, Francisco Sabatini, Rodrigo Salcedo, and Laura Blonda. 2006. "Malls en Santiago: Luces y claroscuros." *ARQ* 62: 48–53.

Cairns, Kate, and Josée Johnston. 2015. *Food and Femininity.* London: Bloomsbury.

Calarco, Jessica McCrory. 2018. *Negotiating Opportunities: How the Middle Class Secures Advantages in School.* New York: Oxford University Press.

Caldeira, Teresa. 2000. *City of Walls: Crime, Segregation, and Citizenship in São Paulo.* Berkeley: University of California Press.

Campos Medina, Luis. 2012. "El consumo cultural: Una actividad situada." In *La trama social de las practices culturales: Sociedad y subjetividad en el consumo cultural de los chilenos*, edited by Pedro Güell and Tomás Peters, 51–82. Santiago: Ediciones Universidad Alberto Hurtado.

Canales, Manuel, Cristián Bellei, and Víctor Orellana. 2016. "¿Por qué elegir una escuela privada subvencionada? Sectores medios emergentes y elección de escuela en un sistema de mercado." *Estudios Pedagógicos* (Valdivia) 42(3): 89–109.

Carrasco, Alejandro, Macarena Hernández, Ngaire Honey, and Juan de Dios Oyarzún. 2021. "School Admission in Chile, New Rules of the Game, and the Devaluation of Middle-Class Capitals." *British Journal of Sociology of Education* 42(2): 179–195.

Carrasco, Alejandro, Gabriel Gutierrez, and Carolina Flores. 2017. "Failed Regulations and School Composition: Selective Admission Practices in Chilean Primary Schools." *Journal of Education Policy* 32(5): 642–672.

Castillo, Juan Carlos, Daniel Miranda, and Ignacio Madero Cabib. 2013: "Todos Somos Clase Media: Sobre el estatus social subjetivo en Chile." *Latin American Research Review* 48(1): 155–173.

Castillo, Mayarí. 2014. "Clases medias y trabajadores frente a la política: Sobre el ascenso electoral de la derecha en Chile." *Universum (Talca)* 29(2): 65–82.

Castillo, Mayarí. 2016. "Fronteras simbólicas y clases medias. Movilidad social en Chile." *Perfiles latinoamericanos* 24(48): 213–241.

Centro Cultural La Florida. 2020. "Quienes Somos." https://www.culturalaflorida.cl/nosotros/ (accessed June 1, 2020).

Chile, Ministerio de Educación. 2015a. "Listado comunal: comuna Ñuñoa." http://www.mime.mineduc.cl/mime-web/mvc/mime/listado (accessed August 16, 2015).

Chile, Ministerio de Educación. 2015b. "Listado comunal: comuna La Florida." http:/ /www.mime.mineduc.cl/mime-web/mvc/mime/listado (accessed August 16, 2015).

Church of St. Helena. 2021. "Saint Joseph Calasanz (1557–1648) Founder of the Piarist Fathers." https://churchofsthelena.com/calasanz (accessed September 6, 2021).

Ciper. 2016. "Liceo Manuel de Salas: Desalojo de una toma ejemplar." June 18, 2016. https://www.ciperchile.cl/2016/06/17/liceo-manuel-de-salas-desalojo-de-una-toma-ejemplar/.

Clapham, David. 2005. *The Meaning of Housing: A Pathways Approach.* Bristol, UK: Policy Press.

Colegio Calasanz. 2022. "Historia del colegio." https://calasanz.cl/wpnew/historia/ (accessed March 8, 2022).

Colegio Particular COEDUC. 2009. "Ranking de Colegios total país, según promedio PSU 2009." https://www.coeduc.cl/files/ranking2009.pdf (accessed September 2, 2019).

Colegio Raices Altazor. 2022. "Proyecto Educativo Institucional Colegio Raíces Altazor." https://colegioraicesaltazorcl.files.wordpress.com/2022/01/proyecto-educativo-institucional-colegio-raices-altazor-actualizacion-2022-2.pdf (accessed March 8, 2022).

Colegio Raimapu. 2022. "Reseña histórica." http://www.raimapu.cl/historia.php (accessed March 8, 2022).

Colegio Rosario Concha. 2022. "Nosotros." http://colegiorosarioconcha.cl/nosotros/resumen.html (accessed March 8, 2022).

Collier, David, and Ruth Berins Collier. 1991. *Shaping the Political Arena: Critical Junctures, the Labor Movement, and Regime Dynamics in Latin America.* Princeton, NJ: Princeton University Press.

Consejo Nacional de la Cultura y el Arte (CNCA). 2018. *Encuesta Nacional de Paricipación Cultural 2017.* Santiago: CNCA.

Constable, Pamela, and Arturo Valenzuela. 1991. *A Nation of Enemies: Chile under Pinochet.* New York: Norton.

Contreras, Dante, Paulina Sepúlveda, and Sebastián Bustos. 2010. "When Schools Are the Ones That Choose: The Effects of Screening in Chile." *Social Science Quarterly* 91(5): 1349–1368.

Contreras, Randol. 2013. *The Stickup Kids: Race, Drugs, Violence, and the American Dream.* Berkeley: University of California Press.

Corporación Cultural de Ñuñoa. 2020a. "Quienes Somos." http://ccn.cl/quienes-somos/ (accessed June 1, 2020).

Corporación Cultural de Ñuñoa. 2020b. "Casa de la Cultura." http://ccn.cl/quienes-somos-casa-de-la-cultura/ (accessed June 1, 2020).

Coser, Lewis A. 1954. *The Functions of Social Conflict.* Glencoe, IL: The Free Press.

Csikszentmihalyi, Mihaly, and Eugene Rochberg-Halton. 1981. *The Meaning of Things: Domestic Symbols and the Self.* Cambridge: Cambridge University Press.

Cuadra, Álvaro. 2020. "Protesta Social en Chile, 2019–2020: Fracaso de un modelo económico." *Textos y Contextos* 20: 37–50.

Cunningham, E. Christi. 2002. "Identity Markets." *Howard Law Journal* 45(3): 491–596.

Cutts, David, and Paul Widdop. 2017. "Reimagining Omnivorousness in the Context of Place." *Journal of Consumer Culture* 17(3): 480–503.

Davis, Diane. 2010. "The Sociospatial Reconfiguration of Middle Classes and Their Impact on Politics and Development in the Global South: Preliminary Ideas for Future Research." *Political Power and Social Theory* 21: 241–67.

Davis, Mike. 1990. *City of Quartz: Excavating the Future in Los Angeles.* New York: Verso.

Dayton-Johnson, Jeff. 2019. "Global Middle Classes." In *The Palgrave Handbook of Contemporary International Political Economy,* edited by Timothy M. Shaw, Laura C. Mahrenbach, Renu Modi, and Xu Yi-chong, 169–182. London: Palgrave Macmillan.

De Cea, Maite. 2018. "The Role of Public Sociology in the Development of Cultural Policies in Chile: A Transformation of Cultural Expertise." *International Journal of Politics, Culture, and Society* 31: 145–159.

DeShazo, Peter. 1983. *Urban Workers and Labor Unions in Chile, 1902–1927.* Madison: University of Wisconsin Press.

Desmond, Matthew. 2016. *Evicted: Poverty and Profit in the American City.* New York: Broadway Books.

Donoso, Sofía. 2013. "Dynamics of Change in Chile: Explaining the Emergence of the 2006 *Pingüino* Movement." *Journal of Latin American Studies* 45(1): 1–29.

Drake, Paul. 1978. *Socialism and Populism in Chile, 1932–1952*. Urbana: University of Illinois Press.

Dreier, Peter, John Mollenkopf, and Todd Swanstrom. 2014. *Place Matters: Metropolitics for the Twenty-First Century*. 3rd ed. Lawrence: University Press of Kansas.

Duneier, Mitchell. 1999. *Sidewalk*. New York: Farrar, Strauss & Giroux.

Ekiert, Grzegorz. 2010. "The End of Communism in Central and Eastern Europe: The Last Middle-Class Revolution?" *Political Power and Social Theory* 21: 99–123.

Elacqua, Gregory, and Cristóbal Aninat. 2013. "Chile's Pragmatic Middle-Class Voter." *Americas Quarterly* 7(1): 38.

Elacqua, Gregory, and Humberto Santos. 2013. "Preferencias reveladas de los proveedores de educación privada en Chile: El caso de la Ley de Subvención Escolar Preferencial." *Gestión y Política Pública* 22(1): 85–129.

Elacqua, Gregory, Mark Schneider, and Jack Buckley. 2006. "School Choice in Chile: Is It Class or the Classroom?" *Journal of Policy Analysis and Management* 25(3): 577–601.

Elias, Norbert, and John L. Scotson. 1994. *The Established and the Outsiders: A Sociological Enquiry into Community Problems*. 2nd ed. London: Sage.

El Mercurio. 2008. "Resultados del Simce: Carmela Carvajal y La Girouette logran los mejores puntajes." https://www.emol.com/noticias/nacional/2008/05/26/305852/re sultados-del-simce-carmela-carvajal-y-la-girouette-logran-los-mejores-puntajes .html (accessed September 2, 2019).

Errázuriz, Luis Hernán. 2009. "Dictadura militar en Chile: Antecedentes del golpe estético-cultural." *Latin American Research Review* 44(2): 136–157.

Errázuriz, Luis Hernán, and Gonzalo Leiva Quijada. 2012. *El golpe estético: Dictadura militar en Chile, 1973–1990*. Santiago: Editorial Ocho Libros.

Erickson, Bonnie. 1996. "Culture, Class and Connections." *American Journal of Sociology* 102(1): 217–251.

Erickson, Robert, and John Goldthorpe. 1992. *The Constant Flux: A Study of Class Mobility in Industrial Societies*. Oxford: Clarendon Press.

Escuelas Pias—Colegio Calasanz. 2022. "Historia del Colegio." https://calasanz.cl/ wpnew/historia/ (accessed March 8, 2022).

Espinoza, Vicente, and Javier Núñez. 2014. "Movilidad ocupacional en Chile, 2001–2009: Desiguladad de ingresos con igualdad de oportunidades?" *Revista Internacional de Sociología* 72(1): 57–82.

Ferreira, Francisco H.G., Julian Messina, Jamele Rigolini, Luis-Felipe López Calva, María Ana Lugo, and Renos Vakis. 2013. *Economic Mobility and the Rise of the Latin American Middle Class*. Washington, DC: The World Bank.

Firey, Walter. 1945. "Sentiment and Symbolism as Ecological Variables." *American Sociological Review* 10(2): 140–148.

Fishman, Robert M., and Omar Lizardo. 2013. "How Macro-historical Change Shapes Cultural Taste: Legacies of Democratization in Spain and Portugal." *American Sociological Review* 78(2): 213–239.

Fleet, Michael. 1985. *The Rise and Fall of Chilean Christian Democracy*. Princeton, NJ: Princeton University Press.

Fleet, Michael, and Brian H. Smith. 1997. *The Catholic Church and Democracy in Chile and Perú*. Notre Dame, IN: University of Notre Dame Press.

Flemmen, Magne, Vegard Jarness, and Lennart Rosenlund. 2019. "Class and Status: On the Misconstrual of the Conceptual Distinction and a Neo-Bourdieusian Alternative." *British Journal of Sociology* 70(3): 816–866.

Flores, Carolina, and Alejandro Carrasco. 2013. "(Des)igualdad de oportunidades para elegir escuelas: Preferencias, libertad de elección, y segregación escolar." Documento de Referencia 2. *Espacio Público*. https://www.espaciopublico.cl/wp-con tent/uploads/2016/05/8.pdf (accessed September 1, 2020).

Ford, Janet, Julie Rugg, and Roger Burrows. 2002. "Conceptualising the Contemporary Role of Housing in the Transition to Adult Life in England." *Urban Studies* 39(13): 2455–2467.

Franco, Rolando, and Arturo León. 2010. "Clases medias lationamericanas: ayer y hoy." *Estudios Avanzados* 13: 59–77.

Fridman, Daniel. 2016. *Freedom from Work: Embracing Financial Self-Help in the United States and Argentina*. Palo Alto, CA: Stanford University Press.

Friedman, Sam. 2012. "Cultural Omnivores or Culturally Homeless?" Exploring the Shifting Cultural Identities of the Upwardly Mobile." *Poetics* 40: 467–89

Friedman, Sam, and Daniel Laurison. 2019. *The Class Ceiling: Why It Pays to Be Privileged*. Bristol, UK: Policy Press.

Fuentes, Luis, and Oscar Mac-Clure. 2019. "The Middle Classes and the Subjective Representation of Urban Space in Santiago de Chile." *Urban Studies* 57(13): 2612–2627.

Fundación Pablo Neruda. 2022. "Biography." https://fundacionneruda.org/en/bio graphy/ (accessed March 9, 2022).

Funk, Robert L. 2010. "Parties, Personalities, and the President: The Challenges of the Bachelet Government's Political Narrative." In *The Bachelet Government: Conflict and Consensus in Post-Pinochet Chile*, edited by Silvia Borzutsky and Gregory Weeks, 50–66. Gainesville: University Press of Florida.

Gárate Chateau, Manuel. 2012. *La revolución capitalista en Chile (1973–2003)*. Santiago: Ediciones Universidad Alberto Hurtado.

Garcia-Bryce, Iñigo. 2012. "A Middle Class Revolution: The APRA Party and Middle-Class Identity." In *The Making of the Middle Class: Toward a Transnational History*, edited by A. Ricardo López and Barbara Weinstein, 235–252. Durham, NC: Duke University Press.

García Canclini, N. 2001. *Consumers and Citizens: Globalization and Multicultural Conflicts*. Translation and introduction by George Yúdice. Minneapolis: University of Minnesota Press.

Garreton, Manuel A. 1989. *The Chilean Political Process*. Boston: Unwin Hyman.

Gayo, Modesto. 2011. "La estructuración política del gusto." In *Chile 2010. Percepciones y actitudes sociales: Informe de la sexta encuesta nacional UDP*, edited by Maite de Cea, 89–97. Santiago: ICSO/UDP.

Gayo, Modesto. 2017. "Exploring Cultural Disengagement: The Example of Chile." *Cultural Sociology* 11(4): 468–488.

Gayo, Modesto, María Luisa Méndez, and Berta Teitelboim. 2016. "La terciarización en Chile. Desigualdad cultural y estructura ocupacional." *Revista CEPAL* 119: 187–207.

Gayo, Modesto, and Berta Teitelboim. 2009. "Localismo, cosmopolitismo y gustos musicales." In *Encuesta UDP: Chile 2008—Percepciones y Actitudes Sociales*, edited by Claudio Fuentes, 111–120. Santiago: ICSO/UDP.

Gayo, Modesto, Berta Teitelboim, and Maria Luisa Mendez. 2009. "Patrones culturales de uso del tiempo libre en Chile: una aproximación bourdieuiana." *Universum* 24(2): 42–72.

Gayo, Modesto, Berta Teitelboim, and Maria Luisa Mendez. 2013. "Exclusividad y Fragmentación: los perfiles culturales de la clase media en Chile." *Universum* 28(1): 97–128.

Gayo Cal, Modesto, Gabriel Otero Cabrol, and María Luisa Méndez. 2019. "Elección escolar y selección de familias: reproducción de la clase media alta en Santiago de Chile." *Revista Internacional de Sociología* 77(1): 1–16.

Gieryn, Thomas F. 2000. "A Space for Place in Sociology." *Annual Review of Sociology* 26(1): 463–496.

Glaser, Barney, and Anselm Strauss. 1967. *The Discovery of Grounded Theory: Strategies for Qualitative Research*. Chicago: Aldine.

Gonzalez, Débora De Fina, and Francisca Figueroa Vidal. 2019. "Nuevos 'campos de acción política' feminista: Una mirada a las recientes movilizaciones en Chile." *Revista Punto Género* 11: 51–72.

González, Juan Pablo. 2016. "Nueva Canción Chilena en dictadura: divergencia, memoria, escuela (1973–1983)." *Estudios Interdisciplinarios de America Latina y el Caribe* 27(1): 65–81.

González López, Felipe. 2018. "Crédito, deuda y gubernamentalidad financiera en Chile." *Revista Mexicana de Sociología* 80(4): 881–908.

Gouldner, Alvin. 1979. *The Future of Intellectuals and the Rise of the New Class*. London: Macmillan.

Gubbins Foxley, Verónica. 2014. "Estrategias educativas de familias de clase alta: un estudio exploratorio." *Revista Mexicana de Investigación Educativa* 19(63): 1069–1089.

Halle, David. 1993. *Inside Culture: Art and Class in the American Home*. Chicago: University of Chicago Press.

Hayes, Sharon. 1991. *The Cultural Contradictions of Motherhood*. New Haven, CT: Yale University Press.

Hegewisch, Ariane, and Heidi Hartmann. 2014. "Occupational Segregation and the Gender Wage Gap: A Job Half Done." Institute for Women's Policy Research. https://digitalcommons.ilr.cornell.edu/cgi/viewcontent.cgi?article=2593&context=key_workplace (accessed January 26, 2020).

Heiman, Rachel, Carla Freeman, and Mark Liechty. 2012. "Introduction: Charting an Anthropology of the Middle Classes." In *Global Middle Classes: Theorizing through*

Ethnography, edited by Rachel Heiman, Carla Freeman, and Mark Liechty, 3–30. Santa Fe, NM: School for Advanced Research Press.

Heiss, Claudia. 2020. "Chile: entre el estallido social y la pandemia." *Análisis Carolina* 18: 1–13.

Hipsher, Patricia. 1998. "Democratic Transitions and Social Movement Outcomes: The Chilean Shantydwellers' Movement in Comparative Perspective." In *From Contention to Democracy*, edited by Marco Giugni, Doug McAdam, and Charles Tilly, 149–167. Lanham, MD: Rowman & Littlefield.

Hochstenbach, Cody, and Willem R. Boterman. 2015. "Navigating the Field of Housing: Housing Pathways of Young People in Amsterdam." *Journal of Housing and the Built Environment* 30(2): 257–274.

Hofflinger, Alvaro, and Paul T. von Hippel. 2020. "Does Achievement Rise Fastest with School Choice, School Resources, or Family Resources? Chile from 2002 to 2013." *Sociology of Education* 93(2): 132–152.

Holt, Douglas B. 1998. "Does Cultural Capital Structure American Consumption?" *Journal of Consumer Research* 25(1): 1–25.

Hölzl, Corinna. 2018. "The Spatial-Political Outcome of Urban Development Conflicts: Emancipatory Dynamics of Protests against Gentrification in Peñalolén, Santiago de Chile." *International Journal of Urban and Regional Research* 42(6): 1008–1029.

Hopewell, John, and Jamie Lang. 2019. "Chile Works the Movie-TV Crossover." *Variety*, March 11, 2019. https://variety.com/2019/film/festivals/chile-works-the-movie-tv-crossover-1203159910/.

Hsieh, Chang-Tai, and Miguel Urquiola. 2006. "The Effects of Generalized School Choice on Achievement and Stratification: Evidence from Chile's Voucher Program." *Journal of Public Economics* 90: 1477–1503.

Huneeus, Carlos. 2001. *El régimen de Pinochet*. Santiago: Editorial Sudamericana.

Hutchison, Elizabeth Quay, and María Soledad Zárate Campos. 2017. "Clases medias en Chile: estado, género, y prácticas políticas." In *Historia Política de Chile (Tomo Prácticas Políticas)*, edited by Ivan Jaksic and Juan Luis Ossa, 271–300. México: Fondo de Cultura Económica.

Irby, James. 1967. "Cortázar's *Hopscotch* and other Games." *Novel: A Forum on Fiction* 1(1): 64–70.

Jackson, Emma, and Michaela Benson. 2014. "Neither 'Deepest, Darkest Peckham' nor 'Run-of-the-Mill' East Dulwich: The Middle Classes and Their 'Others' in an Inner-London Neighbourhood." *International Journal of Urban and Regional Research* 38(4): 1195–1210.

Jarness, Vegard. 2017. "Cultural vs. Economic Capital: Symbolic Boundaries within the Middle Class." *Sociology* 51(2): 357–373.

Jarness, Vegard, Magne Paalgard Flemmen, and Lennart Rosenlund. 2019. "From Class Politics to Classed Politics." *Sociology* 53(5): 879–899.

Johnson, John J. 1958. *Political Change in Latin America: The Emergence of the Middle Sectors*. Palo Alto, CA: Stanford University Press.

Jordán, Laura. 2009. "Música y clandestinidad en dictadura: la represión, la circulación de músicas de resistencia y el casete clandestino." *Revista Musical Chilena* 63(212): 77–102.

Kharas, Homi. 2010. "The Emerging Middle Class in Developing Countries." Working Paper No. 285. Paris: Organization for Economic Cooperation and Development.

Kimelberg, Shelley McDonough. 2014a. "Middle-Class Parents, Risk and Urban Public Schools." In *Choosing Homes, Choosing Schools*, edited by Annette Lareau and Kimberly Goyette, 207–236. New York: Russell Sage Foundation.

Kimelberg, Shelley McDonough. 2014b. "Beyond Test Scores: Middle-Class Mothers, Cultural Capital, and the Evaluation of Urban Public Schools." *Sociological Perspectives* 57(2): 208–228.

Kochhar, Rakesh. 2020. "A Global Middle Class Is More Promise Than Reality." In *The Middle Class in World Society: Negotiations, Diversities, and Lived Experiences*, edited by Christian Suter, S. Madheswaran, and B. P. Vani, 15–48. London: Routledge.

Kubal, Mary Rose. 2010. "Challenging the Consensus: The Politics of Protest and Policy Reform of Chile's Educational System." In *The Bachelet Government: Conflict and Consensus in Post-Pinochet Chile*, edited by Silvia Borzutsky and Gregory Weeks, 117–135. Gainesville: University Press of Florida.

Labarca, Amanda. 2009. "Apuntes para estudiar la clase media en Chile." *Atenea (Concepción)* 500: 337–350.

Lacy, Karyn. 2007. *Blue-Chip Black: Race, Class, and Status in the New Black Middle Class*. Berkeley: University of California Press.

Lahire, Bernard. 2016. "Cultural Dissonances: The Social in the Singular." In *Routledge International Handbook of the Sociology of Art and Culture*, edited by Laurie Hanquinet and Mike Savage, 312–323. London: Routledge.

Lamont, Michèle. 1992. *Money, Morals, and Manners: The Culture of the French and the American Upper-Middle Class*. Chicago: University of Chicago Press.

Lamont, Michèle. 2000. *The Dignity of Working Men: Morality and the Boundaries of Race, Class, and Immigration*. New York: Russell Sage Foundation.

Lara-Lara, Fernando. 2019. "Hacia una educación del Sumak Kawsay a través de la propuesta artística de Oswaldo Guayasamín." *Arte, Individuo, y Sociedad* 31(1): 9–26.

Lareau, Annette. 2003. *Unequal Childhoods: Class, Race, and Family Life*. Berkeley: University of California Press.

Lareau, Annette. 2014. "Schools, Housing, and the Reproduction of Inequality." In *Choosing Homes, Choosing Schools*, edited by Annette Lareau and Kimberly Goyette, 169–206. New York: Russell Sage Foundation.

Larson, Jeff, and Omar Lizardo. 2007. "Generations, Identities, and the Collective Memory of Che Guevara." *Sociological Forum* 22(4): 425–451.

La Tercera. 2022. "¿Cómo avanza la redacción de la nueva Constitución?" https://www.latercera.com/como-avanza-la-nueva-constitucion-chilena/ (accessed March 20, 2022).

Laumann, Edward O., and James S. House. 1970. "Living Room Styles and Social Attributes: The Patterning of Material Artifacts in a Modern Urban Community." In *The Logic of Social Hierarchies*, edited by Edward O. Laumann, Paul W. Siegel, and Robert W. Hodge, 189–203. Chicago: Markham Publishing Company.

Lechner, Norbert. 2002. *Las sombras del mañana: La dimension subjetiva de la política*. Santiago: LOM.

Lees, Loretta, Hyun Bang Shin, and Ernesto López-Morales. 2015. "Conclusion: Global Gentrifications." In *Global Gentrifications: Uneven Development and Displacement*, edited by Loretta Lees, Hyun Bang Shin, and Ernesto López-Morales, 441–452. Bristol, UK: Policy Press.

Leguina, Adrian, Sara Arancibia-Carvajal, and Paul Widdop. 2017. "Musical Preferences and Technologies: Contemporary Material and Symbolic Distinctions Criticized." *Journal of Consumer Culture* 17(2): 242–264.

Leiva, di Bruno Aste. 2020. "Estallido social en Chile: la persistencia de la Constitución neoliberal como problema." *DPCE Online* 42(1): 1–17.

Lena, Jennifer C., and Richard A. Peterson. 2011. "Politically Purposed Music Genres." *American Behavioral Scientist* 55(5): 574–588.

Leyton, Daniel, and María Teresa Rojas. 2017. "Middle-Class Mothers' Passionate Attachment to School Choice: Abject Objects, Cruel Optimism and Affective Exploitation." *Gender and Education* 29(5): 558–576.

Liceo Experimental Manuel de Salas. 2018. "Hacia una educación no sexista y con enfoque de género en el liceo Manuel de Salas." July 3, 2018. https://www.lms.cl/hacia-una-educacion-no-sexista-y-con-enfoque-de-genero-en-el-liceo-manuel-de-sal as/ (accessed January 9, 2019).

Liceo Experimental Manuel de Salas. 2020. "Quiénes somos." https://www.lms.cl/nuestro-liceo/quienes-somos/ (accessed August 4, 2020).

Lin, Jan. 2019. *Taking Back the Boulevard: Art, Activism, and Gentrification in Los Angeles*. New York: New York University Press.

Lipset, Seymour Martin. 1959. "Some Social Requisites of Democracy: Economic Development and Political Legitimacy." *American Political Science Review* 53(1): 69–105.

Lloyd, Richard. 2010. *Neo-bohemia: Art and Commerce in the Post-industrial City*. 2nd ed. New York: Routledge.

López-Calva, Luis F., and Eduardo Ortiz-Juarez. 2014. "A Vulnerability Approach to the Definition of the Middle Class." *Journal of Economic Inequality* 12(1): 23–47.

López-Morales, Ernesto. 2015. "Assessing Exclusionary Displacement through Rent Gap Analysis in the High-Rise Redevelopment of Santiago, Chile." *Housing Studies* 31(5): 540–559.

López-Morales, Ernesto. 2016. "Gentrification in Santiago, Chile: A Property-Led Process of Dispossession and Exclusion." *Urban Geography* 37(8): 1109–1131.

López-Morales, Ernesto, Ivo Gasic Klett, and Daniel Meza Corvalán. 2014. "Actores sociales y políticas contestando un modelo de urbanismo pro-empresarial: el lado B de la renovación urbana en Santiago." Conference paper, XIII Coloquio Internacional de Geocrítica: el control del espacio y los espacios de control, Barce-

lona (5–10 de mayo): 17 pages. http://www.ub.edu/geocrit/coloquio2014/Ernesto%
20Lopez%20Morales.pdf (accessed August 18, 2021).

López-Morales, Ernesto, and Daniel Meza-Corvalán. 2015. "Regulaciones públicas y explotación de renta de suelo: el boom inmobiliario de Ñuñoa, Santiago, 2000–2010." *Economía, Sociedad y Territorio* 15(48): 301–332.

López-Pedreros, A. Ricardo. 2019. *Makers of Democracy: A Transnational History of the Middle Classes in Colombia.* Durham, NC: Duke University Press.

Loveman, Brian. 1986. *Chile: The Legacy of Hispanic Capitalism.* New York: Oxford University Press.

Loveman, Mara. 1998. "High-Risk Collective Action: Defending Human Rights in Chile, Uruguay, and Argentina." *American Journal of Sociology* 104(2): 477–525.

Mac-Clure, Oscar. 2012. "Las nuevas clases medias en Chile: Un análisis de cohortes." *Revista CEPAL* 108: 169–182.

Mac-Clure, Oscar, Emmanuelle Barozet, and Cristóbal Moya. 2015. "Juicios de las clases medias sobre la élite económica: ¿Crítica a las desigualdades en Chile?" *Polis: Revista Latinoamericana* 41: 1–22.

Madigan, Ruth, and Moira Munro. 1996. "'House Beautiful': Style and Consumption in the Home." *Sociology* 30(1): 41–57.

Marambio Tapia, Alejandro. 2018. "Endeudamiento 'saludable,' empoderamiento y control social." *Polis. Revista Latinoamericana* 49: 79–101.

Marín, Víctor Hernán, Javier Ruiz-Tagle, Ernesto López Morales, Hernán Orozco Ramos, and Sadia Monsalves. 2019. "Gentrificación, clase y capital cultural: transformaciones económicas y socioculturales en barrios pericentrales de Santiago de Chile." *Reis: Revista Española de Investigaciones Sociológicas* 166: 107–134.

Márquez, Francisca. 2020. "Anthropology and Chile's *Estallido Social.*" *American Anthropologist* 122(3): 667–675.

Márquez, Francisca B., and Francisca P. Pérez. 2008. "Spatial Frontiers and Neo-communitarian Identities in the City: The Case of Santiago de Chile." *Urban Studies* 45(7): 1461–1483.

Martínez, Javier, and Alvaro Díaz. 1996. *Chile: The Great Transformation.* Washington, DC: Brookings Institution.

Martínez, Javier, and Eugenio Tironi. 1985. *Las clases sociales en Chile: Cambio y estratificación, 1970–1980.* Santiago: Ediciones SUR.

Mau, Steffen. 2015. *Inequality, Marketization, and the Majority Class: Why Did the European Middle Classes Accept Neo-liberalism?* Houndmills: Palgrave Macmillan.

Mayol, Alberto. 2020. "Protestas y disrupción política y social en Chile 2019: Crisis de legitimidad del modelo neoliberal y posible salida política por acuerdo de cambio constitucional." *Asian Journal of Latin American Studies* 33(2): 85–98.

McAdam, Doug. 1986. "Recruitment to High-Risk Activism: The Case of Freedom Summer." *American Journal of Sociology* 92(1): 64–90.

McAdam, Doug. 1989. "The Biographical Consequences of Activism." *American Sociological Review* 54(5): 744–760.

McCracken, Grant. 1988. *Culture and Consumption: New Approaches to the Symbolic*

Character of Consumer Goods and Activities. Bloomington: Indiana University Press.

McCracken, Grant. 2005. *Culture and Consumption II: Markets, Meaning, and Brand Management.* Bloomington: Indiana University Press.

Memoria Chilena. 2020. "José Manuel Parada." http://www.memoriachilena.gob.cl/602/w3-article-98137.html (accessed June 22, 2020).

Méndez, María Luisa. 2008. "Middle Class Identities in a Neoliberal Age: Tensions between Contested Authenticities." *Sociological Review* 56(2): 220–237.

Méndez, María Luisa. 2018. "Neighborhoods as Arenas of Conflict in the Neoliberal City: Practices of Boundary Making Between 'Us' and 'Them.'" *City & Community* 17(3): 737–753.

Méndez, María Luisa, and Modesto Gayo. 2019. *Upper Middle Class Social Reproduction: Wealth, Schooling and Residential Choice in Chile.* Cham, Switzerland: Palgrave Macmillan.

Méndez, María Luisa, Gabriel Otero, Felipe Link, Ernesto Lopez Morales, and Modesto Gayo. 2021. "Neighbourhood Cohesion as a Form of Privilege." *Urban Studies* 58(8): 1691–1711.

Micco, Alejandro, Eric Parrado, Bernardita Piedrabuena, and Alessandro Rebucci. 2012. "Housing Finance in Chile: Instruments, Actors, and Policies." *IDB Working Paper Series,* 312. https://papers.ssrn.com/sol3/papers.cfm?abstract_id=2080393 (accessed September 1, 2020).

Mizala, Alejandra, and Florencia Torche. 2012. "Bringing the Schools Back in: The Stratification of Educational Achievement in the Chilean Voucher System." *International Journal of Educational Development* 32(1): 132–144.

Mizala, Alejandra, and Florencia Torche. 2017. "Means-Tested School Vouchers and Educational Achievement: Evidence from Chile's Universal Voucher System." *Annals of the American Academy of Political and Social Science* 674(1): 163–183.

Molina, Paula. 2020. "Plebiscito histórico en Chile: 4 claves para entender la consulta en la que ganó la opción de cambiar la Constitución de Pinochet." *BBC News,* October 26, 2020. https://www.bbc.com/mundo/noticias-america-latina-54630310.

Money, Annemarie. 2007. "Material Culture and the Living Room: The Appropriation and Use of Goods in Everyday Life." *Journal of Consumer Culture* 7(3): 355–377.

Montes, Rocío. 2022. "La Convención de Chile presenta un proyecto de Constitución con cambios profundos a la institucionalidad." *El País,* May 16, 2020. https://elpais.com/chile/2022-05-16/la-convencion-de-chile-presenta-un-proyecto-de-constitucion-con-cambios-profundos-a-la-institucionalidad.html.

Moor, Liz, and Sam Friedman. 2021. "Justifying Inherited Wealth: Between 'the Bank of Mum and Dad' and the Meritocratic Ideal." *Economy and Society* 50(4): 618–642.

Mosoetsa, Sarah, Joel Stillerman, and Chris Tilly. 2016. "Precarious Labor, South and North: An Introduction." *International Labor and Working-Class History* 89: 5–19.

Moulian, Tomás. 1997. *Chile: Anatomía de un mito.* Santiago: LOM.

Moulian, Tomás. 1998. *El consumo me consume.* Santiago: LOM.

Mujeres Bacanas. 2021. "Isabel LeBrun (1845–1930)." https://mujeresbacanas.com/isabel-le-brun-1845-1930/ (accessed July 21, 2021).

Muñoz, Andrés, and Antonia Fava. 2020. "Fuera de la institucionalidad: quién es Víctor Chanfreau, vocero de la Aces y líder de las 'funas.'" *La Tercera*, January 7, 2020. https://www.latercera.com/la-tercera-pm/noticia/la-institucionalidad-quien-victor-chanfreau-vocero-la-aces-lider-las-funas/964312/.

Muñoz, Daniela. 2017. "El 40% de los colegios no ha iniciado los trámites para ser sin fines de lucro." *La Tercera,* October 29, 2017. http://www.latercera.com/noticia/40-los-colegios-no-ha-iniciado-los-tramites-sin-fines-lucro/.

Murray, Marjorie, and Sebastián Ureta. 2005. "Un país de poetas? Una mirada comparada al consumo de productos mediales y artísticos en la ciudad de Santiago." In *Consumo Cultural en Chile: Miradas y Perspectivas*, edited by Carlos Catalán and Pablo Torche, 41–58. Santiago: Instituto Nacional de Estadísticas, Consejo Nacional de Cultura y el Arte.

Notimex. 2014. "José Donoso, pieza clave del 'boom latinoamericano.'" https://www.20minutos.com.mx/noticia/b221543/jose-donoso-pieza-clave-del-boom-latinoamericano/ (accessed June 1, 2020).

Núcleo de Sociología Contingente. 2020. *Informe de Resultados Oficial: Encuesta Zona Cero.* Santiago: Núcleo de Sociología Contingente, Facultad de Ciencias Sociales, Universidad de Chile. https://nudesoc.cl/wp-content/uploads/2020/03/Informe-Resultados-OFICIAL.pdf (accessed September 5, 2021).

Ocejo, Richard. 2014. *Upscaling Downtown: From Bowery Saloons to Cocktail Bars in New York City.* Princeton, NJ: Princeton University Press.

Ollivier, Michèle. 2008. "Modes of Openness to Cultural Diversity: Humanist, Populist, Practical, and Indifferent." *Poetics* 36(2–3): 120–147.

Ossandón, José. 2014. "Sowing Consumers in the Garden of Mass Retailing in Chile." *Consumption Markets & Culture* 17(5): 429–447.

Oxhorn, Phillip. 1995. *Organizing Civil Society: The Popular Sectors and the Struggle for Democracy in Chile.* University Park: Pennsylvania University Press.

Ozarow, Daniel. 2019. *The Mobilization and Demobilization of Middle-Class Revolt: Comparative Insights from Argentina.* New York: Routledge.

Palacios-Valladares, Indira. 2016. "Internal Movement Transformation and the Diffusion of Student Protest in Chile." *Journal of Latin American Studies* 49: 579–607.

Parker, David S. 2012. "Siúticos, Cursis, Arribistas and Gente de Medio Pelo: Social Climbers and the Representation of Class in Chile and Perú, 1860–1930." In *The Making of the Middle Class: Toward a Transnational History*, edited by A. Ricardo López and Barbara Weinstein, 336–354. Durham, NC: Duke University Press.

Parkin, Frank. 1968. *Middle Class Radicalism: The Social Basis of the British Campaign for Nuclear Disarmament.* New York: Praeger.

Parraguez, Leslie, 2016. *The Chilean Student Movement: A Family Matter. The Intimate and Conflicting Construction of Revolution in a Post Dictatorial Country.* PhD diss. Chicago: Loyola University.

Pereyra, Omar. 2015. *Contemporary Middle Class in Latin America: A Study of San Felipe.* Lanham, MD: Lexington Books.

Pérez, Miguel. 2017. "Reframing Housing Struggles: Right to the City and Urban Citizenship in Santiago, Chile." *City* 21(5): 530–549.

Pérez, Miguel. 2019. "'Uno tiene que tener casa donde nació.' Ciudadanía y derecho a la ciudad en Santiago." *EURE* 45(135): 71–90.

Peters, Tomás. 2012. "La afinidad electiva entre consumo cultural y percepción sociocultural: el caso de Chile." In *La trama social de las practices culturales: Sociedad y subjetividad en el consumo cultural de los chilenos*, edited by Pedro Güell and Tomás Peters, 109–147. Santiago: Ediciones Universidad Alberto Hurtado.

Peterson, Richard, and Roger Kern. 1996. "Changing Highbrow Taste: From Snob to Omnivore." *American Sociological Review* 61(5): 900–907.

Pierce, Joseph, Deborah G. Martin, and James T. Murphy. 2011. "Relational Place-Making: The Networked Politics of Place." *Transactions of the Institute of British Geographers* 36(1): 54–70.

Poduje, Iván. 2008. "Participación ciudadana en proyectos de infraestructura y planes reguladores." *Pontificia Universidad Católica de Chile: Vicerectoría de Comunicaciones y Asuntos Públicos.* Working Paper 3, 22. Santiago: Pontificia Universidad Católica de Chile: 1–17.

Poggio, Teresio. 2008. "The Intergenerational Transmission of Home Ownership and the Reproduction of the Familialistic Welfare Regime." In *Families, Ageing, and Social Policy*, edited by Chiara Saraceno, 59–87. Cheltenham, UK: Edward Elgar.

Portes, Alejandro.1989. "Latin American Urbanization during the Years of the Crisis." *Latin American Research Review* 24(3): 7–44.

Programa de las Naciones Unidas Para el Desarrollo (PNUD). 2002. *Nosotros los chilenos: Un desafío cultural*. Santiago: United National Development Program.

Programa de las Naciones Unidas Para el Desarrollo (PNUD). 2010. *Desarrollo Humano en Chile 2010. Género: Los desafíos de la igualdad*. Santiago: PNUD.

Programa de las Naciones Unidas Para el Desarrollo (PNUD). 2017. *Desiguales. Orígenes, cambios y desafíos de la brecha social en Chile*. Santiago: Programa de las Naciones Unidas para el Desarrollo.

Pugh, Alison. 2009. *Longing and Belonging: Parents, Children, and Consumer Culture*. Berkeley: University of California Press.

Raczynski, Dagmar, Daniel Salinas, Loreto de la Fuente, Macarena Hernández, and Miguel Lattz. 2010. "Hacia una estrategia de validación de la educación pública-municipal: imaginarios, valoraciones y demandas de las familias. Informe Final Proyecto Fondo de Desarrollo e Investigación en Educación." Santiago: Gobierno de Chile, Departamento de Estudios y Desarrollo, División de Planificación y Finanzas, Ministerio de Educación.

Rasse, Alejandra. 2015. "Juntos pero no revueltos. Procesos de integración social en fronteras residenciales entre hogares de distinto nivel socioeconómico." *EURE* 41(122): 125–143.

Rasse, Alejandra, Rodrigo Salcedo, and Juan Pardo. 2009. "Transformaciones económicas y socioculturales: ¿cómo segmentar a los chilenos hoy?" In *El arte de clasificar a los chilenos: Enfoques sobre los modelos de estratificación en Chile*, edited by Pedro Guell and Alfredo Joignant, 17–36. Santiago: Ediciones Universidad Diego Portales.

Raveaud, Maroussia, and Agnes van Zanten. 2007. "Choosing the Local School: Middle Class Parents' Values and Social and Ethnic Mix in London and Paris." *Journal of Education Policy* 22(1): 107–124.

Ray, Raka. 2010. "'The Middle Class': Sociological Category or Proper Noun?" *Political Power and Social Theory* 21: 313–322.

Reay, Diane, Gill Crozier, and David James. 2011. *White Middle-Class Identities and Urban Schooling*. Houndmills, UK: Palgrave.

Revista Don. 2020. "Las mejores obras del 'boom latinoamericano.'" http://www.revis tadon.com/28542/las-mejores-obras-del-boom-latinoamericano-literatura-cien -anos-de-soledad-garcia-marquez (accessed June 1, 2020).

Rey, Jeanne, Matthieu Bolay, and Yonatan N. Gez. 2020. "Precarious Privilege: Personal Debt, Lifestyle Aspirations and Mobility among International School Teachers." *Globalisation, Societies and Education* 18(4): 361–373.

Reyes, Victoria. 2019. *Global Borderlands: Fantasy, Violence, and Empire in Subic Bay, Philippines*. Palo Alto, CA: Stanford University Press.

Reyes Päcke, Sonia, and Isabel Margarita Figueroa Aldunce. 2010. "Distribución, superficie y accesibilidad de las áreas verdes en Santiago de Chile." *EURE* 36(109): 89–110.

Richards, Patricia. 2010. "Of Indians and Terrorists: How the State and Local Elites Construct the Mapuche in Neoliberal Multicultural Chile." *Journal of Latin American Studies* 42(1): 59–90.

Riquelme, Pedro. 2018. "Construcción identitaria en jóvenes participantes de la cultura otaku en Chile." *Ultima década* 26(49): 101–127.

Ríos, Marcela. 2021. "Convención Constitucional de Chile: Un triunfo de la inclusión." Santiago: UNDP https://www.latinamerica.undp.org/content/rblac/es/home/blog /2021/chile-s-constitutional-convention--a-triumph-of-inclusion.html (accessed March 10, 2022).

Rivera, Lauren. 2015. *Pedigree: How Elite Students Get Elite Jobs*. Princeton, NJ: Princeton University Press.

Roberts, Kenneth M. 1998. *Deepening Democracy? The Modern Left and Social Movements in Chile and Perú*. Stanford, CA: Stanford University Press.

Roberts, Kenneth M. 2011. "Chile: The Left after Neoliberalism." In *The Resurgence of the Latin American Left*, edited by Steven Levitsky and Kenneth M. Roberts, 325–347. Baltimore, MD: Johns Hopkins University Press.

Roberts, Kenneth M. 2017. "Chilean Social Movements and Party Politics in Comparative Perspective: Conceptualizing Latin America's 'Third Generation' of Antineoliberal Protest." In *Social Movements in Chile: Organization, Trajectories, and Political Consequences*, edited by Sofia Donoso and Marisa von Bülow, 221–248. New York: Palgrave Macmillan.

Rodríguez-Merino, Pablo Adriano. 2018. "Fuera de foco: un análisis estratégico de la campaña guerrillera del Che Guevara en Bolivia (1966–67)." *Revista de Pensamiento Estratégico y Seguridad CISDE* 3(2): 53–62.

Rojas, María Teresa. 2018. "Inclusión social: miradas de los docentes y apoderados frente a la mixtura social en sus escuelas." *Estudios Pedagógicos* 44(3): 217–234.

Romero, Martín. 2011. "Raimapu, el colegio de Camila Vallejo: 'alternativo' y semillero de líderes." *La Segunda*, September 2, 2011. http://www.lasegunda.com/Noticias/ Nacional/2011/09/677847/raimapu-el-colegio-de-camila-vallejo-alternativo-y-se millero-de-lideres.

Rosemblatt, Karin Alejandra. 2000. *Gendered Compromises: Political Cultures and the State in Chile, 1920–1950.* Chapel Hill: University of North Carolina Press.

Rosemblatt, Karin Alejandra. 2013. "Welfare States, Neoliberal Regimes, and International Political Economy: Gender Politics of Latin America in Global Context." *Journal of Women's History* 25(4): 149–162.

Roy, Rianka. 2021. "Precarious Privilege: Globalism, Digital Biopolitics, and Tech-Workers' Movements in India." *The European Legacy* 26(7–8): 675–691.

Roy, William G. 2010. *Reds, Whites, and Blues: Social Movements, Folk Music, and Race in the United States.* Princeton, NJ: Princeton University Press.

Rozas Bugueño, Joaquín, and Antoine Maillet. 2019. "Entre marchas, plebiscitos e iniciativas de ley: innovación en el repertorio de estrategias del movimiento No Más AFP en Chile (2014–2018)." *Izquierdas* 48: 1–21.

Ruiz-Tagle, Javier. 2016. "La persistencia de la segregación y la desigualdad en barrios socialmente diversos: un estudio de caso en La Florida, Santiago." *EURE* 42(125): 81–108.

Sabatini, Francisco, and Gonzalo Cáceres. 2004. "Los barrios cerrados y la ruptura del patrón tradicional de segregación en las ciudades latinoamericanas: el caso de Santiago de Chile." In *Barrios cerrados en Santiago de Chile: entre la exclusion y la integración residencial*, edited by Gonzalo Cáceres and Francisco Sabatini, 9–43. Santiago: Lincoln Institute of Land Policy and Pontificia Universidad Católica de Chile, Instituto de Geografía.

Sabatini, Francisco, Alejandra Rasse, Pia Mora, and Isabel Brain. 2012. "¿ Es posible la integración residencial en las ciudades chilenas? Disposición de los grupos medios y altos a la integración con grupos de extracción popular." *EURE* 38(115): 159–194.

Sabatini, Francisco, and Rodrigo Salcedo. 2007. "Gated Communities and the Poor in Santiago, Chile: Functional and Symbolic Integration in a Context of Aggressive Capitalist Colonization of Lower-Class Areas." *Housing Policy Debate* 18(3): 577–606.

Sagaris, Lake. 2014. "Citizens' Anti-highway Revolt in Post-Pinochet Chile: Catalyzing Innovation in Transport Planning." *Planning Practice and Research* 29(3): 268–286.

Salcedo, Rodrigo. 2004. *Towards a Reconceptualization of Post-Public Spaces.* PhD diss., Political Science. Chicago: University of Illinois at Chicago.

Santibáñez, Dimas, Tamara Hernández, and Manuela Mendoza. 2012. "Edades y consumos culturales: industrias culturales, oferta y diversificación de mercados." In *La trama social de las practices culturales: Sociedad y subjetividad en el consumo cultural de los chilenos*, edited by Pedro Güell and Tomás Peters, 109–47. Santiago: Ediciones Universidad Alberto Hurtado.

Santos, Humberto, and Gregory Elacqua. 2016. "Socioeconomic School Segregation in Chile: Parental Choice and a Theoretical Counterfactual Analysis." *Cepal Review* 119: 123–37.

Savage, Mike. 2014. "Cultural Capital and Elective Belonging: A British Case Study." In *Social Capital, Social Identities: From Ownership to Belonging*, edited by Dieter Thomä, Christoph Henning, and Hans Bernhard Schmid, 29–54. Berlin: Walter de Gruyter.

Savage, Mike, Gaynor Bagnall, and Brian J. Longhurst. 2005. *Globalization and Belonging*. London: Sage.

Savage, Mike, James Barlow, Peter Dickens, and Tony Fielding. 1992. *Property, Bureaucracy and Culture: Middle-Class Formation in Contemporary Britain*. London: Routledge.

Savage, Mike, Niall Cunningham, Fiona Devine, Sam Friedman, Daniel Laurison, Lisa McKenzie, Andrew Miles, Helene Snee, Paul Wakeling. 2015. *Social Class in the 21st Century*. London: Penguin UK.

Savage, Mike, and Modesto Gayo. 2011. "Unravelling the Omnivore: A Field Analysis of Contemporary Musical Taste in the United Kingdom." *Poetics* 39: 337–57.

Schielke, Samuli. 2012. "Living in the Future Tense: Aspiring for World and Class in Provincial Egypt." In *Global Middle Classes*, edited by Rachel Heiman, Carla Freeman, and Mark Liechty, 31–57. Santa Fe, NM: School of Advanced Research Press.

Schlack, Elke, and Neil Turnbull. 2015. "Emerging Retail Gentrification in Santiago de Chile: The Case of Italia-Caupolicán." In *Global Gentrifications*, edited by Loretta Lees, Hyun Bang Shin, and Ernesto López-Morales, 349–375. Bristol, UK: Policy Press.

Schneider, Cathy. 1995. *Shantytown Protest in Pinochet's Chile*. Philadelphia: Temple University Press.

Schönstatt Sisters of Mary. 2022. "Our History." https://schoenstattsistersofmary.us/our-history/ (accessed March 9, 2022).

Sehnbruch, Kirsten. 2006. *The Chilean Labor Market: A Key to Understanding Latin American Labor Markets*. Houndmills, UK: Palgrave Macmillan.

Sehnbruch, Kirsten. 2010. "Unresolved Conflicts within the Consensus: Bachelet's Inheritance of Labor and Employment Issues." In *The Bachelet Government: Conflict and Consensus in Post-Pinochet Chile*, edited by Silvia Borzutsky and Gregory Weeks, 136–157. Gainesville: University Press of Florida.

Sehnbruch, Kirsten. 2014. "A Precarious Labor Market." In *Democratic Chile: The Politics and Policies of a Historic Coalition, 1990–2010*, edited by Kirsten Sehnbruch and Peter Siavelis, 263–280. Boulder, CO: Lynne Rienner.

Sepúlveda, Bastien, and Paulina Zúñiga. 2015. "Geografías indígenas urbanas: el caso mapuche en La Pintana, Santiago de Chile." *Revista de Geografía Norte Grande* 62: 127–149.

Serrano, Sol. 2018. *El liceo: Relato, memoria, política*. Santiago: Taurus/Random House.

Servicio Nacional del Patrimonio Cultural. 2015. "En más de 40 obras: Mario Carreño revela su sorprendente y colorido universo creativo." https://www.patrimoniocultural.gob.cl/noticias/mario-carreno-revela-su-sorprendente-y-colorido-universo-creativo (accessed February 11, 2022).

Sherman, Rachel. 2017. *Uneasy Street: The Anxieties of Affluence*. Princeton, NJ: Princeton University Press.

Siavelis, Peter. 2010. "What It Takes to Win and What It Takes to Govern: Michelle Bachelet and the Concertación." In *The Bachelet Government: Conflict and Consensus in Post-Pinochet Chile*, edited by Silvia Borzutsky and Gregory Weeks, 27–49. Gainesville: University Press of Florida.

Siavelis, Peter. 2014. "From a Necessary to a Permanent Coalition." In *Democratic Chile: The Politics and Policies of a Historic Coalition, 1990–2010*, edited by Kirsten Sehnbruch and Peter Siavelis, 15–42. Boulder, CO: Lynne Rienner.

Silva, Eduardo. 2007. "The Import-Substitution Model: Chile in Comparative Perspective." *Latin American Perspectives* 34(3): 67–90.

Silva, Eduardo, and Patricio Rodrigo. 2010. "Contesting Property Rights: The Environment and Indigenous Peoples." In *The Bachelet Government: Conflict and Consensus in Post-Pinochet Chile*, edited by Silvia Borzutsky and Gregory Weeks, 181–214. Gainesville: University Press of Florida.

Silva, Elizabeth B., and David Wright. 2009. "Displaying Desire and Distinction in Housing." *Cultural Sociology* 3(1): 31–50.

Silva, J. Pablo. 2000. *White-Collar Revolutionaries: Middle-Class Unions and the Rise of the Chilean Left*. PhD diss. Chicago: University of Chicago.

Simmel, Georg. 1955. *Conflict and the Web of Group Affiliations*. Translated by Kurt H. Wolff and Reinhard Bendix. New York: The Free Press.

Small, Mario Luis. 2009. "'How Many Cases Do I Need?' On Science and the Logic of Case Selection in Field-Based Research." *Ethnography* 10(1): 5–38.

Snow, David A., and Leon Anderson. 1987. "Identity Work among the Homeless: The Verbal Construction and Avowal of Personal Identities." *American Journal of Sociology* 92(6): 1336–1371.

Solimano, Andrés. 2012. *Chile and The Neoliberal Trap: The Post-Pinochet Era*. New York: Cambridge University Press.

Srivastava, Sanjay. 2012. "National Identity, Bedrooms, and Kitchens: Gated Communities and New Narratives of Space in India." In *Global Middle Classes*, edited by R. Heiman, C. Freeman, and M. Liechty, 57–84. Santa Fe, NM: School of Advanced Research Press.

Statista. 2021a. "Elecciones presidenciales en Chile: resultados del voto en la primera vuelta de 2021." November 22, 2021. https://es.statista.com/estadisticas/1277306/resultados-elecciones-presidenciales-primera-vuelta-chile-candidato/.

Statista. 2021b. "Elecciones presidenciales en Chile: resultados del voto en la segunda vuelta de 2021." December 20, 2021. https://es.statista.com/estadisticas/1282172/resultados-elecciones-presidenciales-segunda-vuelta-chile-candidato/.

Stern, Claudia W. 2021. *Entre el cielo y el suelo: Las identidades elásticas de las clases medias (Santiago de Chile, 1932–1962)*. Santiago: RIL Editores.

Stillerman, Joel. 2003. "Space, Strategies and Alliances in Mobilization: The 1960 Metalworkers' and Coal Miners' Strikes in Chile." *Mobilization: An International Journal* 8(1): 65–85.

Stillerman, Joel. 2004. "Gender, Class, and Generational Contexts for Consumption in Contemporary Chile." *Journal of Consumer Culture* 4(1): 51–78.

Stillerman, Joel. 2012. "Chile's Forgotten Consumers: Poor Urban Families, Consumption Strategies, and the Moral Economy of Risk in Santiago." In *Consumer Culture in Latin America*, edited by John Sinclair and Anna Pertierra, 67–80. Houndmills, UK: Palgrave.

Stillerman, Joel. 2016. "Educar a niñas y niños de clase media en Santiago: capital cultural y segregación socioterritorial en la formación de mercados locales de educación." *EURE* 42(126) mayo: 169–186. https://dx.doi.org/10.4067/S0250-71612016 000200008.

Stillerman, Joel. 2017. "Housing Pathways, Elective Belonging, and Family Ties in Middle Class Chileans' Housing Choices." *Poetics* 61 (April): 67–78.

Stillerman, Joel, and Rodrigo Salcedo. 2012. "Transposing the Urban to the Mall: Routes, Relationships and Resistance in Two Santiago, Chile Shopping Centers." *Journal of Contemporary Ethnography* 41(3): 309–336.

Straubhaar, Joseph D. 2007. *World Television: From Global to Local*. Thousand Oaks, CA: Sage.

Svampa, Maristella. 2001. *Los que ganaron: La vida en los countries y barrios privados*. Buenos Aires: Editorial Biblios.

T13. 2021. "Elecciones 2021: Revisa los resultados comuna por comuna de la segunda vuelta presidencial." *Teletrece*, December 21, 2021. https://www.t13.cl/noticia/eleccio nes-2021/politica/elecciones-2021-revisa-resultado-comuna-comuna-segunda-vuel ta-boric-kast-20-12-2021.

Tavory, Iddo, and Stefan Timmermans. 2014. *Abductive Analysis: Theorizing Qualitative Research*. Chicago: University of Chicago Press.

Teichman, Judith. 2015. "The Role of the Middle Class in Distributional Outcomes: Chile and South Korea." *Studies in Comparative International Development* 50: 1–21

Thieme, Claudio, and Ernesto Treviño. 2013. "School Choice and Market Imperfections: Evidence from Chile." *Education and Urban Society* 45(6): 635–657.

Thumala, María Angélica. 2012. "The Aristocracy of the Will: A Critique of Pierre Bourdieu with Illustrations from Chile." *Social Compass* 59(1): 52–68.

Tilly, Charles. 1998. *Durable Inequality*. Berkeley: University of California Press.

Tinsman, Heidi. 2014. *Buying into the Regime: Grapes and Consumption in Cold War Chile and the United States*. Durham, NC: Duke University Press.

Tomaskovic-Devey, Donald, and Dustin Avent-Holt. 2019. *Relational Inequalities: An Organizational Approach*. New York: Oxford University Press.

Torche, Florencia. 2005. "Unequal but Fluid: Social Mobility in Chile in Comparative Perspective." *American Sociological Review* 70: 422–450.

Torche, Florencia. 2007. "Social Status and Cultural Consumption: The Case of Reading in Chile." *Poetics* 35: 75–92.

Torche, Florencia. 2010. "Social Status and Public Cultural Consumption: Chile in Comparative Perspective." In *Social Status and Cultural Consumption*, edited by Tak Wing Chan, 109–138. Cambridge: Cambridge University Press.

Torche, Florencia, and Luis López-Calva. 2013. "Stability and Vulnerability of the Latin American Middle Class." *Oxford Development Studies* 41(4): 409–435

Torche, Pablo. 2005. "El consumo y la creación cultural: el impacto creativo de la conformación de las audiencias." In *Consumo Cultural en Chile*, edited by Carlos

Catalán and Pablo Torche, 141–152. Santiago: Instituto Nacional de Estadísticas, Consejo Nacional de Cultura y el Arte.

Torres-Salinas, Robinson, Gerardo Azócar García, Noelia Carrasco Henríquez, Mauricio Zambrano-Bigiarini, Tatiana Costa, and Bob Bolin. 2016. "Desarrollo forestal, escasez hídrica, y la protesta social mapuche por la justicia ambiental en Chile." *Ambiente & Sociedade* 19(1): 121–145.

Un Techo Para Chile. 2021. "Un poco de historia." https://www.techo.org/chile/que-es -techo/ (accessed September 15, 2021).

Üstüner, Tuba, and Douglas Holt. 2010. "Toward a Theory of Status Consumption in Less Industrialized Countries." *Journal of Consumer Research* 37: 37–56.

Valenzuela, J. Samuel, and Nicolas Somma. 2018. "Resilience and Change: The Party System in Democratized Chile." In *Party Systems in Latin America: Institutionalization, Decay and Collapse*, edited by Scott Mainwaring, 135–163. Cambridge: Cambridge University Press.

Valenzuela Levi, Nicolas. 2021. "¿Cuáles son las claves territoriales de la victoria de @ gabrielboric?" https://twitter.com/valenzuelalevi/status/1474097956487893004 (accessed January 26, 2022).

Van Bavel, René, and Lucía Sell-Trujillo. 2003. "Understandings of Consumerism in Chile." *Journal of Consumer Culture* 3(3): 343–362.

Van Dyke, Nella, Doug McAdam, and Brenda Wilhelm. 2000. "Gendered Outcomes: Gender Differences in the Biographical Consequences of Activism." *Mobilization: An International Quarterly* 5(2): 161–177.

Vega, Constanza. 2013. "El Colectivo de Acciones del Arte y su resistencia artística contra la dictadura chilena (1979–1985)." *Revista Divergencia* 2(3): 37–48.

Vela Castañeda, Manolo E. 2021. "Nuevas perspectivas sobre militancias de alto riesgo: Ciudad de Guatemala, 1980–1985." *Latin American Research Review* 56(4): 831–843.

Villalobos-Ruminott, Sergio. 2020. "Chilean Revolts and the Crisis of Neoliberal Governance." *Radical Philosophy* 2: 9–16.

Villegas, Celso. 2010. "Revolution 'From the Middle': Historical Events, Narrative, and the Making of the Middle Class in the Contemporary Developing World." *Political Power and Social Theory* 21: 299–312.

Von Bülow, Marisa, and Germán Bidegain Ponte. 2015. "It Takes Two to Tango: Students, Political Parties, and Protest in Chile (2005–2013)." In *Handbook of Social Movements across Latin America*, edited by Paul Almeida and Allen Cordero Ulate, 179–194. Dordrecht, Netherlands: Springer.

Walker, Louise. 2013. *Waking from the Dream: Mexico's Middle Classes After 1968*. Palo Alto, CA: Stanford University Press.

Wang, Georgette, and Jan Servaes. 2000. "Introduction." In *The New Communications Landscape: Demystifying Global Media*, edited by Georgette Wang, Jan Servaes and Anura Goonasekera, 1–18. London: Routledge.

Warde, Alan, David Wright, and Modesto Gayo. 2007. "Understanding Cultural Omnivorousness: Or, the Myth of the Cultural Omnivore." *Cultural Sociology* 1(2): 143–164.

Warren, Sarah D. 2017. "Indigenous in the City: The Politics of Urban Mapuche Identity in Chile." *Ethnic and Racial Studies* 40(4): 694–712.

Weber, Max. 1978. *Economy and Society: An Outline of Interpretive Sociology*, 2 vols. Edited by Guenther Roth and Claus Wittich. Berkeley: University of California Press.

Weeden, Kim A., and David B. Grusky. 2012. "The Three Worlds of Inequality." *American Journal of Sociology* 117(6): 1723–1785.

Weinberger, Michelle F., Jane R. Zavisca, and Jennifer M. Silva. 2017. "Consuming for an Imagined Future: Middle-Class Consumer Lifestyle and Exploratory Experiences in the Transition to Adulthood." *Journal of Consumer Research* 44(2): 332–360.

Wherry, Frederick. 2008. *Global Markets and Local Crafts*. Baltimore, MD: Johns Hopkins University Press.

Wherry, Frederick. 2012. *The Culture of Markets*. Cambridge, UK: Polity Press.

Williams, Christine. 1995. *Still a Man's World: Men Who Do "Women's Work."* Berkeley: University of California Press.

Winn, Peter. 1986. *Weavers of Revolution: The Yarur Workers and Chile's Road to Socialism*. New York: Oxford University Press.

Woodward, Ian. 2001. "Domestic Objects and the Taste Epiphany: A Resource for Consumption Methodology." *Journal of Material Culture* 6(2): 115–136.

Woodward, Ian. 2003. "Divergent Narratives in the Imagining of the Home amongst Middle-Class Consumers: Aesthetics, Comfort and the Symbolic Boundaries of Self and Home." *Journal of Sociology* 39(4): 391–412.

World Bank. 2021. *The Gradual Rise and Rapid Decline of the Middle Class in Latin America and the Caribbean*. Washington, DC: International Bank for Reconstruction and Development / The World Bank.

Zancajo, Adrian. 2019. "Education Markets and Schools' Mechanisms of Exclusion: The Case of Chile." *Education Policy Analysis Archives* 27(130): 1–37.

Zavisca, Jane. 2012. *Housing the New Russia*. Ithaca, NY: Cornell University Press.

Zeitlin, Maurice, and Richard Earl Ratcliff. 1988. *Landlords and Capitalists: The Dominant Class of Chile*. Princeton, NJ: Princeton University Press.

Zelizer, Viviana. 1989. "The Social Meaning of Money: 'Special Monies.'" *American Journal of Sociology.* 95(2): 342–377.

Zelizer, Viviana. 2005. "Culture and Consumption." In *Handbook of Economic Sociology*, 2nd ed., edited by Neil Smelser and Richard Swedberg, 331–354. Princeton, NJ, and New York: Princeton University Press and Russell Sage Foundation.

Zimmerman, Seth D. 2019. "Elite Colleges and Upward Mobility to Top Jobs and Top Incomes." *American Economic Review* 109(1): 1–47.

Zukin, Sharon. 2012. "The Social Production of Urban Cultural Heritage: Identity and Ecosystem on an Amsterdam Shopping Street." *City, Culture and Society* 3(4): 281–291.

Index

86, 94, 202; economic policies of, 19, 216; electoral defeat of, 20; human rights abuses by, 19-20

Police (rock group), 179

Portugal, 14–15, 211

pragmatists, 7, 205; activists' tensions with, 57, 115; aesthetic tastes of, 31, 142, 144, 146–147, 158–161, 199; downward mobility of, 5, 16; earnings of, 37; entrepreneurialism among, 49, 50, 54, 57; housing and school choices of, 30, 36–37, 40, 60, 64, 66, 71–72, 75, 81, 85, 102, 105–106, 109, 111, 112, 116, 170, 204, 207; leisure and cultural activities of, 32, 174, 188–192, 195-196, 209; microaggressions resented by, 31, 114, 125, 190, 207, 210; moderate Catholics' tensions with, 57, 124–125, 135; poor people avoided by, 10, 31, 57, 60, 75, 79–80, 106, 107, 116, 118, 135, 181, 203, 206, 210, 214; student protests opposed by, 128, 133, 134, 135; work ethic of, 6, 16; youngsters' tensions with, 57, 124–125, 135

precarious privilege, 15, 16, 23, 32, 142, 169, 199, 203, 205; aesthetic tastes linked to, 147; anti-materialism linked to, 28, 136; cultural consumption constrained by, 174; defined, 9–10; downgraded employment linked to, 29; housing choices constrained by, 59, 64, 66-67, 81; identity investments shaped by, 61, 202; leisure activities constrained by, 173, 174; qualitative research and, 27; school choices constrained by, 85, 91, 97, 107, 110-111; symbolic boundaries linked to, 9–10, 11

Preferential Educational Subvention law (SEP, 2008), 86

Presley, Elvis, 179

progressive cosmopolitanism, 31, 142, 146, 150–151, 161, 166, 181, 182, 208

Providencia (neighborhood), 78, 98

Puente Alto, 60, 63, 80, 243n32

Queen (rock group), 179

Quilapayún (musical group), 171, 178–179, 187

racism, 8, 93, 102, 105, 210, 211

Radical Party (PR), 17–18, 90

Rafael (educational consultant), 39, 54, 94, 109, 163

Raíces Altazor (La Florida school), 88, 103–104, 118, 122–124, 169, 223; characteristics of, 224; diverse student body of, 101, 102, 116–117, 124; inclusive culture of, 116, 207; leadership of, 101–102, 124; parents' weak ties to, 116, 170, 182, 207

Raimapu (La Florida school), 88, 115, 118, 152, 169, 222; activism and polarization at, 128–131, 136; characteristics of, 224; growth of, 98; as liberal enclave, 98, 99–100, 201, 205, 206–207; informality of, 121–122; old timers vs. newcomers at, 113; parental friendships at, 116, 178, 181-182, 207; Raíces compared with, 101–103, 117; student and parent activism at, 208, 212, 215

reggaeton, 172, 187, 188, 195, 196

Rembrandt van Rijn, 152

reproductive housing pathway, 64

Rerum Novarum, 19

research design and methods, 221–228

Ricardo (judge and former history teacher): as bibliophile, 194; coworkers' frictions with, 51; household aesthetics of, 163, 165; housing and school choices of, 65, 78, 99-100; political sympathies of, 151–152; as Raimapu parent, 130, 131; schooling of, 38, 41

Roberto (La Florida resident), 196

Robson, Garry, 68

CULTURE AND ECONOMIC LIFE

Diverse sets of actors create meaning in markets: consumers and socially engaged actors from below; producers, suppliers, and distributors from above; and the gatekeepers and intermediaries that span these levels. Scholars have studied the interactions of people, objects, and technology; charted networks of innovation and diffusion among producers and consumers; and explored the categories that constrain and enable economic action. This series captures the many angles in which these phenomena have been investigated and serves as a high-profile forum for discussing the evolution, creation, and consequences of commerce and culture.

Making Sense: Markets from Stories in New Breast Cancer Therapeutics
Sophie Mützel
2022

Supercorporate: Distinction and Participation in Post-Hierarchy South Korea
Michael M. Prentice
2022

Black Culture, Inc.: How Ethnic Community Support Pays for Corporate America
Patricia A. Banks
2022

The Sympathetic Consumer: Moral Critique in Capitalist Culture
Tad Skotnicki
2021

Reimagining Money: Kenya in the Digital Finance Revolution
Sibel Kusimba
2021

Black Privilege: Modern Middle-Class Blacks with Credentials and Cash to Spend
Cassi Pittman Claytor
2020

Global Borderlands: Fantasy, Violence, and Empire in Subic Bay, Philippines
Victoria Reyes
2019

The Costs of Connection: How Data is Colonizing Human Life and Appropriating It for Capitalism
Nick Couldry and Ulises A. Mejias
2019

The Moral Power of Money: Morality and Economy in the Life of the Poor
Ariel Wilkis
2018

The Work of Art: Value in Creative Careers
Alison Gerber
2017

Behind the Laughs: Community and Inequality in Comedy
Michael P. Jeffries
2017

Freedom from Work: Embracing Financial Self-Help in the United States and Argentina
Daniel Fridman
2016

The authorized representative in the EU for product safety and compliance is:
Mare Nostrum Group
B.V Doelen 72
4831 GR Breda
The Netherlands

www.ingramcontent.com/pod-product-compliance
Lightning Source LLC
Chambersburg PA
CBHW020504270326
41926CB00008B/727